ARCHAEOLOGY OF CAMBR
VOL. 1: SOUTH WEST CAMBRIDGESHIRE

View of Coton Cross, drawn by R. Relhan in the early 19th century. © Cambridge Antiquarian Society.

Archaeology of Cambridgeshire

VOL 1 : SOUTH WEST CAMBRIDGESHIRE

Alison Taylor

Series Editor: Christopher Taylor

Published in 1997 by Cambridgeshire County Council, Resources Unit, 19 Gordon Avenue, March, Cambs., PE15 8AL. Printed by Burlington Press (Cambridge) Limited, 1 Station Road, Foxton, Cambridge CB2 6SW Tel. (01223) 870266 Fax (01223) 872113.
Layout and design by Pen to Print, 196 Lincoln Road, Peterborough PE1 2NQ Tel/Fax (01733) 706675.

ISBN 1 870724 84 4

Contents

To Tim, Rose and Nesta,
and all who have worked on the archaeology of Cambridgeshire

Foreword

The main aim of this book is to give the people who live in the villages it describes an understanding of the history of this area from prehistoric times. It is important to realise that we are heirs to a landscape that is many thousands of years old. This landscape has been moulded and changed numerous times but it still exhibits evidence from many periods of this history. In today's increasingly mobile society, people need to have some connection with the past, and there is no better way of achieving this than through an appreciation of the local environment. Young people in particular need to know about their localities, and I hope that teachers and pupils will use materials and sources found in this book in their own studies.

Another aim is more ambitious: to provide an overview of the archaeology of this part of Cambridgeshire, drawing on the author's twenty years of personal experience in the County. The last definitive attempt to do this was in 1923, when Sir Cyril Fox published *The Archaeology of the Cambridge Region*. Since then, and in particular over the last twenty years, there has been an explosion of information from the County. Many individuals and organisations have contributed to this expansion of knowledge: English Heritage has funded several surveys, most notably the Fenland Survey, led by David Hall; Cambridge University is involved in many aspects of research, and particularly through the work of its archaeological unit adds greatly to the County's archaeological record and its understanding; the Cambridge Antiquarian Society and other local societies keep the public informed about new discoveries; district councils protect archaeological sites through planning controls and help fund excavations. For the area covered in this volume, the published works of the Royal Commission on the Historical Monuments of England and the Victoria County History are a major benefit.

The County Council is especially proud of the role that it has played over these years in ensuring that everything that it has discovered is included in the Sites and Monuments Record for the benefit of all who are interested in archaeology, today and in the future. It is also proud of the lead that it has been able to take in the protection, excavation and wider understanding of Cambridgeshire's archaeological heritage. Alison Taylor was the County Archaeologist throughout this time and so is in a unique position to describe and make sense of the discoveries of these years. She has been helped in this by Christopher Taylor, one of Britain's leading landscape historians, who has lived and worked in South Cambridgeshire since the 1960s and has an incomparable knowledge of the development of villages in the area.

The enormous archive that is the Sites and Monuments Record is the basis for the present publication, and much of the information from it is being published for the first time. New facts and ideas that flow from the Record give different pictures of the past to those seen before; much more remains to be discovered, but at least the outlines are clear. The past of Cambridgeshire is now better understood than ever before, and those that read this book will start to look at their surroundings in a very different way.

Councillor James McKay

Chairman of Cambridgeshire County Council

Notes on Illustrations

The following illustrations have been used throughout the text for decorative purposes:

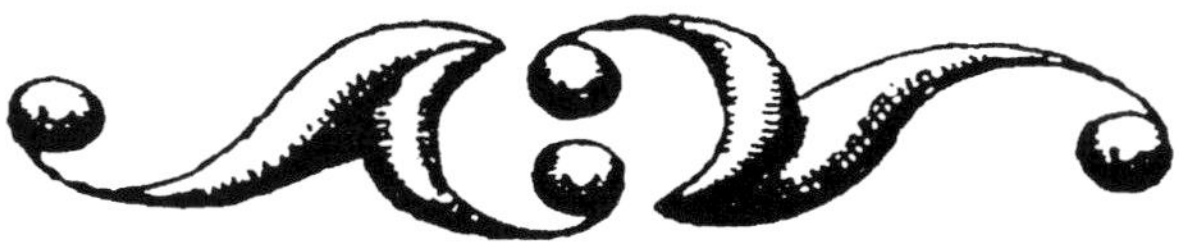

Embossed design on an Early Iron Age bronze ring found at Abington Pigotts.

Potter's mark found on several Samian cups and flat dishes found at Litlington. This pointed leaf was frequently used by the Romans, often as a point in the verbal division of an inscription.

Front Cover

An early Anglo-Saxon brooch, made of gilded bronze and set with garnets and blue glass, from the cemetery at Edix Hill, Barrington.

Title Page

Vignette of the Roman cemetery at Heaven's Walls, Litlington excavated in 1821, with the Icknield Way, Limbury Hill, and Barrow, in the distance.

Contents Page

Roman iron key, with bronze handle, found at Ickleton. Length: 120mm.

Acknowledgement Page

Roman glass and pottery vessels found in a Roman cemetery at Girton.

Maps

On village maps, the lighter shading represents the original village and the darker shading later development.

Unless otherwise credited, all photographs were taken by the author in 1996. As topographical records, they are printed as taken, without computer-generated alterations. The maps were drawn by and are the copyright of Sarah Wroot. Copyright ownership of all other illustrations remains with Cambridgeshire County Council unless indicated in the list of illustrations on page 136. Any enquiries regarding reproduction of illustrations should be directed to the Sites and Monuments Record, Cambridgeshire County Council, Shire Hall, Castle Hill, Cambridge CB3 0AP.

Acknowledgements

This book could not have been written without information being readily available from many sources. Some of these are published, and I owe a huge debt to works such as the volumes of the Victoria County History and the Royal Commission on Historical Monuments, to Cyril Fox's *Archaeology of the Cambridge Region* and Christopher Taylor's *The Making of the Cambridgeshire Landscape,* which are outstanding overviews of Cambridgeshire's archaeology, and also to the innumerable village histories and archaeological reports in which this region is so rich. Also invaluable are the records which the County Council keeps on archaeological and historical matters. The Sites and Monuments Record has descriptions of many of the sites discussed in the text; historic buildings are included in the Department of the Environment Lists held in the Conservation Section; the County Record Office has indexed the historic maps and other records of the County, and the Cambridgeshire Collection has compiled a superb library of local works and cuttings that are unobtainable elsewhere. Just as important as the collections are the people who look after them and provide help for the users. My personal gratitude goes to the staff in the Record Office, to Mike Petty, Chris Jakes and staff in the Cambridgeshire Collection and to Rob Walker and Chris Godfrey in the Conservation Section.

Many archaeologists and historians have been extremely generous in answering questions and supplying information in advance of publication. Details of the latest discoveries have been supplied by Tim Malim and his staff in the Archaeological Field Unit and by Christopher Evans and the Cambridge Archaeological Unit. Without these up-to-date reports it would be impossible to discuss many aspects of Cambridgeshire's past. The work of amateur groups and individuals who have reported their discoveries over the years has also been essential to anyone trying to piece together the odd fragments that archaeologists have to work with, and I hope very much that this book will encourage more people to report finds and observations to archaeologists in the County Council or to a museum.

Much advice on historic buildings and their present condition has been supplied by Beth Davis and John Selby of South Cambridgeshire's Conservation Section, and Michael Monk of South Cambridgeshire's Planning Department provided descriptions of the recent planning histories of the villages. Susan Oosthuizen gave me advance copies of her discussions on some villages, and Margaret Spufford helped with understanding population figures and other aspects of medieval history. The Godwin Institute for Quaternary Research supplied dendrochronological dates as soon as their computer could print them, well before they could be published. Cambridge University Museum of Archaeology and Anthropology was very helpful in checking descriptions and provenances of artefacts and supplying photographs, and the Cambridge University Committee for Air Photography not only provided prints from their vast collection but helped with selecting the best views. Kind permission was given by the British Library for the use of the Cole drawings and an extract of a map of the Chishills in 1769, by Cambridge University Library for the Childerley map of 1808, and Downing College for that of East Hatley in 1750. I am also very grateful to many owners of historic houses who allowed me to visit and photograph their homes and who always knew more about the buildings than I did. In addition, of course, this book owes an enormous amount to the map illustrator, Sarah Wroot, and above all to the editor, Christopher Taylor, who has contributed several sections to the text as well as supplying ideas and criticism throughout.

Cambridgeshire County Council gratefully acknowledges the financial support made towards this publication by South Cambridgeshire District Council.

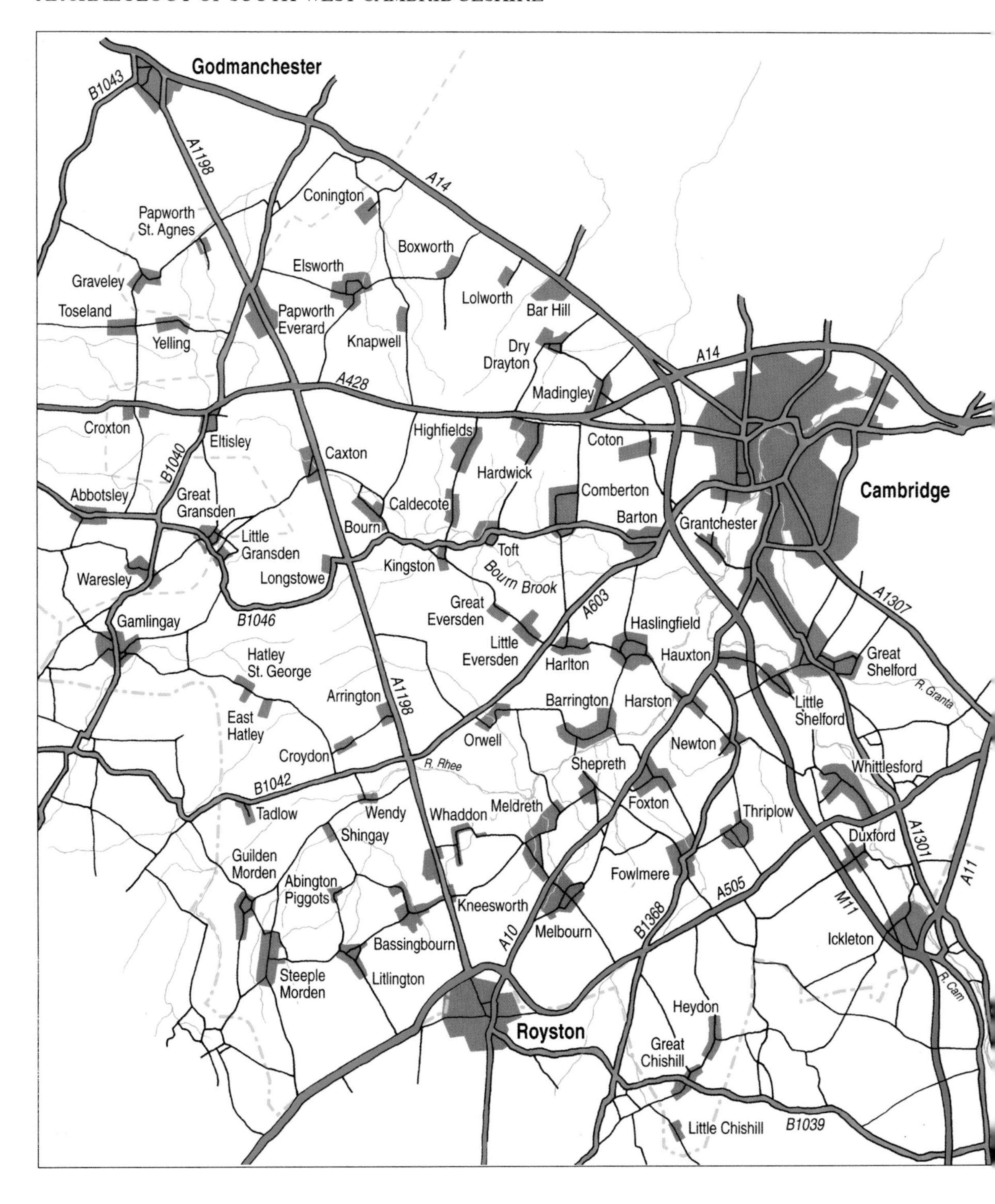
Godmanchester
B1043
A1198
A14
Conington
Papworth
St. Agnes
Boxworth
Elsworth
Graveley
Lolworth
Bar Hill
Toseland
Papworth
Everard
Yelling
Knapwell
Dry
Drayton
A14
A428
Madingley
Croxton
Eltisley
Highfields
Coton
B1040
Caxton
Hardwick
Cambridge
Comberton
Abbotsley
Great
Gransden
Caldecote
Barton
Little
Gransden
Bourn
Grantchester
Toft
Kingston
Waresley
Longstowe
Bourn Brook
A1307
Great
Eversden
A603
Gamlingay
B1046
Haslingfield
Little
Eversden
Hauxton
Great
Shelford
Harlton
Hatley
St. George
R. Granta
Arrington
A1198
Barrington
Harston
Little
Shelford
East
Hatley
Orwell
Newton
Croydon
Whittlesford
R. Rhee
Shepreth
B1042
Foxton
Meldreth
Tadlow
Wendy
Whaddon
Thriplow
Duxford
Shingay
A1301
Guilden
Morden
Fowlmere
A11
A505
Abington
Piggots
M11
Kneesworth
B1368
A10
Melbourn
Ickleton
Bassingbourn
Steeple
Morden
Litlington
R. Cam
Heydon
Royston
Great
Chishill
Little Chishill
B1039

Introduction

South-west Cambridgeshire today is a prosperous rural area with good communications to the outside world and between its villages, much as it has been throughout its history. It is well-served by towns close by on each side, but there have never been more than country markets within its borders, and, apart from the short-term upheavals of coprolite mining in the late 19th century and modest pottery kilns in Roman times at Harston, industrial activity has been restricted to serving the needs of the local population. Fortifications exist, but the Iron Age and Saxon dykes, (Mile Ditches and Bran Ditch), have been ploughed away, and the castles at Bourn, Caxton, Bassingbourn and especially at Knapwell are hardly imposing monuments. What we *are* able to see and study in this area, however, are the effects of stable agricultural populations who have filled even inhospitable tracts of land, and who, over the last five millennia, have left distinctive traces of every culture whose people have travelled, fought, worshipped, buried their dead, hunted, ploughed, fed their animals and, above all, created the living villages which are their best memorial.

Geology

The region is generally well-watered by the Cam, the Rhee, the Bourn Brook and many tributaries of these rivers. Spring-lines between chalk and clay sub-soils where most of the tributaries begin are favoured areas for settlement, and so, to an even greater extent are the river valleys. Here, light gravel and alluvial soils and good communications at crossing places have led to concentrations of farms and villages from prehistoric times until the present day. Chalk soils in the south were settled only where water supplies were available, but the open aspect of this countryside was valuable for sheep grazing, for which it was famous until the mid 19th century, and above all it enabled long-distance travellers and traders to cross the region from east to west,

Icknield Way at Heydon.

using numerous parallel tracks that are known collectively as the Icknield Way, the long-distance route that linked Berkshire to the Wash from prehistoric times. Clay soils in the north and west of the region are naturally less hospitable than river gravels, but as populations rose in Late Iron Age and Roman times their potential for agriculture could not be ignored, and sites along routeways and streams were opened up. By the time Domesday Book was compiled in 1086 these clay uplands contained as many villages as any other areas, and some, such as Bourn and Wimpole, were among the most populous.

Transport

Rivers in this area were only navigable for very small craft, and the most important transport systems were roads and tracks. As we shall see in discussions on the early forms of many villages, the trackways that were used from prehistoric times could become decisive elements in the creation of medieval settlements and hence our modern distribution pattern. The major roads the Romans built for military and economic purposes continued to be important highways through the Middle Ages, were turnpiked in the 18th century and have become modern trunk roads. There is an important distinction in the effects of major and minor roads: villages (as opposed to towns) *avoid* major roads at all periods until overriding factors force their removal to road-side sites, but minor roads *attract* development, especially where they cross either each other or a watercourse. Once settlements are in place, networks of tracks are created for local needs, but the long-distance tracks and drove-roads that preceded them still had a role. In common with at least three-quarters of old routeways, many of these ceased to be recognised except as footpaths after 19th century Enclosure Acts.

Prehistoric

Our earliest archaeological finds are flint axes and other tools of Palaeolithic and Mesolithic hunter-gathering societies. These are now being found in surprising numbers, probably because the number of people able to recognise them has increased. In areas such as Gamlingay and Duxford collections of flint tools in fresh condition dating to Mesolithic times suggest groups of people stayed for some time, but usually there are only single finds. In Neolithic times, however, when agriculture and more settled communities existed, scatters of flint tools and waste flakes resulting from their manufacture are commonly found, most notably along the chalk grasslands around the Icknield Way, in river valleys and on patches of light soil such as the greensands of Gamlingay. So far, no house-sites have been found in the region, but at Melbourn there is a 'causewayed camp', probably a communal monument and meeting-place. At Bassingbourn another monument that may also be of this date has been noted from the air.

Distribution of sites in the Bronze Age is similar to that in the Neolithic. However, new types of artefact, most notably bronze tools, are found and round burial mounds or barrows are a common monument. Surviving barrows of this date can be seen at Ickleton and Melbourn, but several hundred more would once

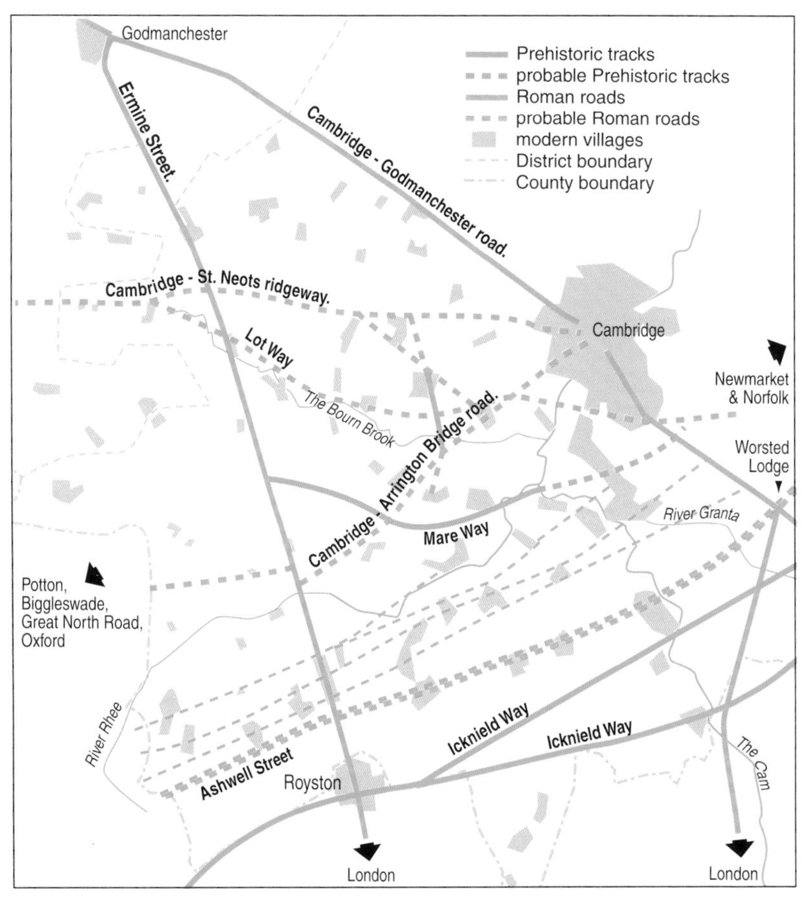

have stood on land that was of little use for agriculture, both in flood-plains of rivers and on the highest and driest areas in the region, along the ridges of chalk along the Icknield Way. These have almost all been ploughed flat, mostly in Roman times in the valleys and in the 19th or 20th century on the uplands. They can only be identified by the ditches which once surrounded them, as these can be seen from the air as marks known as 'ring-ditches', showing up in a ripening crop or as dark ditch-fill contrasting with pale chalky soil. Clusters of ring-ditches and hoards of bronze tools, perhaps left by travelling smiths, are common features along the Icknield Way. This is not just because of its use by travellers and the availability of uncultivated land, but also because the tract of open passable chalk countryside functioned rather like a river in the way it improved communications along its route but acted as a boundary to tribal groupings on either side, as it was to do again in Iron Age and Saxon times. It therefore naturally attracted statements of 'belonging' such as burial mounds though these may be distant from settlement areas.

During the Iron Age, areas suitable for farming, notably in the river valleys, filled up with innumerable settlements that are revealed on aerial photographs as sprawling complexes of rectangular enclosures, trackways, circular huts and ditches of unknown purpose. Some of these 'sites' cover as much as a hundred hectares and were in use over several centuries. Many span the years before and after the Roman conquest, though others seem to belong either to Iron Age or Roman times, for farming methods changed only gradually on this type of site. These large open settlements are typical of parishes such as Foxton, Haslingfield, Harston, Great and Little Shelford, Shepreth and Newton. They all appear to be purely agricultural settlements, practising mixed farming, with no indications of the kind of status or wealth which occur elsewhere in the river valleys. Abington Pigotts, Hauxton, Barrington and Grantchester, for example, all have sites where artefacts indicate trade with the Roman world towards the end of the Iron Age, and this provided some classes in society with items of luxury and status, most notably feasting regalia and wine-filled amphorae. These were of great importance in a society where wealth, military power and influence gained through lavish feasting and entertaining all went together. The finest example of this is the burial site at Barton, where amphorae and ornate iron 'fire-dogs' were found with cremations. This site also illustrates continuity of burial practise by the minority who were given ceremonious burial in the Late Iron Age, their cremations accompanied by Romanised feasting equipment, and their successors in the years after the Conquest whose burial practises must have seemed by then almost ostentatiously old-fashioned. This ostentation and deliberate archaism extended to construction of a huge burial mound

Crop marks of ring-ditches, pit-alignment ar Iron Age and Roman features at Harston, 1986 Photograph by Rowland Parker.

Excavation of a Roman barrow at Barton in 1908.

at Barton near the Iron Age cemetery in Roman times, and similar mounds were built by road-sides in Litlington, Bourn, Whittlesford and Girton.

Roman

Farming practises and cultural indicators such as upper class burial ceremonies may have continued in recognisable forms into Roman times, but there were many innovations that had enormous impact. It happens that all the Roman towns in this region, Cambridge, Godmanchester, Sandy and Great Chesterford, are just outside our area, but their effect is obvious in the parishes close to these centres, most notably Girton and Ickleton, and their markets brought prosperity and many new goods to the rural areas. Roads are the lasting legacy of Roman rule, but at the time perhaps the most impressive and influential signs of Roman wealth and innovation were the villas which were at the centre of agricultural estates. Villas excavated at Litlington and Ickleton were particularly large and magnificent examples, and others are known at Comberton, Guilden Morden and Shepreth. Substantial buildings, too, are found in several parishes. Residents of the villas required elaborate styles of burial, and major cemeteries with lavish grave-goods have been excavated at Litlington, Guilden Morden and Foxton. Even individual graves, such as the infant buried with figurines at Arrington, have much to tell us about the cosmopolitan society of the time.

Anglo-Saxon

South Cambridgeshire is one of the principal areas in Britain for the study of the early Anglo-Saxons, thanks to the remarkable series of cemeteries that has been discovered. The living population has proved more difficult to study than the dead, but huts have been excavated at Grantchester, Guilden Morden and Harston, and at least we now have enough evidence to show that Roman sites were often re-occupied or used for burial in Saxon times. Roman roads too must still have been usable, for many settlements and burial sites follow their routes. Anglo-Saxon burials begin in the 5th century, and brooches and other grave-goods of that date have been found in small quantities at Girton, Haslingfield and Barrington, and they became more numerous and richly furnished as the 6th century wore on. Burials of the 7th century are less common, but a few of the Barrington skeletons belonged to this date, and so did the whole cemetery at Melbourn. They differ from Roman burials in many ways and are generally more rewarding to study. For a start, virtually the whole community used the same cemetery, from new-born babies to the very old, and from the wealthy to those who were buried with nothing at all. Even those with diseases such as tuberculosis and leprosy were not excluded. Thus the health and physique of the population as a whole can be assessed. Then, rather than being sent into the next world with a standard set of tableware and little that was personal to their own past lives, the Anglo-Saxons were dressed in their 'best-clothes', i.e. men were accompanied by their normal weapons, mostly spears and shields, and women wore jewellery and had personal items such as spindle-whorls, keys, purses, amulets and even, in two cases at Barrington, their beds. We can therefore study their daily lives more fruitfully from the archaeological evidence than is possible for other periods.

Cemeteries tell us something about the Anglo-Saxon attitude to the historical environment, for they often laid claim to the memorials of older societies by incorporating them into their own burial ritual. Barrington cemetery was built around a Bronze Age barrow, and that at Girton re-used a Roman burial ground. There were probably second-

Contents of a Roman grave at Guilden Morden. © Cambridge University Museum of Archaeology and Anthropology.

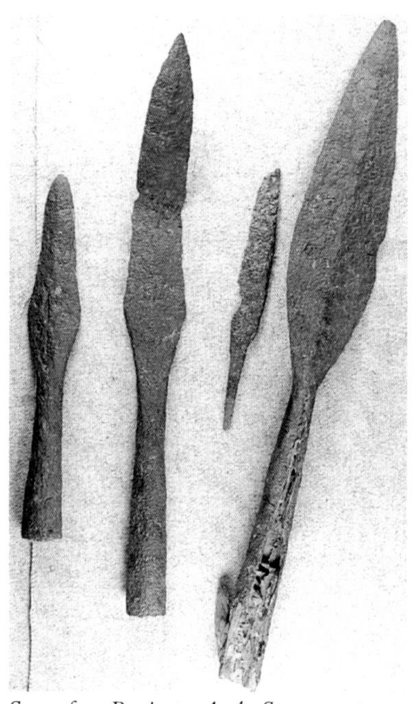

Spears from Barrington Anglo-Saxon cemetery.

ary Anglo-Saxon burials in earlier barrows at Barton, Whittlesford, Melbourn, Steeple Morden, Harston and Dry Drayton, in the cemetery at Guilden Morden and on occupation sites at Abington Pigotts and Wimpole.

Middle Ages

By the time Domesday Book was written in 1086 all the modern villages in our area existed, apart from Bar Hill and Camborne. The great majority of Domesday villages still survive, though Clopton, Shingay and Childerley are exceptions. Quite a few hamlets, however, remained so small that they never acquired a church and these tended to be abandoned. They include Grave in Elsworth, Pincote in Tadlow, Woodbury in Gamlingay, Whitwell in Barton, Wratworth, Whitwell and the other hamlets that once were included in Wimpole, and Malton in Orwell, which became deserted despite having a church. Many other hamlets that were closer to the parent village came to be regarded simply as part of that village, leading to sprawling settlements with many gaps. Most villages have changed size, shape, direction, centre and aspects of their character at various times since their Saxon foundation, but their overall stability and capacity to survive change is perhaps their most remarkable characteristic.

Population Changes

In 1086, when Domesday Book was compiled for William the Conqueror, who required an assessment of all property, including people, be made so that taxes could be collected efficiently, the average village population in this area was about 30 families. Figures ranged from 6 at Papworth St. Agnes and 11 at Caldecote, to 81 at Haslingfield and 76 each at Grantchester and Bourn. Parishes that were established on the clay uplands tended to be smaller in area, but the size of their populations was not generally less. Statistics for a few parishes are missing, and some twin villages are assessed together, but generally we have a remarkably reliable overall picture of society at this date. In 127 the 'Hundred Rolls' were compiled, again for taxation purposes. These are more complicated for historians to use and the figures given can only be approximate, and have not been attempted in several villages. However, those we do have are invaluable, for they record medieval society at its peak, before economic decline and a series of disastrously wet cold summers in the early 14th century led to famines, followed in 1348 and many years thereafter by the Black Death. They show that most villages had doubled their populations, and several had tripled them. Once-small villages such as Caldecote, Hardwick, Papworth St. Agnes and Little Gransden have

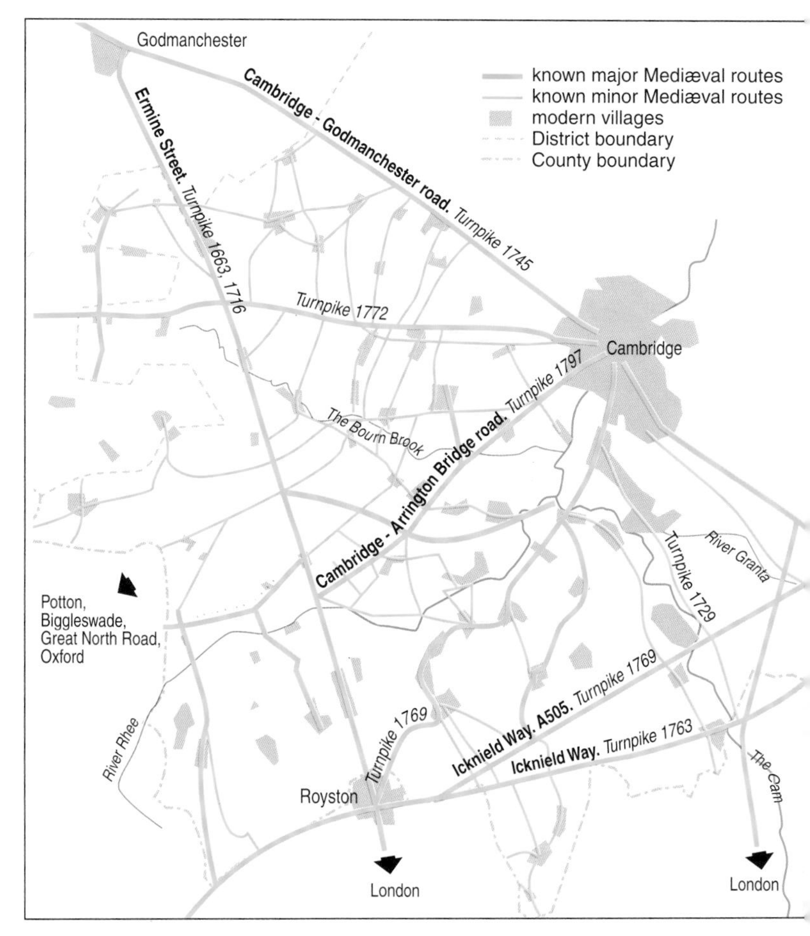

)articularly great percentage
ncreases. The land-hunger that we
ee reflected in documents at this
ime, and the way in which every
crap of land was brought into arable
:ultivation, tell the same story. In
nost cases, the 13th century populat-
on was not reached again until the
9th century, and the gaps we still see
n villages that peaked at this time
re often due to the rapid shrinkage
hat was to follow.

In 1377 a poll-tax of 4d (about
'our days' wages) from everyone over
4 years old was demanded, a tax
:hat was rigorously collected.
)utbreaks of plague had a variable
:ffect on different villages, but the
'igures compiled for this tax-
:ollection show steep and persistent
)verall decline. Now peasants could
afford to walk away from land that
vas hard to plough, as records show
hey did at Dry Drayton, for example,
vhere villagers left standing crops
and their belongings in moonlight
lits to find an easier living. This
mobility means that some villages
appear to suffer disproportionally,
but in fact some of their population
was simply moving to land that was
easier to plough or the landlord was
more generous. Over-population had
been so great in relation to means of
production that no village was
deserted at this time. However, if
labour was in short supply, land could
be converted to sheep pasture, and
sheep, indeed, became such a
profitable crop in the late 15th and
early 16th century that, once the
constraints of the medieval feudal
system had broken down in favour of
free wage-labour, parishes that
happened to fall into the hands of
particularly ruthless and enterprising
landlords certainly could be at risk.
Many complaints against enclosures
of parts of the open fields in villages
such as Kingston, Coton and Orwell
are recorded, and the villages of
Clopton and Childerley were effectively and permanently depopulated.
Less dramatically, many villages
contained successful yeoman farmers
who were able to buy up their
neighbours smallholdings when
prices were favourable, usually
leading to a lower but more
prosperous population later in the

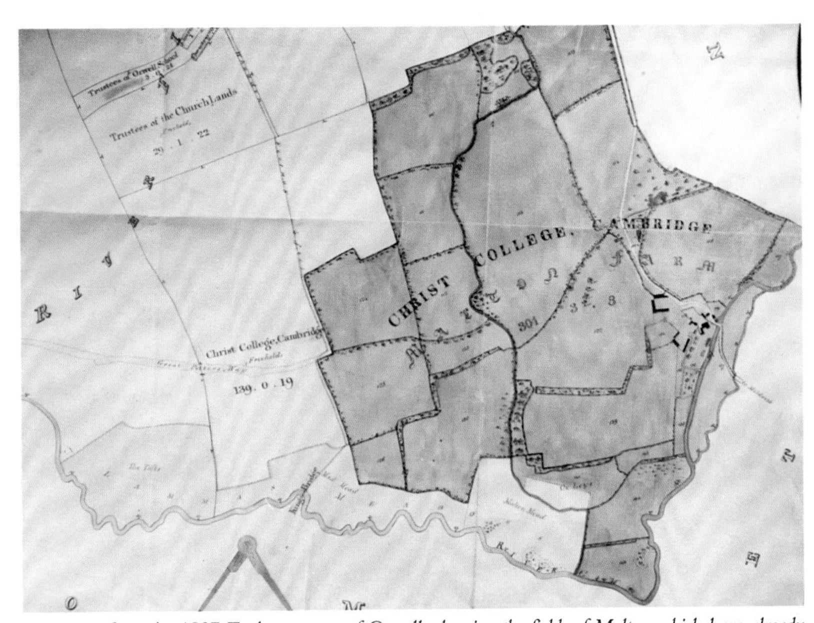

An extract from the 1837 Enclosure map of Orwell, showing the fields of Malton which have already been enclosed.

16th and 17th centuries. We see this process for example at Croxton, where 'ye meane men' re-arranged the earlier village.

Most villages were generally smaller, therefore, in the 16th and 17th centuries. The figures used in the Table (p. 121) are derived from the Subsidy Rolls of 1563, when tax-inspectors were notoriously thorough, and the Hearth Tax of 1664 when a similarly unpopular exercise was carried out. Improvements to crops and markets, and the end of Plague outbreaks after 1666, helped the population to grow a little in the 18th century, though the desire for large empty parks around stately country houses at Wimpole and Hatley St. George led to desertion of struggling settlements there. When the first census returns were made in 1801

Hatley Park, still surrounding an 18th century mansion, retains traces of ridge and furrow from the medieval village that preceded it. Photograph by Geoffrey Robinson.

View of Barton, drawn early in the 19th century by R. Relhan. Note the hedgeless open fields that are still farmed in strips before Enclosure in 1840.

most parishes still had a lower population than they had in 1279, and some were even lower than they had been in Domesday Book.

In the next 50 years there were dramatic changes, however, with most villages doubling in population. There was not necessarily a similar increase in area, for appalling overcrowding of cottages became normal, and the great majority of small properties in Melbourn, for example, housed two large families. An *average* occupancy of ten people per house was not unusual, and scandalous conditions existed in small rural settlements where space should not have been a problem. At Eltisley, even at the end of the 19th century, Rider Haggard recorded 19 people living in four rooms, with no out-buildings. These conditions contrast with medieval houses which were at least spaciously laid out in individual crofts, with single families that were normally of much smaller size. It is important to remember these differences when comparing village sizes through time, for a medieval population would have occupied a much larger area than a similar one in the 19th century.

Arable agriculture flourished in the early 19th century, when the Napoleonic Wars kept corn prices high. Later, though agriculture was usually very badly-paid employment, the population was able to rise, aided by modest improvements to hygiene with the use of soap and washable cotton clothes, and the Poor Laws which aimed to keep most people alive though in great hardship. In some parts of Britain there were now alternatives to a life in agriculture, but Cambridgeshire's towns did not grow until the mid 19th century and there were no large-scale industries until the coprolite boom of the late 19th century, and so the village populations continued to grow. Exceptions to the pattern of growth were some of the villages that were in single ownership, where the lord of the manor was able to prevent the arrival of incomers who may become a charge on the Poor Rate, employing instead labourers who could walk from more populous and less controlled areas.

Coprolites are phosphatic nodules that occur in the sub-soils of many parishes in south-west Cambridgeshire, from Grantchester to Abington Pigotts. They were a valuable fertiliser before artificial kinds were invented, and they could be dug very profitably in deep opencast trenches, a dangerous but well-paid employment. The practice was immensely destructive of archaeological sites, but, conversely, many important discoveries were made. The industry brought short-term prosperity to many villages, which is the reason some reached their population maximum in time for the census in 1871 rather than in 1851, which is nationally more common.

During these years the open-fields of the majority of parishes that were still being farmed in common, as they had been since Saxon times, were enclosed by successive Acts of Parliament. Knapwell was the first in this area, in 1755, and Eltisley was the latest in 1865. The Acts were initiated by the major land-owners in each parish who were able to override any objections by villagers and even institutional landholders such as Cambridge colleges. The great majority of villagers who owned strips in the open fields and had benefited from common rights, usually allowing them free grazing for specified numbers of animals and access to fuel in the countryside, were compensated with a few acres of land which was expensive to fence, and which most soon sold to wealthier neighbours. This radical change in land-ownership meant the end of the traditional peasant class in England, but it also led to many improvements in agricultural methods and productivity, and it coincided with a great increase in the agricultural population, though the various dates for individual Enclosure Acts do not relate to noticeable changes in the villages in question. Real threats to the agricultural community came with repeal of the Corn Laws and other measures that brought cheap food from the colonies into Britain, leading to rural poverty at a time when at last there were alternatives to life in a village. Girls left at an early age to work as maids in London and other towns and often did not return, and single men and families moved either to towns such as London and Cambridge, which more than doubled in size at this time, or migrated to America or Australia. Populations fell everywhere except for commuter settlements such as Great Shelford and Highfields in Caldecote, and this pattern mostly continued through the first half of the 20th century, exacerbated by depressions such as that which followed World War I. After World War II the pattern changed radically, with expansion of all the larger villages to cope with housing needs for a growing population.

Coprolite mining at Barrington in the 19th century.

Andrews' Mill, detail from a plan of land in Great Chishill, 1769.

Village Development

Villages were founded and grew in every part of south-west Cambridgeshire, but the exact location of centres of population within the various parishes was affected by factors such as the need for a water-supply, avoidance of major highways, availability of at least a patch of land that would not be flooded, and above all, it seems, by a favourable situation on the communication network. Many villages, therefore, are situated on either side of river-crossings or at road junctions. Major factors in their early lay-out and development are the existence of the multiple routes of the Icknield Way that ran east-west across the southern part of this area, and the north-south tracks to the north, running from the fens and the Cambridge-St. Neots ridgeway to the valley of the Bourn Brook. These routeways, which were not necessarily all in use at one time, are of great antiquity, particularly along the Icknield Way, where some must have been used in Neolithic times. They were created principally as drove-roads for the passage of animals, and became fossilised most clearly where they are constrained by features such as river-crossings or the avoidance of boggy areas, or where they were marked by historic features such as

Bourn, drawn by R. Relhan in 1819, showing the position of the village at a crossing place of the Bourn Brook. © Cambridge Antiquarian Society.

barrows, temples or later chapels. Where two such routes passed through a favourable site, a village may well have grown up, and as we shall see in discussions of the formations of individual villages, these ancient tracks often have a decisive impact on the design of early settlements.

Later in the Middle Ages there was often a change in the direction of routes that were significant, most typically to an alignment that reflected the increased importance of towns such as Cambridge and Huntingdon and the various roads that ran from London. Because there were already properties obstructing the most direct routes, many villages acquired 'dog-leg' turns, especially on their high streets. Elsewhere, roads had to incorporate balks around furlongs of open fields, leading to rectangular turns in villages such as Grantchester and Toft which have later been interpreted as evidence for a planned gridded lay-out. Small villages such as Knapwell might shift their lay-out completely when changes of route-way occurred, and many villages have late developments on main roads that are separate from the old village, an extreme example being Highfields in Caldecote, where the commuter settlement on the Cambridge-St. Neots road is now far larger than Caldecote itself.

Because all villages have had various periods of growth and contraction it is not usually possible to determine their original form, and in particular whether they have spread out from one nucleated core, or whether the forms we have today are a result of several different centres. Most of our villages now include more than two centres, often known as 'Ends'. In sprawling settlements such as Meldreth and Bassingbourn it is clear these are of medieval origin, though sometimes 19th century expansion and contraction could have a similar effect. Elsewhere, there are early centres further from the main village which have tended to disappear as the nucleated pattern became more normal. As the villages in this area usually belonged to more than one manor, this early pattern of dispersed settlement is unsurprising.

Later in the Middle Ages it is possible to see the direct impact of a lord of the manor upon village development. Apart from extreme examples where a whole settlement might be moved from the view of the manor house, it was common to clear a space for a small park in an area that might be the earliest part of the village, pushing the settlement into another area or permanently reducing the habitable locations in the village. This happened, for example, at Barrington, Dry Drayton, Newton, Haslingfield, Little Shelford and Whittlesford, and on a more ambitious scale at Madingley, Longstowe and Croxton. In other villages the lord obtained a charter to hold a market and fair, in the hope he would benefit from its revenues, and may then need to create a suitable market-place, preferably close to a through-route. This process led to a decisive dislocation of the settlement at Caxton, and also changed the pattern at Kingston and Shepreth.

National trends have also played their part in village development. In the Late Saxon period land in many parishes was given to monastic houses, and these could prove to be energetic landlords who helped develop sizeable villages, including some in unfavourable areas, such as Graveley, Elsworth, Knapwell and Dry Drayton. At the Norman Conquest most manors passed into the hands of Norman lords, some of whom held huge estates based on

An early 19th century drawing by R. Relhan of the classical mansion and park that displaced the medieval village of Dry Drayton. © Cambridge Antiquarian Society.

centres at Bourn and Caxton. In the mid 12th century there was a period of civil war which we know as the Anarchy, when temporary fortifications were needed in parts of Britain, and it is likely that castles at Caxton and Knapwell belong to these campaigns. A very different period of unrest was the short Peasants' Revolt of 1381, following imposition of the Poll Tax. Interestingly, the ring-leaders of this revolt all seem to be minor lords of the manor, and their followers were mostly tradesmen and craftsmen, with few genuine peasants. Records show that their attacks were targeted against popular hate-figures, such as the Knights Hospitaller at Shingay, nuns at Ickleton, John of Gaunt's steward at Guilden Morden and Steeple Morden and the lords John Topcliffe at Meldreth and Thomas Walsingham at Great Eversden rather than at manorial lords in general. Following this revolt, records of which provide many insights into manor houses of the time, the defences of certain moated sites were strengthened or built on new sites.

In the 16th century Henry VIII separated the English church from Rome and used this as an excuse to dissolve all monastic houses, selling their property for his own benefit. Estates that belonged to the Bishop rather than the Abbot of Ely were mostly not affected, although Elizabeth I managed to take some of these before the end of her reign. The Preceptory at Shingay and the nunnery at Ickleton were closed at this time, and many pre-Conquest manors changed hands to the benefit of families such as the Hindes of Madingley and the Wendys of Haslingfield.

The Enclosure Acts of the late 18th and 19th centuries had a major impact, not only on the lives of villagers but on the countryside as a whole. Open fields that had been the basis of agriculture in almost all villages for perhaps a thousand years were replaced with the small hedged fields we tend to think of as traditional, and the road system was changed significantly, the majority of old tracks becoming merely footpaths, while straight roads were built to serve the new needs of each parish. Now that fields were individually owned, rather than each villager having scattered strips, farmhouses could be built away from villages in remote locations. Ancient landscape features such as Thriplow Heath and Fowlmere's Great Moor were lost, together with the sheep-walks that had characterised the region of the Icknield Way, but woodlands were generally safe, for they benefited the hunting activities that became an important part of the economy of the clay uplands. Several village greens, too, were lost at this time.

A defensive moated site at Guilden Morden, built after the Peasants' Revolt during which an earlier manor house had been destroyed.

In the 20th century there have been two world wars during which airfields were built, for example at Graveley and Duxford, together with an impressive cemetery for American airmen at Madingley. This century has also seen huge changes to village life, as the need for agricultural labourers has almost disappeared but the demand for homes for an expanding and mobile population is still relentless. Rural decline and depopulation were halted in the post-War years, and were replaced by the need for public authorities to limit expansion of employment and housing through the planning system, rather than encouraging it. The major factor behind this renewed growth was the car, for this made commuting to work and use of outside facilities possible in every village. Rail travel was also significant, especially later in the century when combined use of car and rail enabled many commuters to work in London. Other important factors in the exceptional growth of certain villages and very limited change in others, however, relate directly to deliberate planning policies. The first of these were expressed in the Holford Report of 1954, which stated that Cambridge's historic character and fabric were too important to permit any significant growth either in industrial development or housing within its boundaries or within a seven mile radius. Instead, population growth should be dispersed to the larger villages which already had good communications and which provided services for their surrounding area. Industrial development should be limited to scientific institutions closely related to the University, and commercial business uses were very restricted.

These principles have broadly been followed in later plans for the area, though the Town Plan of 1957 allowed expansion of a few villages that are close to Cambridge. As population pressures continued to increase, the same principles were used but the ring of villages which could grow was widened in 1965, and a new village was created at Bar Hill, specifically to relieve pressure on Cambridge. The same pattern of large settlements getting larger and small ones staying small was emphasised in the first County Structure Plan of 1980, and was given extra weight by growing appreciation of environmental issues such as protection of Conservation Areas and the rural character and charm of certain villages, most of which were very small, and also by attempts to limit commuting distances. At the same time, non-commercial businesses such as the University and other educational establishments, governmental organisations, public authorities and many other interests were growing or moving to the area, attracted to some extent by the lack of industrial development which should have limited population growth.

In the 1980s, the new Structure Plan allowed some relaxation of these restrictions in favour of high technology industries related to the University. There were also improvements to communications through rail electrification and opening of the M11, and the combined effects fuelled the Cambridge Phenomenon, a period of tremendous opportunities for expansion. In order to lessen journey-times to work there was now only supposed to be growth in a few centres close to Cambridge, but this proved unrealistically restrictive, and once again growth had to be accommodated by much the same villages. There was also said to be potential for two new settlements, but this proved very controversial, and so far, in 1997, only outline permission for one site has been given. At the same time, increased prosperity and demographic changes meant that households became much smaller, and so a village whose housing stock did not expand actually fell in terms of population, and village services were also declining fast. Very small villages were therefore in danger of dying, particularly where many of the houses were in estate ownership and likely to be neglected. There was some relaxation of planning policies linked with tough conservation measures that led to repairs to historic buildings, and these helped in the revival of settlements such as Croxton and Papworth St. Agnes, which had otherwise been on the brink of extinction.

At the end of the 20th century, therefore, the villages of south-west Cambridgeshire are flourishing and prosperous, and many have retained characteristics acquired over the past millennium. There have been dramatic changes in their economic base, ownership and the life-styles of their inhabitants, but their history is still visible in innumerable places and, with care, their individuality should still be strong in the years to come.

Abington Pigotts

Abington Pigotts, a small parish of 500 hectares, lies on almost level land between 25 and 30m above sea level. The northern third is on heavy clay; elsewhere the clay is overlain by chalk. It is mostly bounded by ancient water-courses. The open fields of the parish were enclosed before 1770 without an official Award being made. In Domesday Book its name is simply *Abingtona*, 'Abba's Farm', with 'Pigotts' being added from the 15th century after the acquisition of most of the parish by the family of that name.

Prehistoric, Roman and Anglo-Saxon

The only Iron Age and Roman site known from the parish was discovered in the late 19th century during coprolite mining. A large settlement situated on a local rise in the chalk north of the village, covering about 8.5 hectares, was found, apparently bounded on at least two sides by a bank and ditch. Numerous pits and hut sites were noted, together with finds which included weaving combs, a bronze ring with embossed design, querns, loom weights and spindle whorls, as well as large amounts of Iron Age pottery. Among the more notable discoveries of pre-Roman material were a gold coin of Cunobelin and a Roman coin dated to 9 BC. The site continued to be used in Roman times, and there was a huge scythe and part of a plough from this period, which are some of the very few agricultural implements known in Cambridgeshire. Fragments of human skull and one complete skeleton were noted. Since a knife and spear typical of early Anglo-Saxon grave-goods are also recorded, it is more likely that the burials in fact belong to that period.

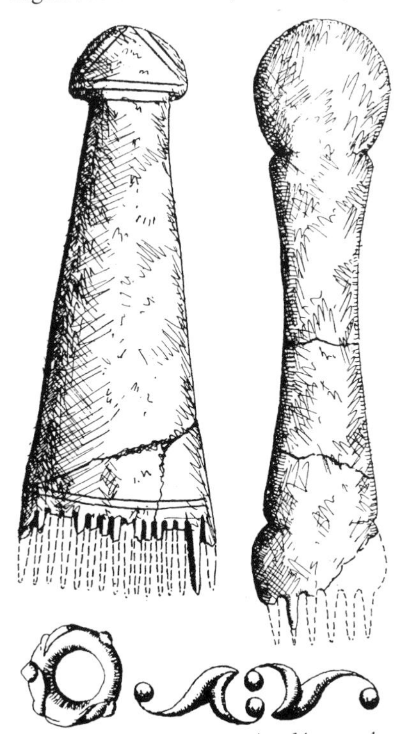

Early Iron Age weavers' combs of bone and a bronze ring with cast embossed ornament.

Middle Ages

Abington Pigotts is notable for its medieval moated sites, all of which appear to have been the centres of manors. Abington Manor, as it was known throughout most of the medieval period, originated as a pre-Norman Conquest estate held by the Bishop of Winchester. It later passed into secular hands and was subsequently acquired by the Pigott family. In the late 13th century, when the moated site was a widow's dowry, it was described as including a fishpond, moated six acre site, walled and moated enclosure, cow house and pig sty. The original manor house probably stood in The Rookery, a large sub-rectangular wet moat, with internal features that are probably due to 18th century landscaping, including a mound on which a summer house once stood.

In the 14th century the Pigotts built themselves a new house, re-using another moated manor house site north of the church. This had also been the site of a pre-Conquest estate, later known as the manor of Feugère. From its location, and the fact that the church lies in its curtilage, it seems likely that this may once have been the site of the original manor of Abington. The house was re-modelled in the 16th and 17th century, and the Manor was reduced to a farmhouse in the 18th century when Granado Pigott moved to Bassingbourn.

The medieval Down Hall Manor was centred on a third moated site well to the south-west of the village. This comprises two adjoining moated enclosures, most of which still survive. The existing farmhouse is of 19th century date, but the most notable aspect of the site is an impressive and highly unusual timber-framed gatehouse at the entrance to the second enclosure. It appears from the type of joints used to be a 15th century structure, but dating of a tie-beam using radiocarbon has given it a date range of 1250 to 1380. This gatehouse is jettied on two sides and has two entrance-ways, one for wagons and one for pedestrians. Down Hall Manor was in existence before the Norman Conquest, belonging to Alwyn, the Kings Crier who continued to hold it after the Conquest. During the Peasants' Revolt in 1381 William de Norton of Down Hall helped arrest rioters who had destroyed a house in Shingay.

Abington Pigotts Gatehouse.

Two other moated sites exist within the parish. One, Moynes Manor also stood in a double sub-rectangular moat, which is still well preserved and lies in Moyne's Wood, north-west of the village. Quarrels with neighbours led to the death of the owner in the mid 14th century, and in 1381 William de Moyne joined the peasants in the Peasants' Revolt, which involved much fighting in this part of Cambridgeshire. His possess-

Gatehouse, Down Hall Farm, Abington Pigotts. Reconstruction by John Bailey.

ions, described at that time, included 'an empty moated plot of 12½ acres'. Boybridge Grove contains yet another sub-rectangular moat, also well preserved and with no trace of internal buildings. This was the centre of an estate which in the 13th and 14th centuries was held by the Bibois family of Litlington.

Village Development

The village of Abington Pigotts, which was described in the 19th century as 'scattered but handsome', is now largely confined to a single street running south-west from Home Farm, with the parish church and Manor Farm well to the north-west. However, traces of former house-sites, paddocks and hollow-ways preserved as slight earthworks between the church and the existing village indicate that the village once lay in that area. It may have been deliberately moved or gradually shifted to its present site as a result of the expansion of enclosed manorial farmland before the 14th century, perhaps aided by the purchase in the early 15th century of most of the parish by John Pigott, a rich wool merchant from Hitchin, Hertfordshire.

The population was only 17 at Domesday, with 78 tax-payers in 1377. In the 16th and 17th centuries 24 and 18 households are recorded. This rose to a total population of 177 in 1801 and a peak of 259 in 1831. After this it fell to 197 in 1871 and 127 in 1931, rising only to 150 in 1996, because its poor service facilities and considerable historical interest and character have meant that planning and conservation policies have prevented growth.

In the late 19th century the parish was the centre of the most extensive coprolite working in the County. Much of the parish was affected, with eleven washing mills working at one time. Many of the back-filled excavations are still recognisable today.

Arrington

Arrington is a small parish of 550 hectares, on land which rises from 25m above sea level on clay soils in the south to a chalk escarpment 80m high in the north. It is bounded by the Rhee on its southern border and Ermine Street on the east. The village is on a spring-line at the base of the escarpment, with four streams flowing to the river. Most of the open fields in the parish were enclosed by the Chicheleys of Wimpole Hall in about 1680, though some fields had been enclosed from an early date. In Domesday Book it is *Aerningetun*, 'the farm of Earninga's people,' a place-name with the same origin as Ermine Street.

Roman

Apart from prehistoric worked flints found near the church the earliest finds from Arrington are Roman. A few pot-sherds were found in the extreme north of the parish and in 1990 a Roman burial was discovered when a trench for a water pipe was cut close to Ermine Street . The burial was that of a baby who suffered from hydrocephalus, wrapped in a pink and blue woollen shawl, lying in a lead-lined wooden coffin in which there were also small lumps of an aromatic resin, possibly myrrh. On top of the coffin a wooden box contained a collection of pipe-clay figurines of animals, children, a god and goddess.

The 'mother goddess' is seated in an upright chair and is a type normally found in Germany. The children are busts of an infant and a curly-haired child, of a type made in Southern Gaul and found quite widely in the Roman Empire. The seated figure of a naked boy pulling a thorn

:xcavation of a Roman child's burial.

rom his foot is a popular classical notif often made in marble. A cloak-ed figure of a god standing next to a ear appears to be Asiatic in origin nd is possibly Orpheus. The animals re two rams and a bullock, manu-actured in central Gaul, perhaps epresenting sacrifices which the :hild might offer on its journey to the Afterlife. The presence of this exotic urial in the Cambridgeshire :ountryside is perhaps to be explain-ed by Ermine Street, a major nation-al thoroughfare that would attract nternational travellers connected with military, commercial and civil service life. There are no settlements known in the immediate area but just to the south in Wimpole there was a Roman posting station for travellers.

Arrington Bridge is at the crossing-place of Ermine Street and the Rhee, which could be forded at this point. During construction of the modern bridge a gravel ford was found from which were recovered Roman pottery, a spear, knife, ox-goad and two hippo-sandals (Roman horseshoes).

Village Development

The village grew along the spring-line around the church, and hollow-ways and irregular earthworks here indicate its original site. It later shifted towards Ermine Street when that road became an important route after about 1200. Land was being enclosed at Arrington from an early date, probably by the Knights Hospitaller of Shingay who were given parts of the parish in the 13th century. In places ridge and furrow lies within small hedged fields, perhaps indicating old enclosures within which ploughing continued. In the 17th century Arrington became part of the Wimpole estate, and 18th century estate cottages, 19th century almshouses and the gates to the Hall were built in this parish.

The Domesday population was a low 17, which grew to 41 households in 1279. This had dropped to 20 families in the late 17th century and the population was still low at 190 in 1801. It peaked at 317 in 1841 and then dropped, before rising rapidly immediately after 1950 when temp-orary accommodation was provided for many families. After this it fell and stabilised at 370 in 1996.

Arable agriculture continued within enclosed fields in the 18th and 19th centuries and sheep also be-came important in the economy. In 1794 Vancouver, who documented the state of agriculture in every parish at this time, records that there was a 'very fair crop of turnips' here, and 'about 500 sheep of the common breed'. No crafts, apart from milling, are known, but in the hey-day of stage-coach travel in the 18th century the Hardwicke Arms served the pass-ing trade it brought and became known as one of the finest inns on Ermine Street.

The ford was probably the meeting-place, or *Moot,* of Arming-ford hundred in Saxon and medieval times, although the first mention of a bridge is around 1285. The bridge itself was essential to the national highway of Ermine Street. John Layer, writing in the early 17th cen-tury, states that 'Arrington Bridge is maintained at the charge of the County and is one of the greatest passages now in the kingdom'. How-ever, it was apparently not always reliable and it was fortunate the river could be forded. In 1662 'travellers and their horses passing that way in the time of the great frost and high waters are forced to go through the river to their great danger'. In 1663 the road between Ware and Hunting-don was the first in Britain to be made a turnpike, and a new bridge was built in Arrington. Two 18th century or early 19th century mile-stones here give the distances to London, Royston and Caxton.

Roman figurines found in child's burial at Arrington, 1990.

Barrington

Barrington, a medium sized parish of 914 hectares, is largely flat and low-lying, though the village is well above the flood-plain of the river which forms its southern border. The Rhee in this area was a serious barrier, for it often flooded and was marshy across about half a mile, so fordable sites near the village made the area attractive to settlers in Anglo-Saxon and earlier times. To the north-west a chalk escarpment topped by clay rises sharply to about 70m, where the ridge is followed by the route of Mare Way, the northern parish boundary. Its open fields were enclosed by an Award made in 1800. In Domesday Book Barrington is known as *Barentona*, or 'the farm of Bara'.

Prehistoric

Some of the oldest finds in Cambridgeshire are the prehistoric animals found in quarries at Barrington between 1879 and 1948. Dating from a period before the last Ice Age, approximately 100,000 BC, they included bones of hyena, bear, lion, wolf, fallow deer, red deer, bison, extinct forms of elephant, giant deer and ox, and the entire skeleton of a hippopotamus. The habitat of these types of animal indicate there was varied vegetation of the type created by the flood-plain of a river cutting through mixed forest. Pollen found with the animals included that of birch, pine, elm, oak, linden, alder, maple, hornbeam, hazel and willow. Small plants were typical of those found in trampled short grassland and damp meadows. In fact, although some of the animals found at Barrington are similar to those of tropical Africa, the vegetation suggests a cool, damp climate like that of today.

Artefacts of much later date include two Neolithic polished stone axes, two Bronze Age axes and a small hoard of two axes and a gouge. A Bronze Age arrow-head was found in a garden in Orwell Road and another was stuck in a wolf's skull. A small Bronze Age burial mound was found during excavations of the Anglo-Saxon cemetery on Edix Hill.

What were probably Iron Age farming enclosures have been noted as crop marks in the extreme north-east corner of the parish, and there are stray finds including five gold coins, an iron currency bar, and an imported 'Arretine' cup which indicate wealth and foreign contacts. It was excavations for coprolites on Edix Hill in the 19th century and recent work on an Anglo-Saxon cemetery there which revealed extensive Iron Age settlement. A wide deep ditch surrounding large pits containing Late Iron Age pottery and bones of ox, sheep, horse and pig was found in the 1880s, and in 1989-1991 numerous storage pits were excavated. These were separate from the area of habitation, and domestic rubbish was noticeably absent from them although there were single finds of a jet ring and a quern. Storage of grain on a large scale is a possible use for these pits. The most extraordinary feature, however, was

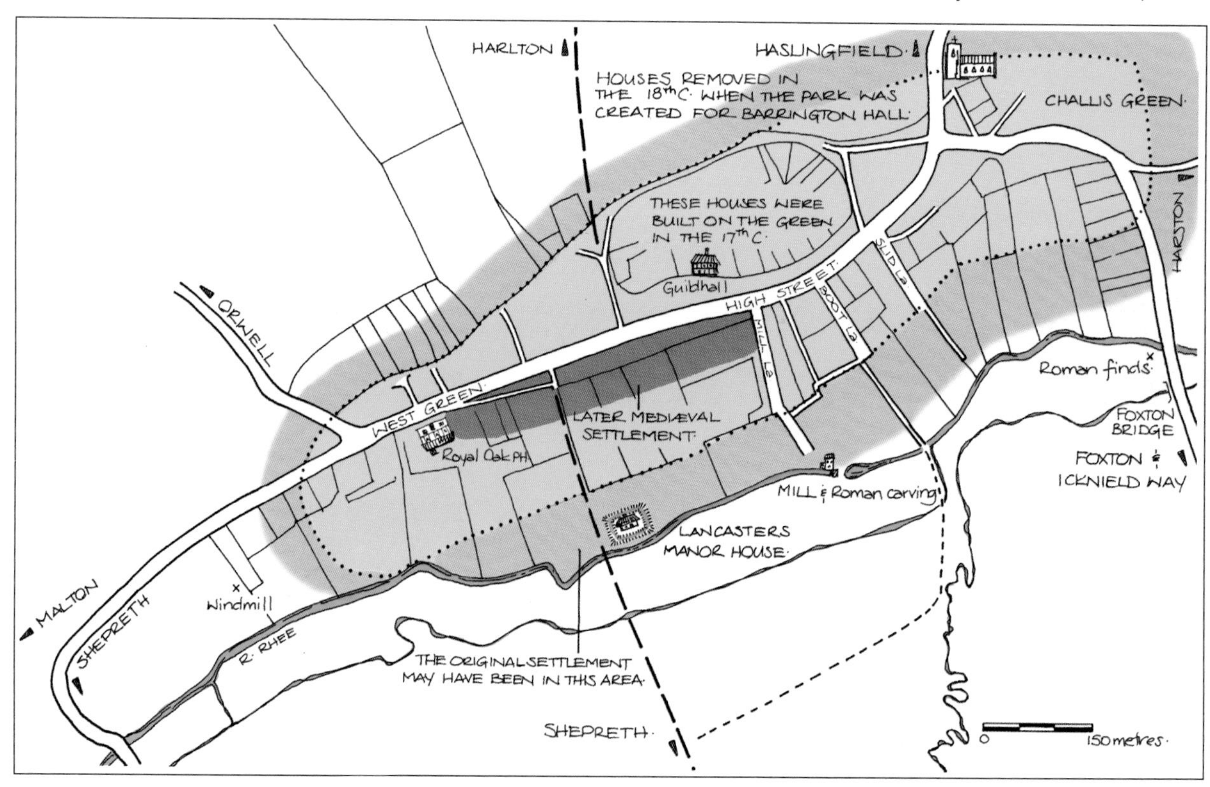

the ritual deposit of a complete dog skeleton, carefully laid out in a pit, with a cattle skull placed over its head. Elsewhere, enclosure ditches, trackways and buildings, with pottery ranging from 150 BC to 50 AD, were found. The scale of the defensive ditches, presumed specialised areas for bulk grain storage and the ritual deposit all point to a site more important than a normal farming settlement.

Roman

There were small amounts of Roman pottery and other artefacts on the surface of the cemetery on Edix Hill, and considerable remains of a Roman settlement were found at Barrington's other Anglo-Saxon cemetery, close to the village. Not far from this site, built into the foundations of a watermill, are carved clunch blocks from some large building.

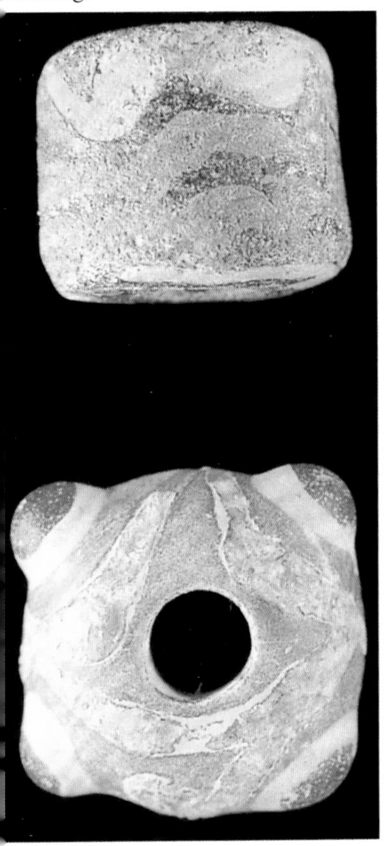

Anglo-Saxon beads from Edix Hill.

Excavating a woman's grave, with brooches and beads.

Anglo-Saxon

Together with its neighbour Haslingfield, Barrington is one of the most outstanding areas in Britain for the study of early Anglo-Saxon burials. Two major cemeteries were discovered in the 19th century and were noted with some care by antiquarians of the time, and one of these, Edix Hill, was recently rediscovered and more fully excavated.

Hooper's Field, just west of the village, contained 114 inhumation graves plus an unknown but probably quite small number of cremations, in addition to many that had been lost before recording began. The artefacts were not described with the graves in which they were found, but it is clear that many women were wearing clothes fastened by bronze brooches, often in pairs on the shoulder, and some also had their long sleeves fastened with pairs of metal wrist-clasps. Necklaces of glass and amber beads were common, and there were occasional bracelets and one silver finger-ring in the Roman style. Apart from belt-buckles, the men hardly ever wore jewellery, but were buried with the weapons they used in life and which indicated their status in society. On this site, fifteen men had spears and two of these also had a sword. Some were buried with their shield, of which only the central iron bosses survived, and some were supplied with food and drink in pottery vessels and wooden buckets. These burials dated from the late 5th to the early 7th century. None of the graves seems exceptionally wealthy but the average number and quality of the grave-goods is high, only about a quarter, including the children, having no surviving objects with them.

Edix Hill, close to the parish boundary with Orwell and on a high-point of the chalk escarpment, has had a long history of exploration starting in 1840. Coprolite mining in the same field must also have disturbed many burials that were not reported. Almost all the graves were furnished with grave-goods similar to those from Hooper's Field. Modern excavations began in 1989 and over the next three years 149 skeletons were found. Again, grave-goods mainly consisted of jewellery worn by women, some of it made with imported precious materials such as amber from the Baltic, garnets and ivory that probably came from India, and crystal from Central Europe. Men were commonly buried with a spear and sometimes with a shield, and often also had small items such as buckles, tweezers and buckets. Children sometimes had a small amount of jewellery or a pot, and most people wore a knife at their waist. There were two extraordinary burials of women lying in wooden beds with iron fittings. One of these women suffered from the earliest case of leprosy known in Britain.

Examination of the bones showed that the Edix Hill population was generally in good health and well-nourished, with average heights of 5ft 8ins for men and 5ft 4ins for women, similar to modern populations up to the 1960s. Practically everyone over 30 had osteoarthritis from their work and the effects of cold and damp in the open air and there was at least one case of cancer and another of tuberculosis. One woman in her 60s suffered from osteoporosis. Four men had head wounds, at least two of these being sword-cuts, and one had a spear wound in his shoulder. All had recovered from these wounds, so hygiene was not impossible. Dental health was good, though abscesses and tooth loss affected older people. Long term ill-health did not affect the status of one's grave-goods, the leper and a man with cancer having some of the most elaborate burials.

Middle Ages

Barrington has two surviving moated sites. One, Lancasters manor house, is south of the village, adjacent to the river, and was inhabited from the 10th to the 14th century, judging by great quantities of domestic refuse, including about 4000 potsherds and an important collection of iron tools, that was dredged from the river here. A moat standing in pasture in the grounds of Barrington Hall was presumably the site of Bendyshe Manor house. This manor originated when a successful local peasant, Thomas in the Willows, was able to buy his freedom in the 14th century. The house was replaced by the present Hall in the 17th century.

Village Development

Barrington's huge oval village green is still one of the largest in England. Originally it was even larger, but an area south of the High Street was built on quite early in the Middle Ages by houses which front onto narrow lanes running down to the river. It is possible that even the church and manor house, sited at the eastern end, were built on part of the older Saxon green. Two remarkable late medieval survivals are the 15th century Royal Oak public house on the southern edge of the green, and a 14th century house on the north. In or before the 17th century a large area was taken out of the northern side, and houses built there, but medieval houses along the northern edge were cleared in later centuries in order to give a more fashionable parkland setting for Barrington Hall.

A considerable settlement of 54 households at Domesday, Barrington had grown to 107 families in 1279 and 256 adults in 1377, though this figure dropped in the 16th century to 81 families. There were 348 people here in 1801, but the population then rose to a peak of 727 in 1871. After this it fell, but doubled in size after 1950 and in 1996 it was 990.

Its communications with neighbouring villages were good, and 13th century deeds record ancient ways to Haslingfield, Harston, Harlton, Newton, Orwell and Shepreth. River crossings, with two major fords and numerous foot-bridges, were an important element in the growth of this village. Foxton Bridge, on the site of a prehistoric ford, was on the route of ancient tracks to Icknield Way, and the Boot Lane foot-bridge led to meadows in Foxton that were used by Barrington cattle.

The village was one of the largest in the area until the 16th century, perhaps benefiting from a market and Michaelmas fair which were granted in 1252 and again in 1335. The market survived into the 19th century and the fair to the 20th century. Also important to the local economy was quarrying for clunch and chalk, recorded from the 14th century to the present day. The cement works opened in 1918, and in 1962 these were extended and have continued to provide employment. Coprolite mining brought temporary prosperity and doubled labourers wages in the late 19th century, one factor in Barrington's growth at this time.

Royal Oak on the village green, Barrington.

Barton

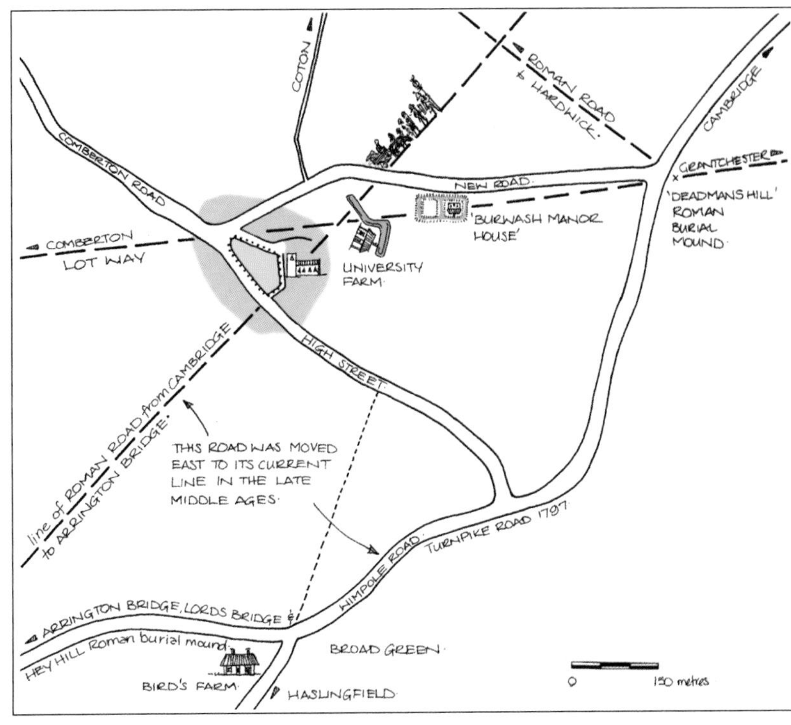

Barton, a parish of 724 hectares, contains a mixture of clay and chalk soils, with a small area of gravel where the oldest part of the village stands. The south of the parish is low-lying, especially in a once-marshy area near the Bourn Brook which forms the southern boundary. North of the village land rises to chalk downland up to 50m above sea level. It then falls into the shallow valley of the Whitwell Brook and rises to the Cambridge-St. Neots ridgeway, the parish's northern boundary. Originally the parish included two settlements, but the Late Saxon village of Whitwell had decayed in the later Middle Ages. The open fields were enclosed by an Award made in 1840. Barton's name in Domesday Book is *Bartona,* or 'Manor Farm'.

Prehistoric

Early finds are scarce, though there is a Mesolithic axe from Barton Hill, and two bronze spear heads come from this parish. Late Iron Age finds, however, are of exceptional interest. At Lord's Bridge, near an old ford across the Bourn Brook, cremations in urns and an imported amphora were discovered in the early 19th century, and iron slave chains and fire-dogs came from the same area. These finds are of a type characteristically found with chieftains' burials in North Hertfordshire, Essex, and South Cambridgeshire, dating to around 50 BC to 50 AD and are part of an exceptionally rich group of cremations characterised by imported luxury wares of pottery and metal, amphorae, and hearth furniture. These burials show the chieftains' close links with the Roman world, which gave them access to symbolically extravagant goods, as well as the more traditional importance of feasting and lavish entertainment as ways of exercising local control. Slave chains are not usually found in this context, but as export of slaves is known to be one way Roman imports were financed, and such an item would be totally alien in a Roman burial, it seems most likely they were in an Iron Age grave. Wheel-made pots and another burial were found near here in the early 20th century, and a bronze bull ornament of the same date came from the village.

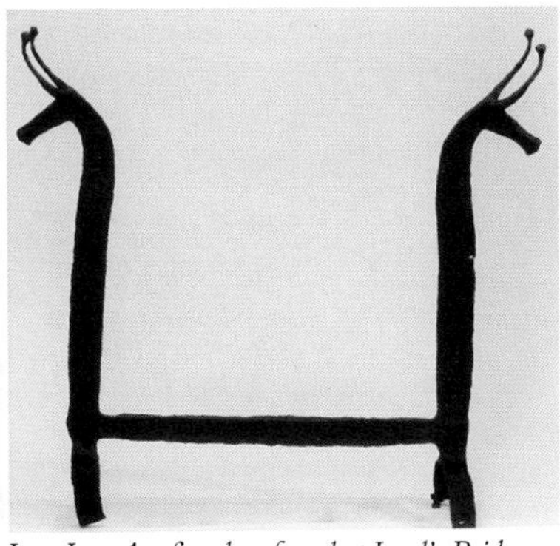

Late Iron Age fire-dogs found at Lord's Bridge.

Roman

The Iron Age cemetery site was re-used for a Roman burial mound, later known as Hey Hill, in which was found a Roman stone coffin containing a young woman with two bone hair pins, bones of a cock and a goose, teeth fragments of sheep and piglet, and fragments of a large urn. Hob-nails were found just outside the coffin. Another burial near the edge of the mound, found without its head, is later, perhaps dating to Anglo-Saxon times. The mound, which was a well-known landscape feature in the mid 19th century, lay at the junction of four parishes on a piece of common land and may have served as an official meeting place or *moot* in Saxon and medieval times.

One kilometre north of Hey Hill was another mound, Deadman's Hill, lying close to a Roman track. The mound was used for a windmill before it was levelled in 1839. Later, the ground beneath it was examined and a few human bones, Roman nails, fragments of iron, and Roman sherds etc. were reported in two separate and inconclusive reports. Other Roman remains from Barton are a bronze figurine of Mercury and finds from the moated site at Burwash Manor.

Two Roman roads cross the village of Barton, and the crossing place of Bourn Brook at Lords Bridge was also significant. Other old trackways through the parish,

Birds Manor Farm, Barton.

probably in use in prehistoric and Roman as well as medieval times, ran from Deadman's Hill to Hardwick, and from Hardwick across to Coton through Whitwell. The northern parish boundary is also on the line of a probable Roman road.

Middle Ages

A moated site consisting of two conjoined enclosures stood in a pasture field near University Farm until it was levelled in 1962. Excavations in the early 20th century produced an early medieval spur, two iron arrowheads, and pottery which indicated that the site was occupied from the 12th century. This was the manor house for the Burwash estate. In the late 16th century it was sold to the Martins, a family who had much land in Barton and Grantchester. Presumably it was this family who built the present house, now known as Burwash Manor Farm, an early 17th century farmhouse, timber-framed and plastered, containing a Jacobean plastered ceiling and fireplace. This house lies within a two-armed moat that was dug as a garden feature at the same date.

Village Development

The village of Barton itself was built around a green just west of a church, which is on the Roman road, in an angle where medieval successors of the Roman roads met. Later in the Middle Ages the Cambridge-Arrington Bridge Roman road was moved further east to the present alignment. Houses were subsequently built along lanes leading out from the green, especially running south onto the shifted road. Bird's Farm, for example, originally a late medieval hall and the earliest surviving house in the village, lies on this road.

In the medieval period there was a separate hamlet in the north of the parish known as Whitwell, which was situated closer to Coton than to Barton. It was arranged around a small green, and was a separate manor before Domesday. It lay on a track running from Coton to Hardwick and was still a separate settlement in the 16th century, with its own field-system. In the 17th century the Martins amalgamated all the fields into a single farm, whose farmhouse was soon the only inhabited building left.

Medieval Barton was a moderate sized village with a Domesday population of 31, growing rapidly to 85 households, 425 people, in 1279. This had declined to 25 families in the mid 16th century and the population only seems to recover by the beginning of the 19th century, with 219 counted in 1801. There was the usual 19th century growth, jumping to 418 in 1871 with an influx of coprolite miners before declining again by 50% in the early 20th century. New housing for Cambridge commuters led to growth, 1930-1970, when it reached 980 but since then the population has been slowly declining, to 810 in 1996. There were no separate figures for Whitwell, which seems to have been assessed with Barton.

Agriculture was the only industry apart from 19th century coprolite mining, even the usual rural crafts being uncommon in the 19th century. Land was nearly all owned by colleges and one family, the Martins, who amalgamated several holdings, which kept the population low after the Middle Ages.

Bassingbourn cum Kneesworth

Bassingbourn cum Kneesworth is a large parish of 1536 hectares, lying mostly on chalk but with clay along its northern edge. The villages are on a spring-line, with streams rising in Bassingbourn and flowing north to the Rhee at Wendy. A stream from a spring south of Kneesworth flows north through the parish and forms part of its boundary with Whaddon. Land rises very gently from 25m in the north, where there is a small area of fenland, to the centre of Bassingbourn village at about 30m and then to 60m along the A505, one of the lines of the Icknield Way, here forming the southern parish boundary. Kneesworth, originally part of Whaddon parish and not described separately in Domesday Book, was a hamlet by the 13th century and was formally joined to Bassingbourn in 1966. The open fields of Bassingbourn were enclosed by an Award made in 1806, and those of Kneesworth in 1842. Bassingbourn's Domesday name is *Basingaburna*,

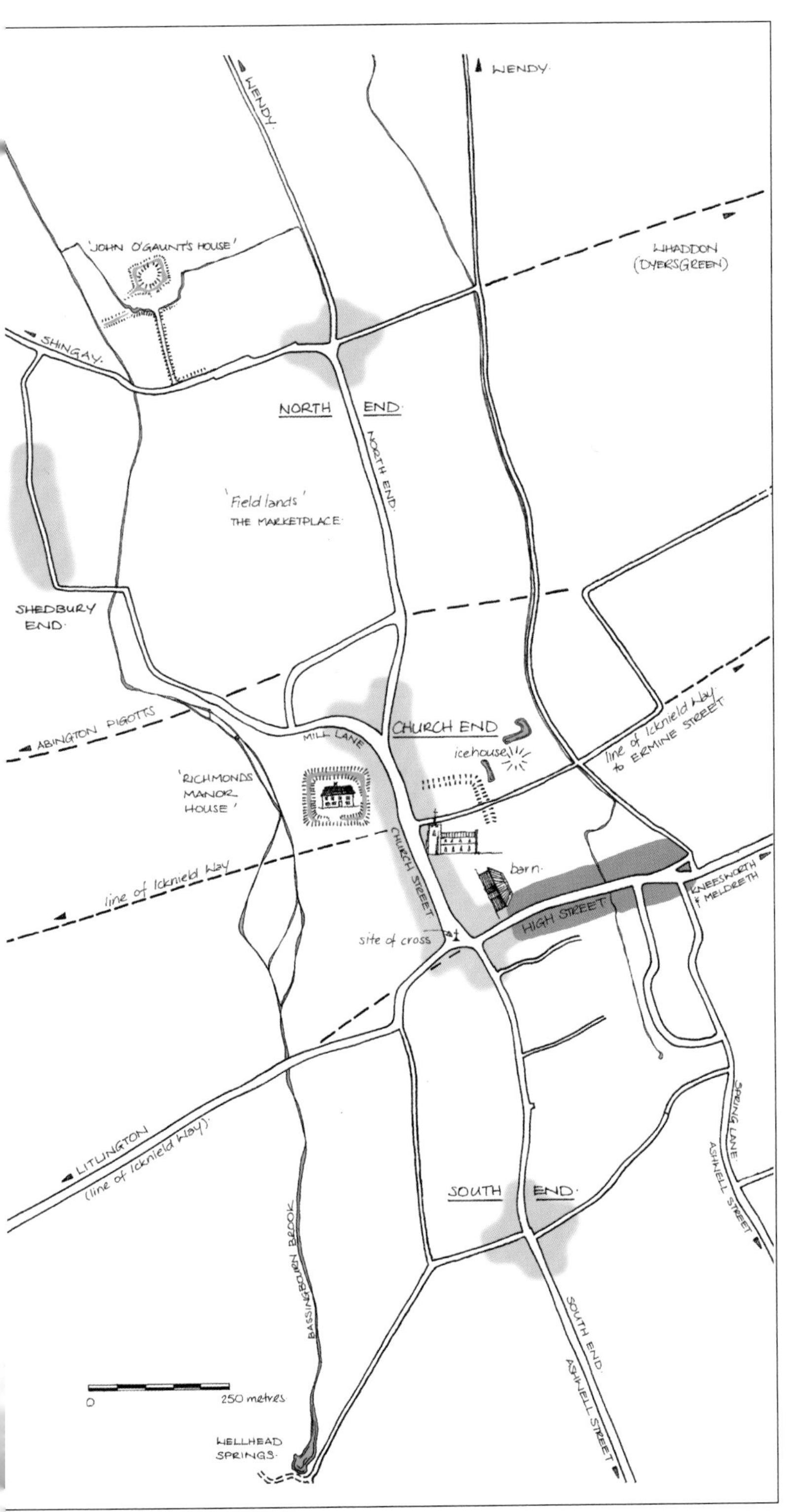

'the stream of the people of Basa'. Kneesworth probably means 'the enclosure of Cen'.

Prehistoric

Bassingbourn cum Kneesworth is crossed by remnants of the various tracks of the Icknield Way, including Ashwell Street which narrows to a single line where it fords streams near the village. These tracks were already in use as trade-routes in the Neolithic period, but the only find of this period is one axe. A site that resembles monuments of Neolithic date is a small elongated enclosure with parallel sides revealed by aerial photography. Bronze Age remains are more recognisable. At least thirteen ring-ditches indicating former burial mounds are known from aerial photography, a small hoard of two bronze axes and lumps of bronze perhaps belonging to an itinerant smith were found on the site of the aerodrome, and a fragment of a bronze rapier came from the north end of the village. Scatters of flint tools and debris from tool manufacture were found during field walking at Clear Farm, near Ashwell Street.

The Mile Ditches are three banks and ditches running roughly north-south that were built at right angles to the Icknield Way and apparently designed to block it. They are Iron Age in date and are similar to others found in Hertfordshire. They extend from an upstanding round barrow on

Soil marks showing the Mile Ditches, 1985.

Therfield Heath in Hertfordshire for about a mile and a half to the springs in Bassingbourn. The ditches, which were silting up from Roman times and were finally levelled in the late 19th century, can now be seen as massive dark parallel lines when the soil is bare. When excavated, before the A505 was dualled in 1978, they proved to be shallow, the largest being 1.2m deep and 3.5m wide, with a dark featureless fill.

Roman

A small collection of bronze objects found near Bassingbourn Mill to the north-west of the village contains a fragmentary hinge from military armour and a belt stud, uncommon finds in this part of Britain. A bronze statuette of Diana, found within the parish, is provincial in style, suggesting, along with other Cambridgeshire examples, the presence of a local workshop. It is a highly unusual example of a native figurine, presumably used in a simple domestic shrine.

Anglo-Saxon

A fragment from a 5th century Anglo-Saxon brooch was found in 1993, and five 8th century coins were discovered in the medieval market area north of the church.

Roman bronze statuette of Diana. Photograph © Cambridge University Museum of Archaeology and Anthropology

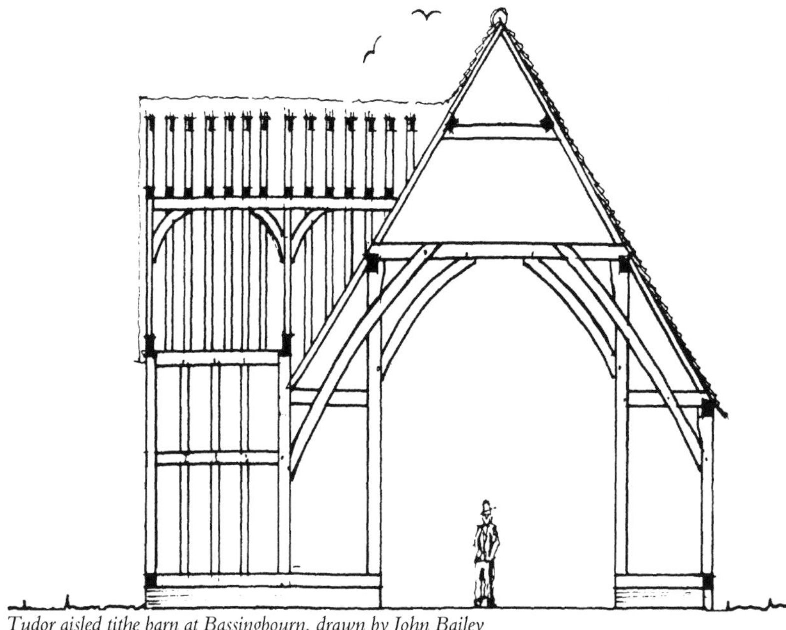

Tudor aisled tithe barn at Bassingbourn, drawn by John Bailey

Middle Ages

The fortified site now known as John of Gaunt's castle in fact belonged to Warin de Bassingbourn. A close friend and supporter of the future Edward I, fighting beside him at the battles of Lewes, Bristol and Evesham, de Bassingbourn was granted a licence to surround his house with a ditch and a wall of stones and to fortify it in 1266. It consisted of a large sub-rectangular inner moat, approached by a long causeway from the village, enclosed by a wide ditch that was filled by Bassingbourn Brook. In 1948 the Victoria County History recorded bastions, traces of banks, and spreads of brick and tile suggesting later buildings. The site had been much damaged by coprolite digging in the late 19th century, and has since been regularly ploughed. The only time that its defences were apparently tested was when it repelled peasants in 1381.

Richmond's, the manor house that actually *was* held by John of Gaunt in the 14th century, though never lived in by him, probably stood in the rectangular moated site north-west of the Church. In the mid 13th century this had been used as a residence by Peter of Savoy, uncle of Queen Eleanor of Aquitaine, and must have surrounded a prestigious dwelling. It was ruinous in 1436. A new house, with re-dug moats and fishponds, was built in the late 15th century and was empty by 1620. The well-restored Tudor tithe barn near the church belonged to this manor.

The area known as the Old Mount, now an infilled pond and rubbish tip, was once an ice house for the Pigott family of Abington Pigotts, who moved to Bassingbourn and rebuilt the parsonage house north of the church in the 1740s.

A fragmentary moated site next to Ermine Street at North Farm, Kneesworth, is all that remains of Chamberlain's manor house. The bankrupt estate was bought in about 1600 by Geoffrey Nightingale, who had acted as both lawyer and steward and was regarded with great and justifiable suspicion by his former clients. He moved the estate centre to Kneesworth Hall, which he substantially rebuilt. His family acquired most of the parish and held it until the 19th century.

Village Development

Bassingbourn is a somewhat scattered settlement with hamlets at North End, South End, Church End and Shadbury End (formerly Shadborough, *'decayed'* by 1640), but the main body of the village, the High Street, is a planned two-row settlement along a track of the Icknield Way. It is on an area marginally higher than surrounding land and was well served by Bassingbourn Brook and numerous springs. Church Street, running north-south, became important later in the Middle Ages, with the growth of the market. In 1395 a cross stood where it met the High Street. A large sub-rectangular field to the north of Richmond's manor house was the site for a market. The grant for this market and for an eight-day fair was given to Peter of Savoy in the 13th century, but the site's commercial use may be considerably older than this. Bassingbourn's large and impressive church also stands near the main manor, north of the village centre.

The hamlet of Kneesworth also originally lay on the line of Ashwell Street, but it seems to have moved west to Ermine Street, and changed its axis to north-west, quite early in the Middle Ages, presumably because of developing traffic along the main road.

Bassingbourn has always had the largest population of villages in its area. At Domesday there were 39 inhabitants recorded, and 347 poll-tax payers in 1377. There were 90 households in the 16th century, rising to about 700 people in 1600. Figures fluctuated greatly after this until 1801, when there were 828, rising to a peak of 1710 in 1871. After this it declined until the 1950s, but then rose rapidly, having good provision of schools, shops and other facilities in addition to Bassingbourn Barracks and a favourable situation for road transport. In 1996 the population, with service families and Kneesworth, but without parts of the parish which were transferred to Royston in 1897, was 3530. Kneesworth had 76 poll-tax payers in 1377, but only about 16 households in the 16th and 17th centuries. In 1801 there were 120 inhabitants, and the population reached a peak of 200 in 1861.

These population figures show that from the later Middle Ages until the 18th century Bassingbourn was growing into a semi-urban centre. Cultural activities, such as the Bassingbourn St. George Play, which involved the whole neighbourhood in preparations and festivities in the early 16th century, and the variety of occupations of villagers in medieval and later times, also show Bassingbourn serving a wide area. In the 17th century, however, its smaller neighbour, Royston, was growing to a similar size, and by 1801 it was considerably larger. Royston had been a planned town from the 12th century, and, although only half the size of Bassingbourn in the early 16th century, its position at the crossing of Icknield Way and Ermine Street and on the County boundary helped its successful medieval markets develop into a fully urban centre. Bassingbourn could not compete with this market and, although it continued to be a large settlement, especially in the later part of the 19th century when coprolite mining provided employment and higher wages, it did not develop urban characteristics.

Bourn

Bourn, a large parish of 1658 hectares, lies mainly on clay and is bisected by the upper reaches of the Bourn Brook, which flows through the centre of the village. The land rises on either side of this brook to 70m, with a high plateau to the north. It is bounded by Roman Ermine Street on the south-west, by the Cambridge-St. Neots ridgeway in the north, and by Porters Way and Kingston Wood in the south-east. The open fields were enclosed by an Award made in 1820. Known in Domesday Book as *Brunna*, Bourn simply means 'stream'.

Roman

There are a number of finds of Roman pottery in the parish and, during the dry summer of 1995, aerial photographs also revealed five sites to the north where crop marks of enclosures indicate farmsteads that are likely to be of this date. The most important Roman sites, however, are three circular mounds known as Moulton Hills, sited at an old cross-roads in the north end of

Bourn Hall in 1990, showing the moat of the Norman castle. Aerial photograph by Geoffrey Robinson.

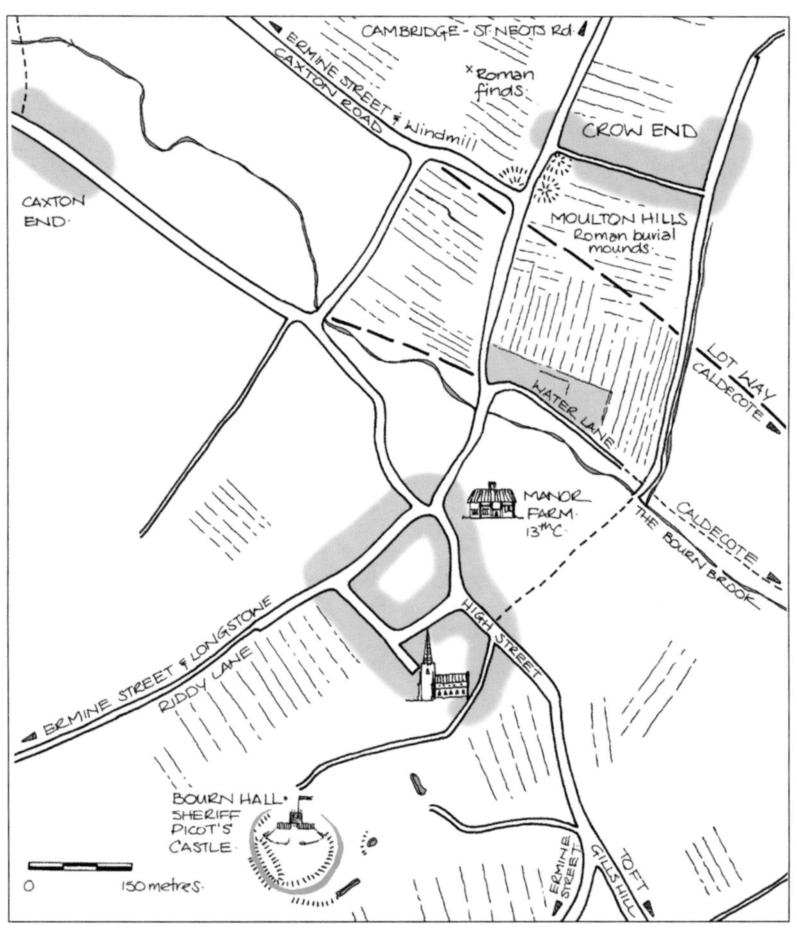

the village. In 1909 two of the mounds were trenched and much Roman material found, including buckles, pins, nails, a knife, animal and human bones, pottery, loom-weights and whetstones, as well as extensive traces of burnt wood. This evidence suggests that these mounds originally contained Roman burials which are consistent with many cremation burials from Eastern England, characterised by their occurrence with nails, bronze fragments and burnt wood (derived from boxes), single Roman coins, animal bones including fowl and 'feasting debris'. However, the excavations also revealed late Saxon pottery and later medieval millstones. These perhaps indicate that at least one of the mounds was re-used for a medieval windmill and that there was also earlier medieval activity in the area.

Finds of Roman coins and pottery nearby might mean there was a Roman settlement in the vicinity.

Another probable Roman cemetery was discovered during the construction of Bourn airfield in the north of the parish in 1941. At least one stone coffin (now at the Cambridge Museum of Archaeology and Anthropology) was recovered and other burials were said to be found with it, all probably close to the Cambridge-St. Neots road.

In addition to the Roman roads which form the parish boundaries, a Roman track, the Lot Way, runs from Grantchester and seems to cross Bourn in an east-west direction, passing Moulton Hills.

Middle Ages

Land in Bourn was given to Ramsey Abbey in about 985, and there may well have been an important estate there, for Bourn was granted to Picot, one of William's leading followers and sheriff of Cambridge after the Conquest, and was used as the centre for his numerous estates in South Cambridgeshire. Not a popular man, he also needed a secure retreat. He built a somewhat unusual type of defensive site, a massive ring-work, or circular rampart, with an attached bailey. Originally both were complete circuits surrounded by banks and ditches and they covered most of a low hill-top. They are now much disturbed by outbuildings of Bourn Hall and ornamental gardens. The ditch, once water-filled, is now mostly dry. Its greatest surviving dimensions are 15m wide by 3m deep and the large ring-work is approximately 150m in diameter. A sketch in a mid-18th century manuscript shows a berm between bank and ditch.

In the 16th century the Haggars, a local family made wealthy through wool, built a grand house on the site, selling it to the Leyalls, who already owned the manors at Haslingfield and Harston, in 1733. Their heirs, the Earls de la Warr, rebuilt Bourn Hall on a grand scale, re-using materials from Haslingfield Hall, which they had demolished, and landscaping the grounds. In the late 19th century the Briscose family undertook more building works, and the Hall was renovated in the 1960s. In 1985 it became Bourn Hall Clinic, well known for work on test tube babies.

An estate in Bourn was given to Barnwell Priory near Cambridge, the

Bourn Post-mill.

:rown giving this to Christ's College .t the Dissolution. Barnwell's manor ouse was at Manor Farm, within vhose brick exterior is a 13th century imber-framed hall, thought to be uilt soon after 1266 when support- rs of Simon de Montfort had burnt he Prior's house.

Probably Bourn's best known nonument is its windmill, the second ldest in England, narrowly beaten y Great Gransden. It is a post-mill, ecorded in 1636 though its machin- ry is 19th century. The mill has been estored several times and is kept in vorking order by Cambridge Preser- ation Society.

Village development

The village of Bourn comprises hree principal elements. The main art, together with the parish church, ies south-west of the stream and has he remains of a simple grid of treets, which might suggest an early nedieval planned origin. To the orth of the stream is Crow End, a amlet of farms and cottages scatter- d along two roughly parallel lanes, while to the west is an irregular group of dwellings known as Caxton End. Evidence of former buildings at oth these latter places suggests they were both once larger.

Bourn was a large village through the Middle Ages. At Domesday it already had 76 households, and by 1279 this had risen to a minimum of 183 families, or about 900 people, which is one reason why there are now so many gaps within the village. There were only 299 adults taxed in 1377, and in 1728 the population was 400, rising, despite some emigration to America, to 973 in 1871. It then fell considerably before squatters used an airfield after World War II, increasing the population to 1050. Some squatters were later housed in new estates in the village, and in 1996 the total population was at the same figure.

In the 16th century much of the parish was consolidated in the hands of the Haggar family, who then lived at Bourn Hall. Arable farming continued the predominant activity, but by the early 16th century the Haggars were also the largest wool-growers in Cambridgeshire. The village was big enough to support several craftsmen and tradespeople, with two blacksmiths, two millers, a butcher, a tailor, a shoemaker, a cooper, a plumber and two shop-keepers recorded in 1851, and the village at this time is described as 'handsome and pleasantly situated, but much scattered'.

On a stretch of Ermine Street near Bourn two merchants were murdered in the 13th century. Major medieval roads such as this had to be cleared back from the road for 200ft to prevent robbers hiding there, a clearance still visible as wood-banks in Bourn Wood, though trees have encroached again near the road.

Boxworth

Boxworth, a medium sized parish of 1053 hectares, lies on clay soil that rises gradually from 14m in the north to a 50m high plateau where the village is situated, and then to 80m in the south. The parish lies between one probable and one definite Roman road, the Cambridge-St. Neots ridgeway and the Cambridge-Godmanchester road. A small stream runs through the village, and water is retained in moats and ponds. Boxworth's open fields were enclosed by an Award made in 1843. Its name in Domesday Book is *Bocheuuord*, or 'Bucc's Enclosure'.

Roman

There is little trace of early settlement in the parish, but a Roman gold coin of the 1st century

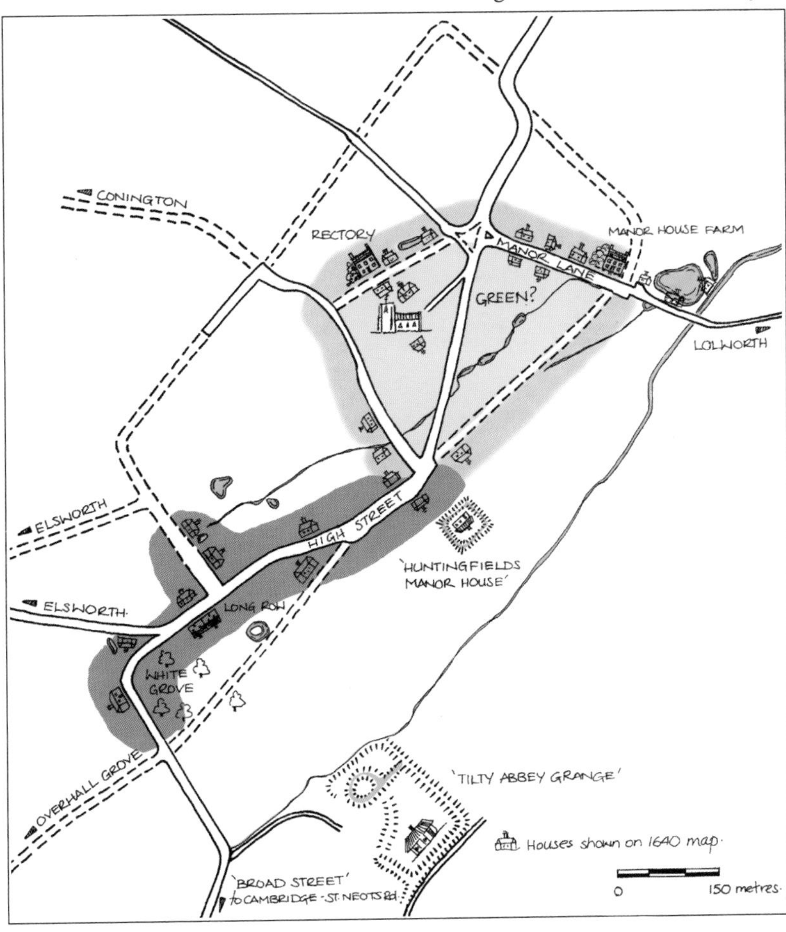

Boxworth church, drawn by R. Relhan in the early 19th century, before extensive restoration work in 1868. © Cambridge Antiquarian Society.

AD was ploughed up in the 19th century, and a 4th century single coin and a hoard of 1st-2nd century date are reported. Possible Roman sherds come from the medieval site of Overhall Grove.

Middle Ages

Overhall Grove is an impressive medieval monument hidden in trees on the edge of the parish, next to Knapwell. The site was the manor house for Overhall, the largest manor in Boxworth, in existence in 1086 although not known by this name until the late 15th century. In the 13th and 14th centuries it was held by the de Boxworth family, who built a chapel and held their manor court here, but it then passed by marriage to a Buckinghamshire family and, judging from the pottery evidence, was no longer an important residence. The antiquarian John Layer describes it as 'a scite decayed' in the early 17th century. The moat is roughly rectangular, with a ditch as much as 3m deep in places and still partly water-filled, with a slight outer bank. It is surrounded on three sides by a double-ditched enclosure, which also encloses two rectangular fishponds. Badgers regularly dig up large sherds of medieval pottery, indicating pits rather than casual rubbish. In recent field-walking some 200 of these sherds were collected, mostly of the 13th to 14th century, including several glazed sherds. In 17th century, when the Cutts family of Childerley, who owned most of Boxworth, had a map made of their estate, Overhall Grove was shown as a wood, with the same boundaries as today.

A smaller well-preserved moat, mostly still wet and, like Overhall Grove, with an outer enclosure, lies in Grange Wood just south of the village. This was the site of the grange of Tilty Abbey in Essex, owners of a small estate in Boxworth. It was first documented in about 1300. Tiles on the site suggest there was also a much later building, but in 1640 it was known as Grange Wood.

Another moat in the village existed until the 1960s but was then in-filled and ploughed. This was the manor house of Huntingfields, named after the family who were lords of a manor here from the early 13th to late 14th century. The land was originally a Saxon estate that was taken over by Picot, sheriff of Cambridge. In the mid 16th century it was sold to Thomas Hutton, with most of the rest of the village. In the 17th century, the manor house was probably moved to the present Manor House Farm, a 17th century brick building that was remodelled in the 18th century.

Village Development

Apart from the out-lying moats in Overhall Grove and Grange Wood, the medieval village, a considerable size at Domesday and in the 13th century but not developing after this, was probably mainly built around a green near the church, with a manor house in Huntingfields Moat in the south-west corner. The High Street ran from present Manor House Farm south of the present High Street to Huntingfields moat. One fork carried on to Overhall Grove and Knapwell and another to the Cambridge-St. Neots road. A road to the west of the village ran behind the church and out to Elsworth. Field roads to Lolworth and Conington can still be traced. The road leading to the Cambridge-Godmanchester road, which became a turnpike road in 1745, was not built until after Enclosure, and its new route within the village cut through the old village green. By the 17th century the village consisted of about a dozen cottages on the north and west side of the green, mostly down Manor Lane, with a few scattered farm-houses along the High Street as far as White Grove.

Remains of ridge and furrow in old enclosures are still visible around the village, and, most impressively, within Overhall Grove, outside the ditched enclosure. Many of the old roads can still be seen as hollow-ways, as the street pattern has changed considerably since Enclosure. House sites, too, can be seen, for example by the Rectory drive, which was previously a road through the northern part of the village, and along Manor Lane.

The population at Domesday was 33, there were 100 landholders, perhaps 500 people in all, recorded in 1279, and 299 poll-tax payers in 1377. In the 16th century this was down to a recorded 17 households, with only 23 houses showing on the 1650 map. In 1801 there were 220 people in the village, rising to 350 in 1871 but then fell considerably. In 1951 the population had risen to 200, but this was too small for many services or facilities to survive, and its growth was restricted to 220 by 1996.

In 1784, when 2120 of its 2602 acres were advertised for auction in the Cambridge Chronicle, Boxworth was described as 'remarkable rich Meadow, Pasture, Arable and Wood', with four farmhouses, '18 cottages, recently built' (which must have included Long Row), 'the lands all within a ring-fence, beautifully formed by nature and in the highest state of agriculture'. It was bought by the Thornhill family, and in 1794 Vancouver described Boxworth as 'a most beautiful village, well situated, and in excellent repair'.

Subsequent squires valued their game, judging by advertisements threatening prosecution for trespass, and it is perhaps partly for this reason Boxworth has retained several areas of woodland, the best known and botanically most important being Overhall Grove, owned by the Wildlife Trust and famous for oxlips and other spring flowers, though its trees have suffered from elm disease.

When the parish was enclosed, 129 acres went to the rector and the remainder to the Thornhill family, all common rights having been extinguished.

Caldecote

Caldecote is a very small parish of 407 hectares which seems to have once been part of the large parish of Bourn. It lies on chalky clay soil which rises steeply from 30m at its southern border, the Bourn Brook, up to 60m in the centre of the parish, and then more gently to 75m on the Cambridge-St. Neots ridgeway, its northern boundary. The only water supply is a stream that rises in Bourn and flows down the western edge of the parish to the Bourn Brook. The open fields were enclosed quite late, following an Award made in 1854. Its place-name, the same in Domesday Book, means 'Cold Cottages', indicating a small, subsidiary and rather uninviting settlement.

Caldecote Church, sited on Lot Way.

Village Development

The parish originated as a hamlet of Bourn and its chapel was only recognised as an independent church in the 12th century. It is a long, linear settlement, strung out along the north-south road known in the Middle Ages as 'Strympole Way', with houses set within crofts, some of which had been enclosed from common fields at an early date. Although there are good earthworks of medieval settlement along the village, particularly in the fields just south of Stinnage Wood, Caldecote must always have had an open and strung-out character. It is possible that this secondary village was set up on a long and narrow strip of wasteland to the east of the fields of Bourn, using a track leading down to the Bourn Brook. The road itself is a hollow-way which is especially obvious near the church, at the extreme south end of the village. The church is located on Lot Way, and is apparently distant from the medieval settlement, the same pattern that is noted in Comberton and Toft.

Highfields settlement was set up in the first decade of the 20th century on the Cambridge-St. Neots road. The land was bought by a speculative builder who divided it into plots for smallholders whom, it was intended, would support themselves by growing produce for Cambridge and St. Neots markets. This succeeded to some extent, but the houses were also well-placed for commuters, and the plots were mostly treated as large gardens or allotments. It is now in the process of becoming part of a new village.

The population of 15 was small at Domesday but was quite high for the size of parish in the 13th and 14th century, with about 62 land-holders in 1279 and 78 tax-payers in 1377, but it then fell to 9 householders in 1554. It stayed very small, with 75 people in 1801, peaked at 144 in 1851, but then it fell again until the development of Highfields in the 20th century. This settlement was chosen for growth in 1965, and the population of the parish rose to 800 in 1996.

Small estates in Caldecote were held by Barnwell Priory, by the Knights Hospitaller at Shingay and by St. John's Hospital (later, St. John's College). Later in the Middle Ages much land was split between rent-paying tenants, especially after the Black Death. This may have led to the enclosure of small fields which are still visible along the village street. In the 17th and 18th centuries much land was owned by Clare and Christ's Colleges and their records show that profits at Caldecote were low and tenants often bankrupt.

Caxton

Caxton is a medium sized parish of 904 hectares on clay, on undulating land between 50 and 75m above sea level. It is intersected by small brooks and dry valleys, and is divided east-west by the Bourn Brook and north-south by Ermine Street. Apart from the Cambridge-St. Neots road in the north its boundaries mainly follow field edges. Fields close to the village were enclosed from the 15th century, and when a map was made of the village in 1750 most of the parish lay in hedged fields. The remaining land was enclosed by an Award made in 1835. Caxton is

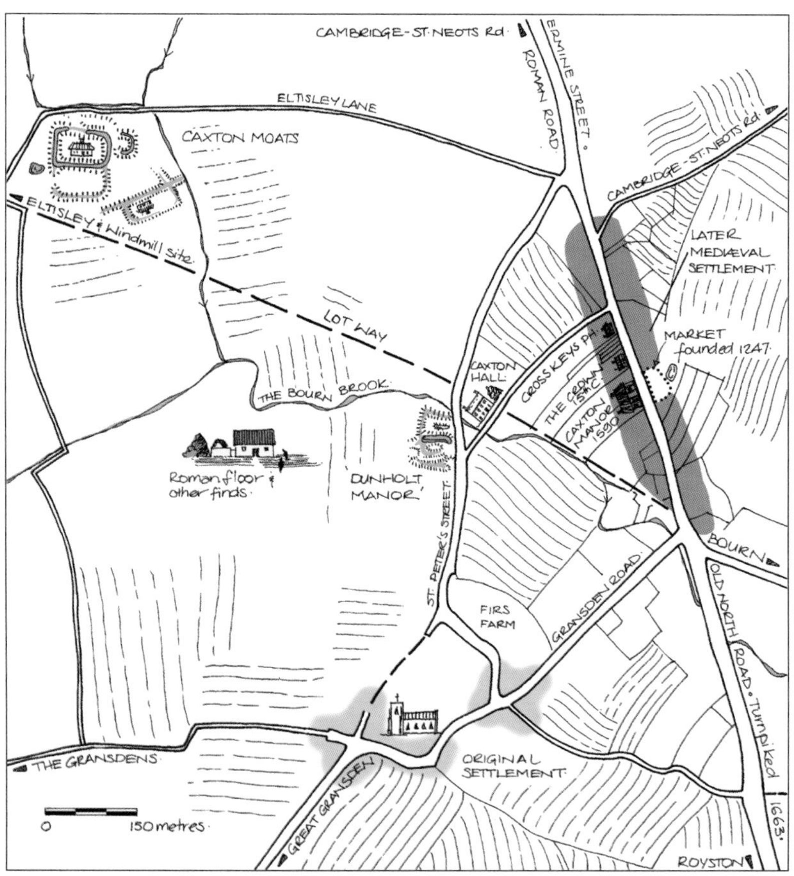

recorded in Domesday Book as *Caustone*, a Scandinavian place-name for 'Kakkr's Farm'

Roman

Roman Ermine Street mostly runs through the centre of Caxton, rather than forming the boundary as in many other parishes. Probable Roman routes ran along the northern parish boundary and also east-west through the village, part of the Lot Way from Grantchester to Eltisley. Roman roads do not normally attract settlement but crossing places do, and it is surprising that, with two cross-roads in Caxton, so little is known from this period. A late 2nd century coin hoard was found near Caxton Common Farm, where a scatter of Roman pottery has been reported, and Roman sherds have been found near Caxton Moats. A Roman floor is said to have been found during drainage work in 1890 west of the village, close to the Bourn Brook, and oyster shells and pottery come from the same area.

Anglo-Saxon

St. Andrew's Church, probably the centre of the Saxon village, contains a fragment of a Late Saxon coffin lid with interlace decoration, part of a Saxon pillar, and other fragments built into the fabric indicating there was a church here before the Conquest, and occasional sherds of Late Saxon St. Neots ware have been found near Caxton Moats and at the north end of St. Peter Street, showing there was widespread settlement at this time. Clearly, there was a substantial and scattered population here which, like other villages along Ermine Street, avoided the actual road itself.

Middle Ages

Caxton Moats consists of a large rectangular wet moat with a defended entrance and internal raised platforms, a dry moated area of similar size, and a small square deep moat, all contiguous. It was a major fortified site in the Middle Ages, blocking the east-west driftway with defences which are comparable to those built to defend the southern fen-edge at Burwell and Rampton in the mid 12th century, on the orders of King Stephen, and it is likely that it too originated as part of that short-lived campaign. It was ineffective in 1264 when rebels from Ely raided the church, and when it is first documented in the late 13th century it had been given to Eleanor de Freville, mother of the heir to de Scalers estate, as a dwelling in her widowhood. There is also an unexplained arrangement of low mounds adjacent to the moats and lying over ridge and furrow where asparagus grew in the late 19th century. These have been trenched by archaeologists with no results and may well have a horticultural origin, perhaps a garden from a later phase of the castle's use.

Caxton Church was at the centre of the village until the 13th century

One of William the Conqueror's principal knights, Hardwin de Scalers, was given the manor of Caxton, along with land in forty Cambridgeshire parishes, and based his centre of administration in Caxton. His main manor may have been Caxton Moats, but it would be

Caxton Moats in 1983. Photograph by Helen Paterson.

unusual to have such a centre in this location, and a more likely site is Dunholt Manor, a moated site in the village, just west of St. Peter Street and opposite the later manor house at Caxton Hall.

Caxton Pastures is a moated site built away from the village on land taken out of open fields. It is on the edge of an area of extensive sheep common, parts of which were ploughed for a time in the Middle Ages and were then converted back to pasture. This large rectangular moat was probably the site of the manor house for Brockholt Manor which had been part of de Scalers manor in the 12th century. The state of the moated site now is due to disturbance by a house and farm buildings that were built within it in the 18th century.

Portions of de Scalers' manor were given to religious houses at Lewes and St. Neots. Land belonging to St. Neots Priory became the separate manor of Swansley, based on the moated site in Swansley Wood Farm which is isolated in the north-east of the parish. 12th and 13th century pottery and cobbled areas have been found on this site, which is now badly damaged and the moat filled in. Documents for this manor, including references to Swansley Wood, which survived until the late 1970s, go back to 1150.

Village Development

Although Caxton today is a linear village built quite compactly along the Roman and medieval road it was in fact originally laid out around the church, well west of the road, where medieval settlement earthworks and pot scatters have been noted. A cluster of lanes from the Gransdens, Eltisley and Bourn all meet at this point. This lay-out shows that the church was in the centre of the original village. The evidence suggests that the village was moved from this church-based centre to Ermine Street, where long, thin and curving building plots still reflect the strips of medieval fields from which they were created.

The impetus for this move was the grant of a market in 1247. This market was held in the centre of the village on the east side of Ermine Street, opposite Caxton Manor, where William Palmer excavated traces of the market stalls in an open place which still exists. The move of the village may have been planned by the lord of Caxton Manor, Baldwin de Freville, in order to take advantage of national traffic which increased after a new bridge in Huntingdon was built. There were inns beside the road in Caxton from at least the 14th century. The Crown, dating to the 15th century, still stands, though it is no longer an inn, and Caxton Manor, built in 1590 opposite the market place, was later used as a public house known as the George.

The population of Caxton was not large, but held up well in comparison with some clay land parishes, thanks to its other sources of employment through trade. The Domesday population is given as 35. In 1279, 83 families were recorded, and there were about 50 houses in the 17th century, probably similar to the total population of 336 in 1801. This rose to a peak of 631 in 1871, though about 100 of these were in the workhouse which served several parishes of the Caxton Union. After this it declined and then stabilised, as it had too few facilities for expansion in the late 20th century, and there were 400 inhabitants in 1996.

Though woodland and meadow were plentiful in 1086, there was arable agriculture over almost all the parish by the 13th century, and its ridge and furrow is still visible from the air as dark curving lines in freshly ploughed soil. In the 14th century sheep became more important, and sheep-walks are also recorded in the 18th century.

Ermine Street, or the Old North Road, part of the first turnpike road in Britain in 1663, became more important as traffic increased in the 16th and 17th centuries, and Caxton was a regular stopping place. There was a post-office in Caxton by the early 17th century and in the mid 18th century it was still the only post-office outside Cambridge. In 1619 John Layer describes it as 'a small village but well known for that it is a post-town and innes for the receipt of travellers'. Thanks to stage-coach traffic in the 18th century, for which The Crown and Cross Keys (where a public house still stands on the same site) were stopping places several times each day, the village developed a distinctive character as a coaching town which faded with the decline of that traffic in the later 19th century.

Caxton gibbet

One of the notable features of Caxton today is the gibbet which stands at the crossing of Ermine Street and the road from Cambridge to St. Neots. This was owned by the Abbot of Ramsey until the Dissolution, when it became a royal gallows. Its timbers are not original and the mound was heightened in the 1980s but the site itself is medieval and its use is graphically documented into the mid 18th century when robbers and murderers were left to hang in iron cages until they died. It stood on common land known as King's Field at the crossing of two main roads, at the junction of the parishes of Caxton, Elsworth, Papworth and Eltisley.

Childerley

Childerley is a very small parish of 433 hectares, lying on clay that rises from 45m in the north to 70m on the Cambridge-St. Neots road, its southern boundary. Its open fields were enclosed in the 16th century by the Cutts family, who owned the whole parish. At Domesday its place-name was *Cildrelai*, 'young men's clearing', perhaps a derogatory reference to the efforts of land-hungry youth from Lolworth, a parish that was divided to create Childerley.

Middle Ages

Roman sherds were found during excavations of the deserted village of Great Childerley, but otherwise the earliest archaeological sites are the deserted villages themselves, Great Childerley, east of the Hall, and Little Childerley to the north-west. Some of the remains of Great Childerley survive as earthworks, including the sites of a church and manor house, cottages, cobbled streets, hollow-ways and quarries. Excavations have revealed 11th-13th century pottery and cobbled yards. Similar earthworks of Little Childerley, consisting of a straight track lined with rectangular house-platforms, were levelled by ploughing in the 1950s. Pottery of the 11th-13th century and cobbles have been found on the surface.

At the extreme south end of the parish, at Childerley Gate on the Cambridge-St. Neots road, are traces of a rectangular moat, probably the manor house of Great Childerley's second manor. The impressive three-sided moat south of Childerley Hall, and the rectangular fish-ponds there, however, are not medieval but are later features associated with formal ornamental gardening of the 17th century around the Hall.

Village Development

These two extremely small parishes were presumably populated from Lolworth at a relatively late date. It is difficult to understand why two such unpromisingly small villages, each complete with a church and manor house, should be set up so close together in an environment that was notorious in later years for its 'somewhat wette and colde' soil. The parishes were separate until the 14th century, and both churches were in use in 1489, when they were first made to share one rector. When they were assessed for tax in 1491 both were too poor to pay.

The combined Domesday population was 23 households, and there were still 76 poll-tax payers in 1377, but by the 16th century there was only one farmer and two labourers apart from the inhabitants of the Hall. In 1801 the population was given as 'about 50', several of whom must have been in the Hall or its outbuildings as there were no more than six houses. Employment rose in the 19th century, but labourers may have lived elsewhere as there were never more than 10 houses, and in 1897 this was down to one. In 1996 there were 30 people living here.

By 1509 both Childerleys had been sold to Sir John Cutts, statesman and treasurer to Henry VII, and the Cutts were to own virtually the whole village and all manorial rights until the late 17th century. The parish has remained in single ownership since that time. The first Sir John Cutts built Childerley Hall, destroying the church and depopulating the villages according to Layer, writing in the early 17th century. However, it is also claimed, particularly by Lysons in 1808, that it was a later Sir John Cutts in the 17th century who depopulated the whole parish and destroyed the church in order to improve his park. Certainly the parishes were being converted to grass by the end of the 15th century, and the first Cutts had converted another large area for this purpose. By 1600 no arable was recorded and it would not have been necessary to have moved anyone else in order to concentrate more on deer and

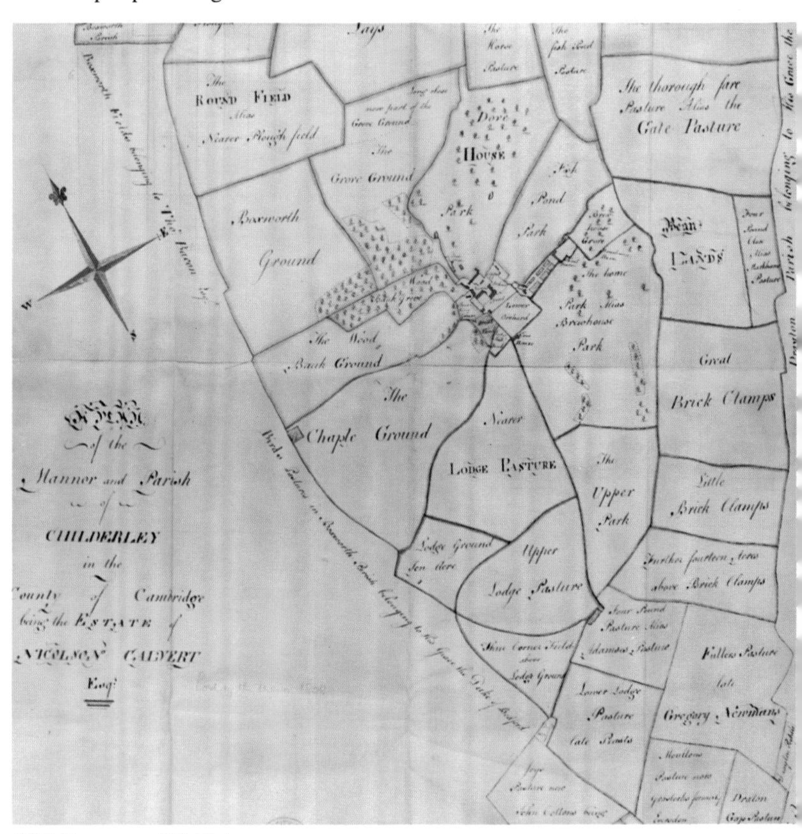

1808 Estate map of Childerley.

Childerley chapel in 1798, drawn by William Cole.

rabbits, creating the 'Parke for deere and conies and sheepe pastures... having wood both for use and ornament' which Layer extols on his friend's land. Both the herd of fallow deer and the rabbits, 'large and exceeding fatt and well relished' in the 17th century, with the warrens still known for black, white and grey rabbits in 1879, were important parts of the Cambridgeshire landscape. On the boundary between Childerley and Boxworth is a double bank and ditch that still survives up to 2m high. These are the remains of a deer-park fence that Cutts built in the 17th century to enclose his park.

Great and Little Childerley churches probably both continued in use until the mid 16th century. In the 17th century Great Childerley church was used as a farm building, and Archbishop Laud failed to prevent Cutts converting tithes to pay a chaplain in the private chapel that he had built. Layer describes this chapel as a 'most neat and delicate chappell' and gives a description of its stained glass windows. In 1748 it too was a barn, though brought back into use for a while in the 19th century.

The 16th century house was enlarged in the 17th century to a mansion with 50 rooms, but much of it was demolished in the 19th century, having ceased to be a 'gentleman's residence' when the Cutts sold it in the late 17th century. However, a point was made of preserving in its original form the room where Charles I stayed as a prisoner, and this is still decorated with frescoes of monkeys, fruit and flowers, which may commemorate the monarch's death, as Layer saw it.

The Chishills

The combined parishes of Great and Little Chishill cover 1300 hectares, which lie across a steep chalk escarpment. The land is far higher than is found elsewhere in Cambridgeshire, rising from about 40m above sea level on the A505, its northern border, to 120m in the villages and 150m in the extreme south. Its hills, sunken lanes and wide views are characteristic of North Essex, of which the parishes were part until 1895. Their open fields were enclosed in 1818. In Domesday Book their place-name is *Chishelle,* meaning 'Gravel Hill', referring to patches of gravel that overlie the chalk on top of the escarpment.

Prehistoric

Routes of the Icknield Way, one now the A505 and another a greenlane, cross the north part of both parishes and they are followed by many signs of land-use in Neolithic and Bronze Age times. At least forty ring-ditches are known from the air, clustering along the Icknield Way, and Neolithic flint blades and scrapers have been found near the A505. None of the ring-ditches have been examined, apart from one unlocated barrow dug into in the mid 19th century, from which only Roman finds were reported. One gold coin of Cunobelin has been found in the parish.

Roman

Though crop marks other than ring-ditches are not common in this area, there are two instances where small, almost square enclosures can be observed with groups of ring-ditches. There is no dating evidence from these, but there was clearly a Roman presence in the area and it is possible that these are rural shrines from Roman times. Two very small settlements, perhaps Roman farmsteads, are visible as crop marks. Roman pottery and illegible coins were ploughed up at one of these sites, near the border with Chrishall. Stray finds of Roman pottery have been reported from various other places, and in the village of Great Chishill a 3rd century coin and a storage jar buried nearly 2m deep, presumably in a rubbish pit, are recorded.

Middle Ages

The Icknield Way continued in use as a long distance route in the Middle Ages. A chapel of St. Mary Magdalene at Shapens, noted by John Layer in the early 17th century and marked as a farm on the Ordnance Survey map of 1887, lay on its

Little Chishill church stands on a promontory near the centre of the village.

route, and there is the possible site of a gallows where the parish boundary between Great and Little Chishill is crossed by the route.

The Stonk is a moated site of unusual form, an incomplete polygonal ditch set within a narrow rectangular moat, surrounding a small 16th century house. Perhaps the most interesting archaeological remains in the Chishills, however, are the strip-lynchets that survive from medieval ploughing. These were a series of terraces following the contours of the steeply sloping land, caused when ploughing on the upper side of each lynchet over many years moved soil down the slope, depositing it at the edge. This led to formation of long sinuous scarps that are still as much as 2.5m high. Though modern ploughing has reduced them, they survive on Chishill Down and the largest of them can still be seen.

A fine monument in Little Chishill is the windmill, still internally complete, standing on the road to Barley. It dates to 1819, using timbers from a mill of 1726, and was last working in 1951.

Village Development

Great Chishill lies around a cross-road, with its church on a particularly prominent knoll in the centre. A map of 1777 shows that at that time, and probably in the Middle Ages, the road system was more complicated than today, with parallel streets to the north and south of the present Chrishall road. The only buildings away from the village centre are the Hall, which was the manor house for Chishill Manor by the 18th century, and the Stonk, both of these being east of the village. In 1795 a fire destroyed many buildings and damaged the roof and belfry of the church, but rebuilding seems to have kept within the same area.

Great Chishill lynchets as they appeared in 1990. Photograph by Helen Paterson.

Little Chishill was at the meeting of three roads, one of which is now the bridle way to Great Chishill. Its manor house stood just south of the church, and its only buildings in the 18th century were close to the church, fronting onto the High Street.

At Domesday, the combined population was a minimum of 28, and in 1327 there were 34 tax-payers. By 1801 there were 309 people in Great and only 71 people in Little Chishill. The population rose to a peak of 532 and 105 in each of the villages in 1851, before falling to 329 in Great Chishill but rising to 115 in Little Chishill in 1901. In 1996 there was a combined population of 620.

Comberton

Comberton is a medium sized parish of 785 hectares, mostly lying on clay, with some chalk in the north and alluvial gravel near the Bourn Brook. The village itself is on gravel, slightly higher than the surrounding land, at a cross-roads. In the south, around the Bourn Brook which is its southern boundary, it is flat and low-lying, rising to 70m on the north edge where the parish border is just beyond the Cambridge-St. Neots ridgeway. Comberton's open fields were enclosed by an Award made in 1840. Its name in Domesday Book, *Cumbertone*, could perhaps translate as 'the Cumbrian's farm'.

Prehistoric

A Neolithic axe and three worked flints have been found on gravel soils near the Bourn Brook. Enclosures visible as crop marks in the same area could be of Iron Age date, but no Iron Age artefacts have yet been found, despite the proximity of Lord's Bridge, Barton, and the unusual value and importance of objects occurring there.

Roman

The Roman road from Cambridge to St. Neots runs immediately

south of the short northern boundary of Comberton and the parish is crossed east-west by the Roman routes later known as Portway and Lot Way. The valley of the Bourn Brook attracted settlement, and Comberton has two major Roman sites, both possibly villas, about half a mile apart. The stone walls of one large villa, with painted wall plaster and a hexagonal room, were found in 1842 by workmen digging gravel on the low ground between Comberton church and the Bourn Brook. The other villa is on the line of Lot Way, and is known only from crop marks which show enclosures, boundary ditches and rectangular buildings. A Roman barrow is marked by the Ordnance Survey in 1836 on the course of Lot Way near the Toft parish boundary, but an excavation here in the early 20th century found nothing. Artefacts discovered near it include a grinder for mixing cosmetics and small bronze bust of a goddess.

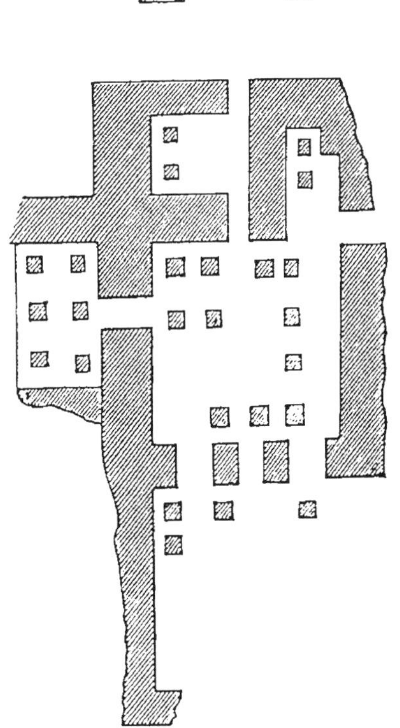

Plan of Roman villa found in 1842 on low ground between Comberton church and the Bourn Brrok.

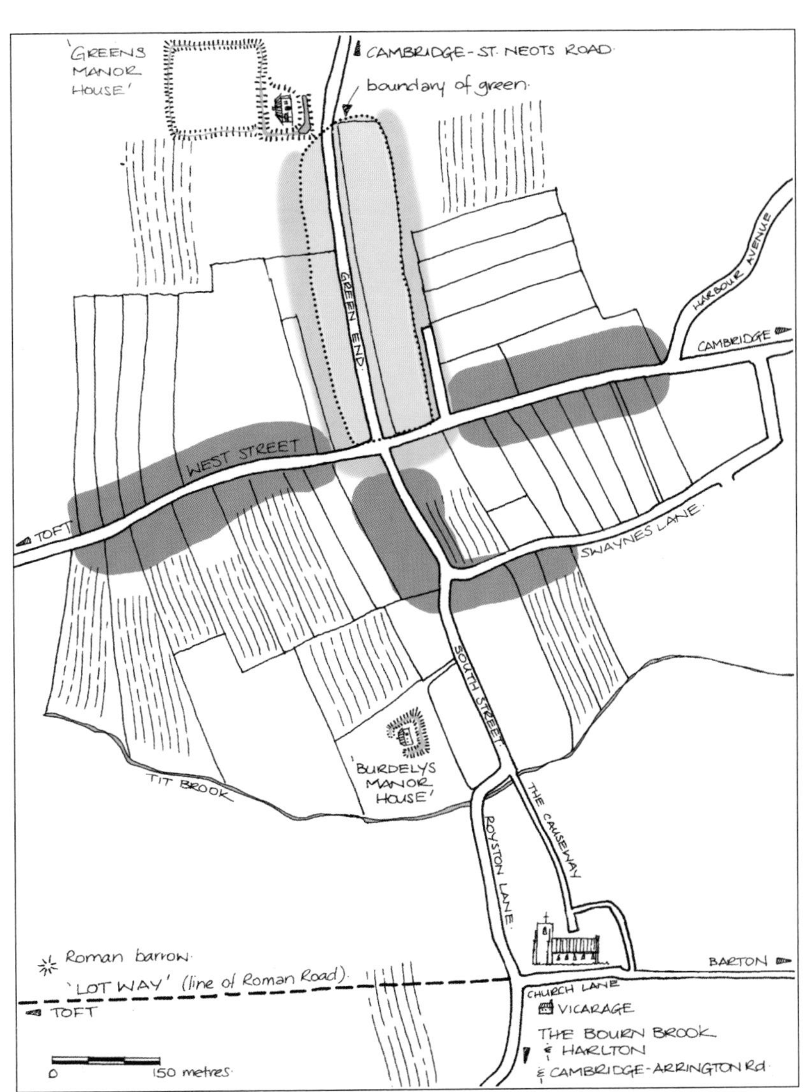

Middle Ages

A square moat with outer enclosure at Green End, now disturbed by gardening and building works, was the site of a manor house which later became the centre of Green's Manor, named after Sir Henry Green, Chief Justice of the King's Bench, who purchased it in the late 14th century. The moated site had probably been built by the Merks family, who held it from 1200 to 1318.

Burdeleys Manor house, near the church, was the centre of the other main manor, and formed part of Sheriff Picot's estate after the Conquest. Hugh Burdeleys married into the Picot family in the 12th century. In the 16th century the manor was sold to the bishop of Winchester as part of an endowment for St.Thomas Hospital, whose governors are still lords of the manor. Its moated site was said to be ruinous in the 14th century and is now a ploughed field, its last ditch being infilled in 1960.

Village Development

Comberton is sometimes cited as a rare example in Cambridgeshire where Roman estate organisation may have continued into Anglo-Saxon and then medieval times. The

Bronze bust of goddess and a grinder for mixing cosmetics, found near a Roman villa in Comberton.

place-name 'Cumbrians' Tun' could translate as 'the farm of the Britons', and, as in its neighbour Harlton, there is a villa but none of the early Anglo-Saxon remains that are so important in nearby villages such as Haslingfield and Barrington. This may suggest that, as there was a well-organised villa-based estate in late Roman times, Anglo-Saxons avoided the area. The church is on a high point completely detached from the medieval village and separated from it by a stream, but it is on or close to a Roman road and near a Roman villa. It may be that these features conditioned its position.

The village itself was built around a cross-roads of some significance, for the Barton Road was the main route from Oxford to Cambridge until the late 18th century when the Cambridge-St. Neots road was turnpiked, and the north-south road ran from the St. Neots road, across Bourn Brook at Fox's Bridge, to Harlton and the Cambridge-Arrington Bridge road. The village built here was remarkable for its large rectangular green and neatly laid out plots which overlie a pre-existing field-system and was perhaps planted in this location in the Middle Ages to take advantage of its good communications. The green was on the north side of the village, and was encroached upon by the 13th century. The roads retained wide grass verges, relicts of common land, until Enclosure. In the early 17th century, John Layer describes 'a cross of stone standing near the very centre and parting of four highways', and there was also a turf-cut maze, probably similar in appearance to the later maze at Hilton, which survived until at least 1925.

Comberton was a considerable village for some of its history, with 43 villagers recorded at Domesday, about 50 households in the 13th century, 152 tax-payers in 1377 and 30 families in the 16th century. It then stayed quite small, rising slowly to a total population of only 295 in 1801. It peaked at 619 in 1871 and then fell before recovering slowly in the first half of the 20th century, then rapidly after the County Council designated it a growth village and built a Village College in 1960. In 1996 there were 2370 inhabitants.

Comberton church lying on a Roman route-way, apart from its medieval village.

Conington

Conington is a small parish of 616 hectares, lying on heavy clay soils, except for a patch of gravel by the church. It is mostly low-lying, under 15m above sea level, rising to about 30m near Boxworth. The northern boundary is the Cambridge-Godmanchester Roman road. Its open fields were enclosed following an Award made in 1804. In Domesday Book, it is *Cunitone*, or 'King's Farm', showing Scandinavian influence on a basically Saxon name.

Roman

Five sites recognised from the air during the dry summer of 1995 show rectangular enclosures and tracks, perhaps indicating farming settlements, though the clay soils generally make it difficult to recognise and interpret crop marks. There was considerable Roman occupation elsewhere in Conington. Excavations for a waste disposal tip near the Cambridge-Godmanchester road, for example, produced much animal bone and pottery, including samian wares, Roman roof-tiles, nails, a key, slag, and glass. Roman coins, including a 1st century BC coin of Julius Caesar, have been found in the parish and a Roman milestone came from the Roman road.

Village Development

There is Saxon evidence in a will for an estate being divided amongst the wife, daughters, servant etc. of a lord called Aefhelm Polga in the late 10th century. As yet there is no archaeological evidence for the location of this settlement, but the original village may have been south of the church, on a local high point of gravel, where irregular low banks are still just visible in a ploughed field within a rectangle bounded by three hollow-ways and the present School Lane. The village seems to have moved north and east, along Town Street and its northward extension towards the Hall which was built in the 17th century. Later still it developed along the present High Street. When the park was extended in the 19th century houses in the old closes in the Hall grounds to the west of the High Street were demolished. Their sites survive as earthworks. They were replaced by model cottages on the opposite side of the road, but all except one were demolished for new housing in the 1970s. Conington eventually became a rather scattered village, especially as the population fell at the end of the 19th century.

The population was only 24 at Domesday, but there were about 65 land-holders, perhaps 325 people in the 13th century, which was reduced to 26 householders recorded in the 16th century. By 1801 it had only risen to 182 in total, and at its peak in the 1850s it was 235. After this it fell to 105 in the 1920s, and in 1996 had only risen to 150.

In the 16th century much land was bought by the Huttons, who were responsible for enclosure of small fields for livestock close to the village. In the 17th century the village was bought by the Cottons of Conington (Hunts), whose younger branch lived here and built the Hall. For fifty years in the 18th century it was the home of Dingley Askham

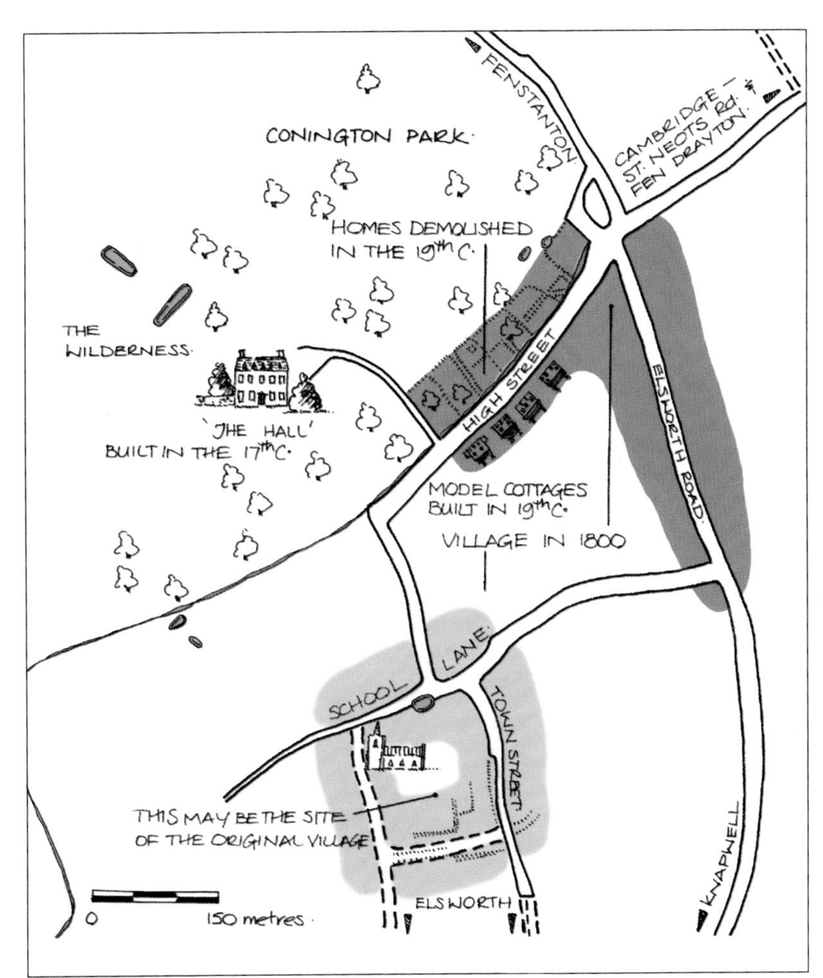

Conington church, now rather isolated in the south of the village but once surrounded by the medieval settlement.

and his wife Frances, whose father Thomas Cotton apparently died of a drunken rage when she married beneath her. This couple made Conington Hall into an ideal country residence which is described in advertisements placed in the Cambridge Chronicle when it was let in the late 18th and early 19th centuries. In 1788, for example, it had 'stables for 20 horses, dog-kennel and all other convenient offices... gardens... fishponds, greenhouses, etc...' Later advertisements include, in addition to these features, 'excellent walled fruit and vegetable gardens, hot-houses, greenhouses and fruit room', forty acres of park and pleasure grounds, orchard and wilderness. Hunting was evidently taken very seriously. Kennels, large stables and hunting and fishing opportunities appear in several advertisements, and, in 1818 trespassers were publicly warned that 'Man-traps, Spring Ginns and Dog Traps are actually set in the rookeries and all the plantations about the premises at Conington'.

By 1800 almost all the parish was held by the Hattons, who then owned but did not usually live at Conington Hall, and at Enclosure most of the land went to that estate, no common rights then existing.

Coton

Coton is a very small parish of 404 hectares, lying on clay. The land rises steeply to 70m above sea level on the Cambridge-Godmanchester road, its northern parish boundary and to 50m at Barton Down in the south. Otherwise the parish is fairly level and low-lying, with the village itself built on the clay/chalk junction north of Coton Brook. Its open fields were enclosed by an Award made in 1803. The place-name, *Cotis* in Domesday Book, means 'cottages', suggesting a small subsidiary settlement, which reflects its probable origins as a satellite of Grantchester.

Prehistoric, Roman and Anglo-Saxon

Early finds from Coton are three Neolithic axes, an ornate Roman brooch decorated with blue and orange enamel, a Roman bracelet and small pot, and an early Anglo-Saxon brooch from a garden in the village.

Middle Ages

There are two moated sites in Coton, one surrounding the Rectory and another to the south of this. The square Rectory moat may have been the manor house of the d'Engaynes. The second moat, at Rectory Farm, only 100m away and fed by the stream that flows out of the other moat, has an unusually irregular shape, of which two arms survive, and may have been in the same ownership.

Village Development

Houses in the village are spread along a single street, a continuation of the old Whitwell Way track, which opens into the remains of a green east of the church, where there is still a village pump and where a smithy owned by churchwardens was mentioned in 1580. In the 16th century much of the land between the High Street and the brook was acquired and enclosed by Richard Angier, a lawyer from Barton who fought many law-suits with the Colleges over possession of land. Straight ridge and furrow in old enclosures is still visible in places.

Wayside Cross, Coton.

Coton was presumed part of Grantchester until at least the 12th century. Its chapel was dependent on Grantchester church, gradually establishing its independence in the 13th century, although no burials were allowed in Coton churchyard until 1348. Coton was also closely linked with Whitwell, a nearby hamlet in the parish of Barton, and they shared the same field-system. Commons were shared with Grantchester until the parish boundary was fixed at Enclosure.

Medieval populations of Coton are not known as they were included with Grantchester. In the 16th century there were 21 families, and this stayed fairly stable, being 126 people in total in 1801. The population reached a peak of 390 in 1871, before declining and then recovering in the first half of the 20th century, growing fast with much new building after 1950, to 710 in 1996.

The two main manors in Coton were Coton D'Engaynes and Maidenburys. D'Engaynes is recorded in 1086, passing to the Huntingdon family of Gidding at the end of the 14th century. In the 15th century the Giddings sold much of their land to townspeople in Cambridge. The Maidenbury family had inherited the manor that was given their name by the end of the 13th century, and held it until the mid-15th century. In 1513 it was sold to St. Catherine's College. Other land in Coton was held by manors in Grantchester that were owned by King's College. At Enclosure, King's was allotted a large estate which formed Manor Farm. St. John's Hospital had been given many small grants of land by villagers in the 13th century, and thus St. John's College, which took over the Hospital's estates, had a sizeable estate in Coton, and Queens College too had acquired land in the 16th century. University influence extended to the church, whose rector was normally a fellow of St. Catherine's. In the early 1930s much of Coton was bought by Cambridge Preservation Society in order to protect countryside and views around Cambridge.

Croxton

Croxton is a relatively small parish of 772 hectares, lying on clay except for a small area of alluvial gravel near the Abbotsley Brook. It rises from about 30m above sea level in the south-west near the Brook, to 60m along the Cambridge-St. Neots ridgeway in the north. Its boundaries include the Abbotsley and Gallow Brooks, and the original course of the Cambridge-St. Neots road. The open fields were enclosed after an Award made in 1818. Its place-name in Domesday Book is *Crochestune*, or 'Crocc's Farm', a Scandinavian personal name.

Prehistoric and Roman

A Bronze Age rapier has been found within Croxton Park, and there is one small Roman site south-west of the Park. Apart from a scatter of Roman sherds, finds included a bronze folding pocket-knife, its handle in the form of a dog chasing a hare, a vase with three holders, and a mosaic workers chisel/anvil. The form of vase is definitely religious, as the knife probably is, and all are unusual objects to find so far from any significant settlement site.

'illage Development

Originally Croxton probably ›nsisted of two centres, Croxton and 'estbury, but there was considerable ıovement, expansion and shrinkage ver the whole settlement area. The :ntre of Croxton was near the ıurch, where the manor house and :ctory stood and where there was a ›ng and narrow village green. Westury hamlet may have started near /estbury Farm, shifting east to the ollow-way, now a track, that leads to 'roxton Manor and the church. roxton village also seems to have ›read north along a road to a milar green situated near the resent North Lodge, both settleıents being attracted to the highway. and that had previously been arable as built upon in quite a haphazard ay. When the population fell in the ıter Middle Ages, it was the older arts in the south that were deserted, ut the fluctuating and mostly land-ss population seems to have moved round considerably within the ındscape.

In the 16th century the main ıedieval Croxton manor was sold to ›r. Edward Leeds who had just :tired as master of Clare College. Ie built a new house on the old ıanor house site, and his family, ıostly merchants or lawyers, held 'roxton until 1818, the present Hall eing built on the same site in 1760, enclosing part of the original manor house, which was discovered during renovations in 1995. The building now known rather confusingly as the Manor House is a late medieval timber-framed house, with a hall and cross-wings, and it was probably a later manor house for Westbury. The original Westbury manor house was presumably at Westbury Farm, another building which incorporates a medieval open hall and which still has traces of its surrounding moat.

In the 17th century, Layer says of Westbury Manor 'this manor was dismembered and now the scite and some landes in one Coosens a yeoman', and it was added to the Leeds estate in the late 18th century. Huntingdon Priory also had an estate that was sold to successful peasant families after the Dissolution, which Layer slightingly describes as being 'in ye handes of meane men'. This land too was eventually sold to the Leeds. Of Croxton Manor, known as Sanzavers, he said 'the old site is decaied being a faire one, but Doctor Leedes built a faire gentlemanlike house upon it'. In other words, the failure of Croxton to grow in the 16th and 17th centuries, and some of its areas of apparent desertion, are due more to the successes of one group of peasants amalgamating their neighbours smallholdings, rather

'he late medieval building known as Croxton Manor was once the manor house for Westbury hamlet.

than to gentrification by an outside family. This is confirmed by tax returns which classify nine men as 'yeomen', a high figure in this small population.

The Domesday population was 23, increasing to 65 tenants recorded in 1279, and 117 poll-tax payers in 1377. In the 16th century there were 25 tax payers and in the 17th century 128 adults. In 1801 there was still only a total of 171 people. Enclosure and creation of the Park actually preceded the only period of growth in Croxton since the early Middle Ages, the population reaching 308 in 1871, but falling subsequently. Many of the houses were allowed to become derelict and the population continued to fall until 1989, but after changes in ownership in the late 20th century, and with encouragement from the local authority, repairs were carried out and a small number of new houses were built. In 1996 there were 130 people living here, just above the Domesday figure.

By the 19th century the Leeds family had been successful in buying up most of the farms, and owned almost all the parish when it was enclosed in 1818. Soon after this the estate was sold to the Newton family, whose descendants lived here until the late 20th century. It was this family that caused the major changes to Croxton's landscape by creating an ornamental park over much of the parish, all houses except the Hall being cleared from the old village near the church, even the Rectory being demolished to make way for an ornamental lake. New landscape features were created over the traces of habitation which have now been fossilised beneath the grass.

Croydon cum Clopton

The two former medieval parishes, which were united in the 16th century, cover 1106 hectares. Clay land rises gently from 25m by the Rhee to 45m, then there is a steep chalk scarp to 75m, beyond which is a clay-covered plateau. Both villages are on a spring-line at the foot of the scarp. The Rhee is the southern boundary of the parishes, other boundaries being zigzag edges of enclosed fields which are crossed by ridge and furrow of earlier open fields. Enclosure of the open fields began in the Middle Ages and was complete by 1600. The place-names of these villages, *Craudene* and *Cloptune* at Domesday, perhaps mean 'valley frequented by crows' and 'hill-farm'.

Prehistoric

Prehistoric finds include Mesolithic and Bronze Age axes, a Late Bronze Age axe from a garden in Croydon village and a Late Iron Age brooch found with Roman material at Valley Farm.

Roman

Evidence of Roman settlement is widespread. Excavations at Valley Farm produced a scatter of Roman items such as a seal-box, finger-ring and brooch as well as much pottery. There is also a small villa near the river where excavated finds included the base of a sandstone pillar, bricks roof-tiles, painted wall-plaster and fragments of red, white and brown mosaic paving. The excavator suggested this was a 1st century villa, later re-settled by peasant farmers from the 2nd to 4th century, but his trenches were too small for clear interpretation. During excavations o the deserted village of Clopton Roman occupation evidence of 2nd to 4th century was found.

Village Development

The deserted village of Clopton i the best and most well-documented site of this kind in Cambridgeshire, a county where many villages saw severe shrinkage, but few once-thriving settlements actually disappeared.

Archaeological excavations from 1961-4 showed that the village was built on a site that had been in use in Roman and Early Anglo-Saxon times, and there was a large Late Saxon settlement. It expanded considerably in the 12th century, and in the 13th century was flourishing sufficiently to need re-organisation c the village. The hill-slope was terraced at that time to give more space the High Street was surfaced with cobbles and re-aligned around the churchyard, and the road to Croydon was improved with terracing and a drainage ditch. Remains of the church and graveyard, the rectory, market-place and roads have all been uncovered during excavations.

Clopton deserted village from the air, 1990. Photograph by Geoffrey Robinson.

One of the manor houses was at the Bury, now an irregular and disturbed roughly circular moat in the north-east of the village that once had a spring-fed ditch, deep enough to drown a child in the 14th century, and with a house where a bishop was entertained. Clopton Bury was owned by Robert Hoo in the late 13th century, and it was he who was granted the right to build mounds, which can still be seen north of the village, to attract rabbits, and also to hold a Friday market. From the late 14th century it passed to various large landowners outside the village, including the St. Georges of Hatley. Other owners included a London fishmonger, and then Robert Clopton, a London draper and lord mayor, who already had village connections through a successful peasant family that had taken their surname from their village. When Robert Clopton sold the manor to John Fisher in the late 15th century he kept the manor house, to Fisher's fury, and his widow, Juliana, held onto this until her death in 1525. The moated site later contained cottages, one of which was still inhabited in the early 20th century.

The other Clopton manor, Rowses, was held by the Bishop of Winchester from before the Conquest until the mid-12th century Anarchy period, when it passed to the Crown. Their tenants, the Rowses, lived at Clopton through the 13th century. Like Clopton Bury it was held by the Haseldens in the late 14th century and was purchased by the Cloptons in the mid 15th century, sharing the same ownership and fate thereafter. The manor house stood south of the village in Rowses Wood, adjacent to the river in a moat with outer enclosures, where 13th and 14th century sherds have been found.

Clopton reached its peak in the 14th century, becoming one of the larger villages in the area with 104 tax-payers in 1377. A new church was dedicated in 1352. There are no particular signs of decline in the 15th century and open fields, where ridge and furrow is still visible in places, were cultivated until the 1490s. At that time, however, much of the village was bought by the Fisher family, who saw the economic benefits of converting arable land to pasture at a time when grain prices were low, wool prices high and labour was expensive. John Fisher and his son both had legal backgrounds and were willing to use endless litigation to force their neighbours from their land. Notorious cases included lawsuits when the rector tried in vain to keep his glebe, and Fisher even had Robert and Juliana Clopton imprisoned at one stage because they would not give up the manor house. It is obvious that no ordinary villager would have had any hope of holding onto common rights in this situation. In 1525 there were only five labourers left at Clopton, and in 1561 the village, with just two houses left, was officially declared extinct and combined with Croydon. The church was then already ruinous. It was left to decay until it was demolished in the early 18th century.

Moated sites of Tailboys Manor (now destroyed) and ridge and furrow, at Croydon, 1967. Photograph © Cambridge University Collection of Air Photographs.

The rising Fishers hung on to the estate despite litigation with the Chicheleys of Wimpole, and married into the aristocracy. Clopton thus passed to the Earls of Bedford, who were involved in draining the Fens, was sold to the Downing family and passed with the rest of that estate to Downing College in 1800. There were a handful of scattered houses in 1750 when a map of the parish, which was known as 'Clapton Dairy', was made for the Downing family.

Croydon also had two manors. The house of Tailboys Manor, well documented before its sale in the 16th century, may have stood in two unconnected moats in the south of the village, recorded as wet subrectangular moats in 1968 but now destroyed, or alternatively at Manor Farm, just north-west of the church, which is also filled in. Francis Manor was sold in the 16th century to Anthony Cage of Longstowe whose son built Croydon Wilds, a 17th century moated garden, surrounding a house with a brick tower in the centre which was demolished in the 1950s.

Like Clopton, Croydon shrank considerably from the 15th century and it too retains many well-preserved signs of village shrinkage that can be studied alongside the better known ones at Clopton. The remains include earthworks of house-sites south-west of the church. In 1996, the population of the combined parishes was 200, most of them living in Croydon.

Dry Drayton

Dry Drayton is a medium sized parish of 1008 hectares (including Bar Hill), lying on clay except where chalk is exposed in the north-west corner. The land rises from 15m above sea level on its northern boundary, the Roman road, to 65m on the Cambridge-St. Neots ridgeway, its southern boundary. Two streams run from south to north across the parish, with the village lying between them. The open fields were enclosed by an Award made in 1811. Its place-name in Domesday Book is *Draitona,* or 'the farm by the hill', 'dry' being attached later to differentiate it from Fen Drayton.

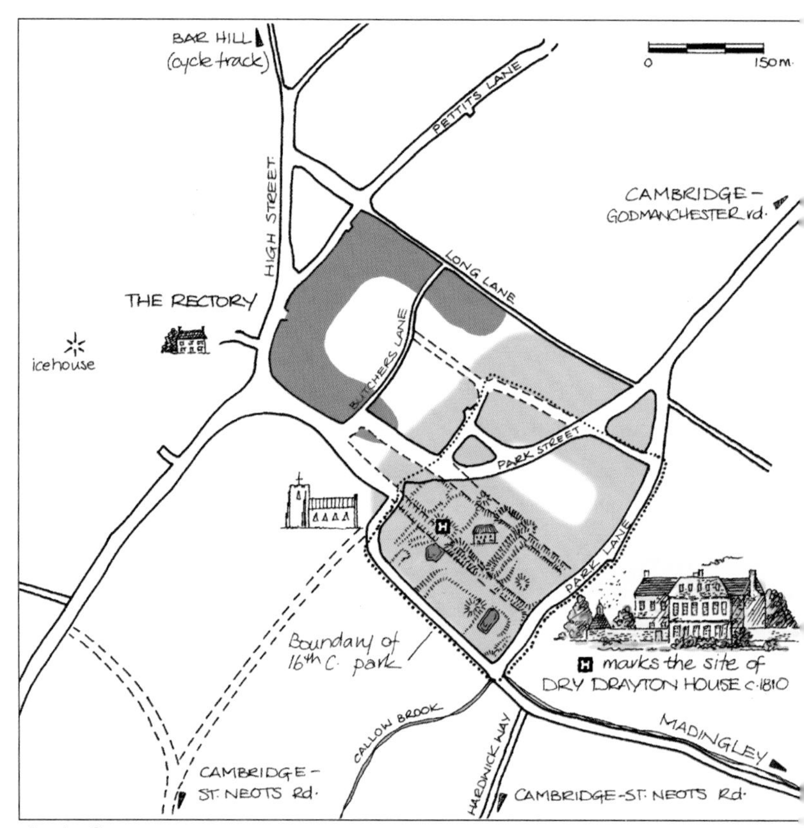

Prehistoric and Roman

Neolithic scrapers and a Bronze Age arrow-head were found near the mound where an Anglo-Saxon beaker was found, an Iron Age coin was discovered at Childerley Gate, and occasional Roman sherds were found by archaeologists excavating at The Park. Roman pottery, including Nene Valley wares, was found on a building site near to Bar Hill.

Anglo-Saxon glass beaker. Photograph @ Cambridge Museum of Archaeology and Anthropology.

Anglo-Saxon

A 7th century beaker of bluish-green and pale yellow glass with trailing decoration was found when the Cambridge-Godmanchester road was dualled in 1977. This beaker is thought to have been in a burial mound that was later used as a medieval gallows and possibly also as a Hundred meeting place, as it stood at cross-roads on a major highway that was also a parish boundary. The original mound was likely to have been Roman, re-used in Early Anglo-Saxon times. A public house and then a farmhouse were built on this site, so no traces survive above ground.

Village Development

Most of Dry Drayton belonged to the Lincolnshire abbey of Crowland from Late Saxon times until the Dissolution, and it was perhaps this institution which created a planned village that already had a high population in 1086. The village was a nucleated settlement, laid out on a grid of lanes within a rectangle, of which two sides were sections of roads which ran between the Cambridge-St. Neots road and the Cambridge-Godmanchester road. Within this rectangle was the moated site, and just outside, in the middle of the south-west side, was the church.

At The Parks, within the original village, Abbot Brichtmer built a manor house in 1032, replacing a previous house that was said to have been burnt by the Danes, and he used this as a summer residence. Rebels supporting Simon de Montfort burnt this house in 1266, after which the Abbot built a new hall, probably in the disturbed moated site that survives. Excavation of the later mansion that stood nearby produced much medieval pottery, including Late St.Neots and Stamford wares, from the 12th to the 14th centuries. One interesting find was a quantity of 15th century religious painted glass that probably originated from the church.

After the Dissolution, the Crown sold Crowland's estate to Thomas Hutton, who already owned other land in Dry Drayton and surrounding parishes. It was probably his son John who made major changes to the village. In order to create a parkland setting for his house, village lanes were officially stopped up, and part of the road past the church seems to have been moved south, creating a dog-leg turn there. Park Street became the route around the Parks, keeping the right-angled bends that were the old close boundaries until 1968. He rebuilt the manor house on a slightly different site, together with an ornamental 3-sided moat, stone-walled courtyard and a garden, all within the parkland area he took out of the village.

In the 1670s the estate was owned by Hugh Weld, who built another house in a grander style, complete with two statues flanking its approach. It is this house that is illustrated in a drawing of 1810. Weld went bankrupt, and his successors, who included the Dukes of Bedford, used the mansion as an occasional residence until the mid 18th century, when it was let as a farmhouse. The Dukes of Bedford sold Dry Drayton to the rector, Dr. Samuel Smith. His son, another Samuel, inherited both the estate and the rectorship, and he pulled down the old mansion in the early 19th century, replacing it with an imposing Georgian rectory with an ice-house in its grounds that now stands at the end of a drive leading off the High Street. The Parks is now a pasture field used for grazing, preserving the earthworks of many periods of activity. Since the Middle Ages the village centre has gradually moved west in the direction of the High Street, leaving Pettits Lane and especially its southern extension to decline, and also leaving clusters of houses on the outside of the old village centre so that, in 1851, Dry Drayton is referred to as 'small and scattered'.

The population at Domesday was high at 52, but was quite moderate thereafter. Nearly half the tenants of Crowland Manor died in the Black Death, and there were complaints about houses being left empty in the later Middle Ages. In 1377 the number of tax-payers was down to 122, and this figure did not change very much in the 16th and 17th centuries. In 1801 there was a total population of 376, rising to 497 in 1851, before falling to 373 in 1931. Since then it has risen to 590 in 1996 in Dry Drayton, in addition to the settlement at Bar Hill.

At Enclosure, the old road to Oakington was kept as a highway, and the major road to the south was partly straightened. North-east routes were reduced to bridle-ways and footpaths, one of which is now the cycle-route to Bar Hill. A private road to Madingley that had been built by the Cotton family was kept, despite objections by villagers whose gardens this route had destroyed.

Large flocks of sheep were kept at Dry Drayton in the Middle Ages, in addition to arable agriculture in three open fields. Common rights included generous provision for grazing sheep, cattle and horses, though these were often exceeded, for example by Swavesey Priory, who at one stage had 120 cattle and 600 sheep on the commons. At Enclosure, remaining common rights were exchanged for old enclosures in or close to the village, most being sold soon after as they were too small to support a family.

Bar Hill is a new village that was built on farmland in the north-west of the parish adjacent to the Cambridge-Godmanchester road, with the intention of reducing development pressures on Cambridge and its surrounding villages. Despite much controversy and opposition, work began in 1965. The village was planned around a central green, with a shopping centre and public buildings (school, church, library and public house) nearby and an industrial estate in the northern corner. It grew rapidly in the 1970s, once cheaper designs and higher densities than had first been used were accepted. Its provision of cheap land on an increasingly important road just five miles from Cambridge helped the light industries and warehouses to flourish, and attracted a large hotel, golf-course and one of the first superstores in the region. It was also well situated for commuters to Cambridge and Huntingdon. In 1996 its population was 4450.

Duxford

Duxford, a large parish of 1310 hectares, lies mostly on chalk except for the tops of some hills which are capped by clay, and near the river where there is gravel and alluvium. It is bounded by the Cam, by the A505, which is the modern route of the Icknield Way, and by furlong boundaries along a route known as Procession Way on its border with Ickleton. The north-west of the parish is flat, between 30 and 50m above sea level, but in the east it rises to Pepperton Hill at about 100m. The village itself is next to the river, built along former lines of the Icknield Way. The open fields were enclosed after an Award made in 1830. Its name in Domesday Book is *Duchesuuorde,* or 'Ducc's Enclosure', rather than being a reference to its fords.

Prehistoric

The parish is crossed by lines of the Icknield Way, which ford the Cam here, and it was attractive for

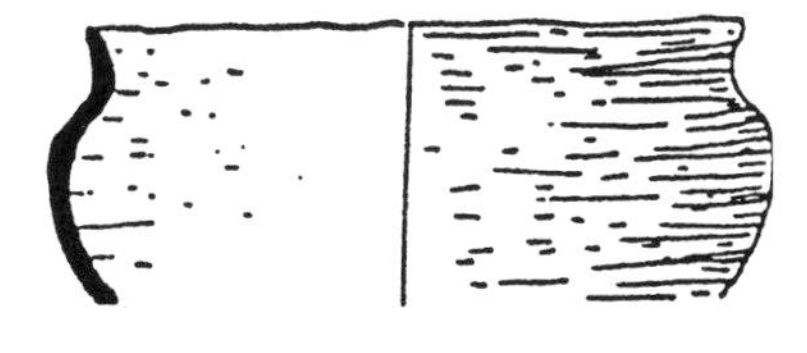

Iron Age pottery found at Duxford.

settlements and other land-uses in prehistoric times. Palaeolithic flints have been found on the heath near Duxford Grange, Mesolithic flints came from Duxford Airfield and, at Duxford Mill, waste flakes of this date were perhaps remains of a fishing expedition. Neolithic activity, including digging pits to mine for flint, was found in recent excavations near the A505, and scatters of tools such as scrapers and blades occur over wide areas of heath around Duxford Grange. Bronze Age flints have been found in similar areas, and there are four possible round barrow sites. A Bronze Age axe and spear-head come from the site of the airfield. Evidence for actual settlement in the Iron Age came from a gas pipe-line on Pepperton Hill, where a farming settlement was discovered dating to about 600-300 BC. There were several food storage pits, and others which were clay-lined and suitable for tanning leather and for water storage. One straight-sided cylindrical pit held a post, and a horse-skull had been placed on the bottom, probably for religious reasons. A deep pit with a human skeleton found in a previous gas pipe trench may belong to this period.

Roman

Pepperton Hill, a local high point with wide views, was used again in the Roman period, and this may have been for a temporary military camp. The pipe trench revealed a steep V-shaped military-style ditch which geophysical survey showed surrounded a playing-card shaped enclosure of about one hectare. A hollow nearby had been used to bury broken pottery, animal bones and nails, presumably when the soldiers left. A clay-lined hearth with fire-bars suggests more sophisticated cooking than most farmsteads enjoyed.

In the south-east corner of the parish, on a ridge of gravel just above the Cam's flood-plain, is a site where substantial Roman buildings survive as crop marks of buildings, trackways, pits and enclosures. Artefacts on the field's surface include bricks and roof-tiles from buildings, as well as pottery. Excavations within the village have found sherds that must have been lying on the ground when later ditches were dug, and there have been occasional metal objects, such as an iron shackle, reported. Excavations and crop marks near the A505 have revealed Roman field-systems. Many areas in Duxford, it seems, have traces of Roman occupation, and crossing-places of the Cam gave access to extensive Roman sites on the opposite banks of the river in Hinxton.

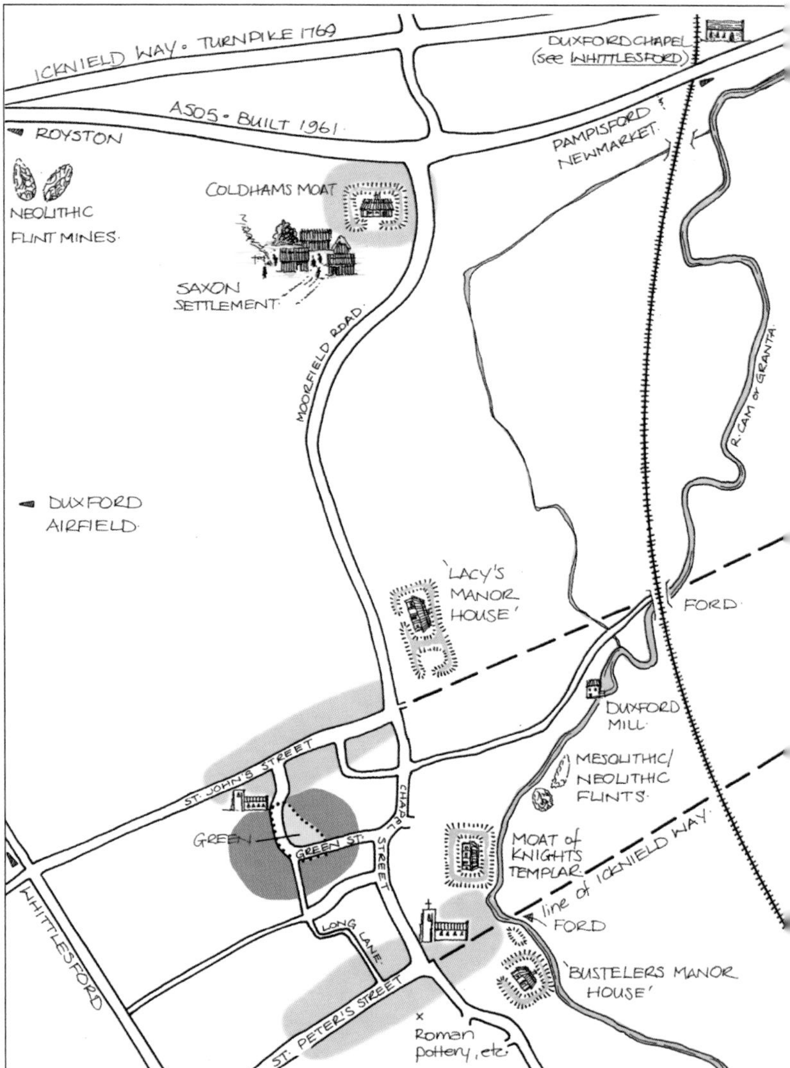

Middle Ages

One moated site formerly existed north of St. Peter's church. This had been the site of the manor house for Temple Manor, named after the Knights Templar to whom it was given in the early 13th century. Previously it had been part of a larger Saxon and medieval estate. The Knights Hospitaller of Shingay took over the manor when the Templars were disbanded in the early 14th century, at which time the manor house included a hall and chamber, and there was a chapel, grange and farm-buildings on the site.

The moated site of Lacy's manor house is the best preserved of Duxford's four moats, though its west side has been destroyed by gardens of adjoining houses. It was a rectangular moat with an extension, and its wide moat was wet until quite recently. The manor belonged to the Lacy family, who held it from the 13th to the late 14th century.

A third moat between the road and the river was the site of Bustelers manor house. Until the 1980s this was a well-preserved rectangular moat fed by a leet from the Cam, which at that time was about 250m east of its present course. Since then it has suffered soil dumping and other interference from building works nearby, and trees have been planted on it. This manor house was the centre of a large estate that was part of the de Scalers of Caxton's land, below whom were the lords of Overhall Grove in Boxworth. Under them, it was occupied by the Goiz family from the late 12th to the early 14th century, when it was sold to the Bustelers of Hildersham. In 1366, when there was no male heir, it was split between the heirs of five sisters, one part being inherited by John Hanchach, who became notorious for his leadership of rebels during the Peasants' Revolt. The whole estate was re-united by the Parys family, who held it until the 17th century.

On the road north of the village was Coldham's Moat, a square moat that has been ploughed flat. Pottery shows that this area was occupied in Late Saxon and early medieval times, but a trial excavation suggested that the moat itself may not have been a medieval feature but could have been built later, when the site was otherwise deserted. Alternatively, it might have been the manor house for half of a Saxon estate that was divided with Lacy's before 1200.

Village Development

The basic lay-out of the village along two parallel routes of Icknield Way is probably Saxon in origin, with two original settlements along St. Peter's Street and St. John's Street, each one leading to a ford across the Cam. Land in Duxford was given to the King in the mid 10th century, and sherds of pre-Conquest Thetford and St. Neots ware have been found in St. John's Street. Each settlement had a church and manor house. The village green between the main streets, with houses built around it, may have been a later planned addition. The settlements grew together into a single village, farming their land together in three open fields in the customary way. In addition, there was the Saxon settlement north of the village around Coldham's Moat, but this went out of use later in the Middle Ages.

Duxford village green, a planned addition to the two Saxon centres, with St John's church in the background.

Duxford is unusual in having two parish churches, each serving distinctive parts of the village. Both contain Norman work, and St. John's has a carved cross which may be Saxon. Both were in use until the late 19th century, when St. John's was closed. It has now been repaired by the Churches Conservation Trust, and during the course of this restoration work exceptional wall-paintings dating from the 12th century onwards were uncovered.

Duxford was quite a large village at Domesday, with 37 inhabitants recorded, and this had grown to about 100 tenants in the 13th century, but had only 104 poll-tax payers in 1377. In the 16th century 58 families paid tax, growing to 86 households in the 17th century. In 1801 the total population was 494, reaching a peak of 881 in 1871 before falling again until the expansion of the Airfield in World War II. It was chosen for expansion after 1950, and in 1996 the population was 1850.

In addition to open fields, the parish included about 8 hectares of heath near Thriplow, which were used for sheep, and extensive areas of meadow near the river where cattle grazed. In fields south of St. Peter's church, between Duxford and Hinxton, there are remains of artificial water-meadows, designed in the 17th or 18th centuries to flood fields in order to have an early crop of grass, an unusual system of water-management in Cambridgeshire. Common grazing rights were generous, and numbers of sheep in particular were always high. When fields were officially enclosed, the majority of the land went to four landowners, with about one third being shared among 70 others.

During the First World War an airfield was opened at Duxford, later rebuilt as part of the pre-World War II expansion of the RAF. It played a major part in the Battle of Britain and the defence of Eastern England, being transferred to the Americans in 1942. It was closed in 1961, but in 1972 it became part of the Imperial War Museum. It is now the home of aircraft and artillery of both World Wars and later exhibits such as Concorde, and an American air museum is at present under construction.

Elsworth

Elsworth is a large parish of 1534 hectares, lying on clay, except for an outcrop of limestone known as Elsworth Rock to the north of the village. The land rises steadily from about 15m in the north, to 30m in the village, and then up to 65m along the ridgeway of the Cambridge-St. Neots road which forms its southern border. Other boundaries are field edges, apart from a stream which divides it from Boxworth. The open fields were enclosed after an Award made in 1803. Its Domesday place-name was *Elesuuorde,* meaning 'Elli's Enclosure'.

Roman

The only early discoveries so far from Elsworth are a Roman coin of Hadrian and part of a quern from gardens in the village. However, crop marks of rectangular enclosures that may be Roman occupation sites were noted in drought conditions at six sites in the south of the parish.

Middle Ages

Fragmentary and disturbed remains of a rectangular moat near the present Manor House are all that survive of the Abbot of Ramsey's manor house. In the 14th century, buildings here included a hall, parlour and kitchen, and there was a chapel that had been licensed in 1254.

Elsworth Wood was in existence in 1086, when it was used by Ramsey Abbey for timbers to repair its manorial buildings. In 1279 it covered five hectares, and was presumably the home of Matheus Atewode, who is mentioned at this time. John Ate Wod in 1327, John Atte Wode in 1420 and Thomas Atewode, who became rector in 1432, may be from the same family, or there may have been many who could be described in this way. The wood itself was coppiced, probably from Saxon times until the 1930s, and this management has been revived by the Wildlife Trust. It increased in size to over sixteen hectares in 1800, but has now been reduced to about half of this.

South of the wood was a small settlement known as Grave, which was a separate hamlet in the late 13th century. It is likely that the name was originally Grove, reflecting its origin as part of the wood. During the Peasants' Revolt its main house was robbed, and in the late 14th and early 15th centuries several of its buildings were reported as ruinous. In the mid 15th century there were 36 holdings here, of which seven were empty. Closes are recorded here on the 1st Edition Ordnance Map in 1836, and there are earthwork remains of paddocks, closes and a hollow-way, although since 1980 this area has been used for motor-bike scrambling and so they are hard to distinguish.

Village Development

Elsworth belonged to Ramsey Abbey from the 10th to the 16th centuries, and it was probably this Abbey which laid out the village with a grid of lanes, the main one of which was built along a brook, at the junction of roads to Boxworth, Knapwell, Papworth St. Agnes, Conington and the Cambridge-St. Neots road. The manor house stood in the north-west of the village, in an otherwise apparently empty area that was a park in the 16th century. The church is on a raised site to the south-east. The present street pattern has not changed much since the early 19th century, and is probably similar to the medieval lay-out. Apart from the isolated hamlet at Elsworth Wood, there are settlements at Broad End, Cawdell End and Brockley End, which may suggest the original village was more scattered than it now appears.

The population was high at Domesday, at 48, and there were about 90 tenants in the 13th century. This had fallen to 209 tax-payers in 1377, and thereafter Elsworth was one of the larger villages in this area of clay upland. In the 16th century 53 households were taxed, and 73 in the 17th century. Only later did this really grow, with 600 people in 1801 and 878 in 1841. This was soon reversed, and by 1931 there were only 441 here, going back up to 600 in 1996.

In 1550 the estate was sold to Thomas Wendy of Haslingfield, and then in 1655 to the Disbrowe family. Samuel Disbrowe was a relative and active supporter of Cromwell, and was MP for Edinburgh under the Commonwealth. He was pardoned in 1660, and from then onwards led a quiet life at Elsworth, the first resident lord of the manor. It was he who built the new manor house in the park, south of the old moated site, and his descendants lived here until the 19th century.

Until the 13th century the Abbey's estate was farmed in hand, its function being to supply the monks with food in addition to cash income. Later the emphasis was on money rents, but provisions, including 2300 eggs a year, were still being sent to Ramsey in the 14th century. Milking cattle were kept, and were moved to graze in the fens in summer months. Sheep were increasingly important, both to the Abbey and to many of the villagers. Common grazing rights were gener-

Elsworth Manor House, built by Samuel Disbrowe in the 17th century, replacing Ramsey Abbey's moated house which lay just to the north. It lay within a small park, part of which is now the recreation ground.

Low Farm in Brook Street, Elsworth was once the medieval guildhall.

ous up to Enclosure, and in 1800, for example, 2200 sheep were recorded in the parish, and there were considerable areas of permanent grassland between Elsworth Wood and Caxton in the south, and between the village and Boxworth in the north. There was a large warehouse, probably for wool, at Avenue Farm, and sheep were dipped in the washpit by the bridge over the brook in Fardells Lane.

Low Farm in Brook Street was once the site of the medieval guildhall, from which social and charitable services were provided on a co-operative basis and where there was a chaplain who educated village boys. At the Dissolution its assets were taken by the Crown, but it still continued as a Town House, where help might be given to the poor, subsequently becoming a workhouse. Recent excavations have shown that the present 16th century house is an alteration of a medieval open hall which had foundations of stone and timbers from an earlier aisled building.

Trades and crafts are recorded in Elsworth in the Middle Ages and later centuries, with a high proportion of the population working as smiths, carpenters, wheel-wrights, tailors, shoemakers, butchers, bricklayers etc in the 19th century, for example. These crafts were concentrated in Brook Street, where buildings can still be seen that were once blacksmiths, wheelwrights, a Post and Telegraph Office, bakehouse, three public houses and a general store.

Eltisley

Eltisley is a medium sized parish of 800 hectares, on clay soil, lying on a plateau at around 60m, at the watershed of small streams which flow west to the Ouse at St. Neots, north to the Ouse at St. Ives and east through Caxton to the Bourn Brook. Its boundaries do not follow any natural or historic features, despite being the County boundary on two sides. Its open fields were not enclosed until a late Award was made in 1868. At Domesday its place-name was *Hecteslei,* 'Wood or clearing of Elti', perhaps indicating a relatively late clearance of woodland.

Middle Ages

Eltisley appears to be the point where the extension to the Lot Way from Caxton, Bourn and villages to the east joins the Cambridge-St. Neots road, but no pre-medieval sites have yet been found here, apart from three rows of undated pits noted during road-works in the extreme west of the parish. This route in the east of the village continued in use in the Middle Ages. Known as Caxton Drift, it was metalled as far as Caxton End, and still continues as a bridle way to Caxton.

A tradition recorded in the 16th century is that in the 9th century a Scottish princess, Pandionia, fled from a proposed marriage to the nunnery at Eltisley where her cousin was abbess, the link perhaps being a Scandinavian landowning family at Eltisley who were involved in campaigns in lowland Scotland. The story goes that she later became abbess herself, and by the 12th century was regarded as a saint. She was supposed to be buried by a holy well but in 1346 her bones were moved to the church which had been dedicated to her. No archaeological trace has been found for this religious house, but it may have been at Papley Grove, where a ruined chapel was confirmed as belonging to 'Lettice the nun and her sisters' by the bishop of Ely in the 13th century. Alternatively, the granting of this manor to the nuns of Hinchingbrooke may have given rise to the tradition of a nunnery here before it moved to Hinchingbrook. Papley Grove, in the

The church of St. Pandionia and St. John.

north of the parish, is a small rectangular wet moat, with a fishpond. Its placename has the same origin as Papworth Everard and Papworth St. Agnes and so it may have been connected in some way with these villages in Saxon times.

An exceptionally well-preserved moated site at Manor Farm to the south-east of the village, where manorial courts were still being held in 1807, is the most likely site for Eltisley's main manor house. The moat now surrounds a farmhouse that is probably 15th century in origin, but with alterations in the 17th and 18th centuries. There are other moated sites, one around a 16th century house, Pond Farm, on the east side of the green, and within Eltisley Wood, where there is a substantial wet, rectangular moat with two outer enclosures. 13th century pottery has been found in the interior of the latter site, which is covered in trees. It is likely that this moated site was connected with a medieval deer park which occupied a large area in the south of the parish, and whose park pale, a long curving bank which surrounded it, can still be seen. To the east of the village, at Caxton End, was a trapezoidal moat that is now ploughed away, where 11th and 12th century pottery occurred and where crop marks indicate there was also settlement round about.

Another apparent moated site is an area of ponds and ditches just south of the church, but in fact these are remains of garden features associated with the large timbered house, the Old House, that was built in 1612 by James Disbrowe. One of Disbrowe's sons was Samuel Disbrowe, who rebuilt the manor house in Elsworth, and another was John, who married Oliver Cromwell's sister and inherited the house here at Eltisley. In the grounds was the holy well of St. Pandionia, which was broken in the late 16th century by the vicar in order to stop superstitious practices.

Village Development

Eltisley now lies largely around a large and magnificent village green, at the cross-roads of two routes, Cambridge to St. Neots and Potton to St. Ives. The church is on the west point of a triangle, a moat is on the east side and the green is surrounded by most of the oldest houses in the village. However, the original village was split between at least two centres, the present green and Caxton End, where there was a smaller green, a moated site and other occupation along Caxton Drift. In the 15th century these settlements were distinguished as 'le Upende' and 'le Estende' respectively. Manor Farm, the most likely site for the village's main manor house, lies between these two centres, and there were also outlying settlements at Papley Grove, in Eltisley Wood, and around Potton End. It was probably not until the later Middle Ages, as the main roads became more important, that the present village took shape.

Pond Farm, Eltisley

The whole parish was part of one Saxon estate, and passed into the hands of the Mowbray family after the Conquest. By 1279 there were two principal manors and it was later broken into smaller estates, with land also given to various religious houses. In the 18th century the Leeds family of Croxton had bought a large estate, and almost all other land was owned by estates outside the village. The land was notoriously poor and rents low, and there was apparently no incentive for Enclosure until very late, in 1868.

The population at Domesday was 27, and there were 136 tax-payers in 1377. There were only 20 families recorded in the 16th century, and 90 adults in the 17th century. By 1801 the population had risen to 250 people in total, and was 504 in 1871. After this it dropped considerably, before rising again to 390 in 1996.

Despite the heavy soil, arable agriculture provided almost all the employment, although extensive woodland also contributed to the economy, and there were strong complaints from villagers and surrounding areas in about 1605, for example, when Thomas Leeds cut down 13 hectares of underwood. Pigs were kept in the wood at Domesday, and quite large numbers of sheep in the late 18th century, but generally livestock were not important. Other trades were insignificant, and little advantage seems to have been taken of the village's excellent communications, even after the main roads both became turnpikes in the 18th century.

The Eversdens

Great and Little Eversden are two small adjoining parishes of 583 and 330 hectares respectively. They lie within a fairly flat clay landscape, about 30m above sea level except for the chalk ridge 85m high along Mare Way, the southern boundary. The parishes are bounded by the Bourn Brook to the north, a stream and a lane to Toft to the west, and the Roman Cambridge-Arrington Bridge road and a minor road to Comberton to the east. Field boundaries divide Great and Little Eversden, and their open fields were enclosed in 1814. In Domesday Book they are *Euresdone,* or 'Boar's Hill'.

Prehistoric and Roman

Apart from two Neolithic flint axes, a reference to Roman pottery occurring near Sing Close in the south of Great Eversden, and a small quantity of Roman pottery at the north end of Little Eversden, no early finds have been reported. The prehistoric track of Mare Way has been undisturbed so long it is renowned for the rare wild flowers that grow upon it.

Middle Ages

A moated site at Manor Farm, Great Eversden, was probably built by the de Andevilles, lords of the manor until the mid 13th century. It was constructed over existing open fields, remains of which can be seen as ridge and furrow on three sides of the site, and it also blocks the village street and forces it to take a sharp right turn. In the late 14th century the manor was given to Sir Thomas Walsingham, a JP and sheriff who was killed by rebels during the Peasants Revolt. His house was pulled down by 'Jn Pepir of Linton and others', and over the following day three more rebels rode to Eversden and other places 'committing felonies'. All four men were later beheaded for this behaviour. Their destruction must have been significant for the goods in Walsingham's house were sold, and it stood empty the following year (when its moat and draw-bridge were recorded). However, by the end of the century it was again the residence of lords of the manor, and an oratory was licensed. John Tiptoft, created Earl of Worcester in the mid 15th century and later executed, was said to have been born here. In the late 15th century the estate was given to Queens College, and the house was rebuilt by John Hale to whom it was leased from about 1500. In the early 17th century, John Layer wrote 'the scite of the manor house remayneth but now a meane house built near to it'. Much of what survives today is 18th century, but there are exposed beams of the 2-storey timber-framed and plastered 'meane' 17th century building. The moat itself is a double rectangle, one arm of the smaller enclosure being destroyed by farm buildings and another widened into an ornamental pond. The moat became dry in the 1970s when a pumping station was built nearby.

Another estate, Rectory Manor, was created in the 12th century by St. Alban's Abbey, which had acquired the church and other land. After the Dissolution this estate was given to Oliver Warner, and his family held it until 1650. The present Rectory Farm is a 17th century house, but an aisled barn with five bays at the same farm is possibly 15th century and exceptionally interesting, displaying several techniques of medieval carpentry. Given that the tithes of Great Eversden were valuable enough to be exchanged for 205 acres of land at Enclosure, it is likely that this barn served as the Abbey's Tithe Barn. By Enclosure the estate had passed to the Earl of Hardwicke at Wimpole.

Great Eversden's 15th century tithe barn, built for St. Alban's Abbey.

There was also a moated site, now destroyed, in the centre of Great Eversden, which has produced 13th century pottery though the later building now standing in the enclosure is 17th century. It, too, lies over open fields. On the boundary of Eversden Wood is a small moat, 15m square, with a substantial ditch and depressions which could either be another enclosure or fishponds. This moat is characteristic of a type noted elsewhere on the edges of ancient woods in Eastern England. The

Manor Farm and moat.The moat around the farm is now dry, due to water extraction nearby.

The Guildhall opposite the church in Great Eversden.

Enclosure map shows part of a moated site at the south end of the village of Little Eversden, of which only one arm survived as a pond in 1968, in an arable field. 14th century and later pottery has been collected there. Medieval pottery has also been found at Sing Close, south of the village, an illustration of scattered settlement in Great Eversden.

Village Development

The Eversdens, which had no lords of the manor before the Conquest, seem to have originated as numerous scattered farmsteads that were attracted to some of the many north-south trackways that linked Mare Way to crossing points of the Bourn Brook from prehistoric times. Great Eversden is on two of these parallel routes, the Wimpole Way and Church Lane, and Little Eversden is on another. Great Eversden later developed along a street to the west, as far as Manor Farm, using land that had previously been within open fields. Areas of the common fields were enclosed before 1600 and in some of these old enclosures ridge and furrow is still visible, both in the village and around Eversden Wood. Its church originally served both villages. It was probably built before the Conquest by the peasant farmers who held the land before it was given Guy de Reimbercourt, who held the majority of both parishes in 1086. This church was sited at the crossing of Church Lane and the village street, both quite long-distance routes, and was close to both settlements. Other communal buildings, such as a guildhall and parish pound were built nearby, but the manorial sites are at a distance. Little Eversden's church, which was in use in the early 13th century was also on a north-south track, at the opposite end of the village to the moated site. Later in the Middle Ages, Great Eversden in particular developed a more rectangular grid of lanes based on access routes to the fields. These disappeared or became footpaths at Enclosure.

The populations were always fairly small. At Domesday the combined population was 26. In Great Eversden there were 148 people taxed in 1377 and only 22 in 1525, with 27 households in 1664. There were 212 people in 1801, rising to a peak of 380 in 1871 when industrial work was available, but it fell in the 20th century and in 1996 was 190. Little Eversden was only half the size of Great Eversden in the Middle Ages, but from the 16th century it was the same or somewhat larger. In 1801 the population was 150, rising to 288 in 1851. It fell by about half in the early 20th century before new buildings after 1950 increased the population to 540 in 1996.

In Great Eversden small-scale quarries provided some employment. Clunch from Great Eversden was used in St. John's College in the 16th century. Small pits were dug for lime or marl at least by the 17th century, and chalk was burnt for lime in quantities large enough for a tramway to be built to Claypit Hill in the late 19th century. There were brickyards at the north end of the village in the 19th century. Small quarries also provided employment in Little Eversden. Clunch quarries at Quarry Farm in the south extremity of the parish produced stone for Corpus Christi and Trinity College in the late 16th-early 17th centuries, and there were 19th century brickyards here also.

Fowlmere

Fowlmere is a medium sized parish of 945 hectares, mostly on chalk, with small areas of gravel in the south-east and north-west corners. The parish contained wide areas of grassland in the south and marshy moorland in the west until the mid 19th century. Its boundaries include Bran Ditch and Old Walden Way, (the old County boundary), and Wallington Brook. The village, at the crossing place of this brook, lies on the border of its parish. Its place name, *Fuelmere* in Domesday, means 'wild birds mere' and is an appropriate description of the parish until about 1850, when the Enclosure Award for the parish was made and the mere known as the Great Moor, that spread for more than 100 hectares around Black Peak, was drained.

Prehistoric

The south of the parish was open chalk downland, crossed by the prehistoric routes of the Icknield

Way and Ashwell Street and it was attractive for early settlement. Many burial mounds here survived into the 19th century thanks to the use of grassland and mere for medieval pasture and common. The oldest stone tools found in the area are a Palaeolithic scraper, cleaver and hand-axe and a Mesolithic axe, all found near Heath Farm. That area of former grassland has also produced several hundred worked flints, including scrapers of many kinds, awls, blades, arrow-heads, axes and cores. During excavations of Bran Ditch in 1993, it was found that the Dyke's bank had protected a layer containing Mesolithic or early Neolithic struck flint flakes in a fresh condition, indicating that it was a tool-production site. Although the sites of at least eleven Bronze Age barrows were landmarks in the 19th century, all are now flattened. Only one was ever investigated, in 1847, and the excavator complained 'it proved, however, a very uninteresting tomb, rich only in its poorness,' though it had the burial of an adult male with 'fragments of light red pottery' (presumably Beaker) and 'several portions of flint knives'. In addition there were Anglo-Saxon secondary burials (below).

Excavations on Bran Ditch also uncovered a small Iron Age enclosure, and there are others visible as crop marks nearby. In the north-east corner of the parish enclosures are probably connected with an Iron Age site excavated at Foxton on the opposite side of the brook.

Roman

Occasional sherds of Roman pottery were also found during excavations of Bran Ditch, derived from a building complex near the Watercress Beds. Pot sherds, tiles, quern fragments and cobbles have been recovered from the fields. Excavations around the Round Moat uncovered small amounts of abraded Roman sherds. Crop marks show the side-ditches of a road leading from the north of Fowlmere to the villa at Shepreth, and it is likely that this extended from Barrington to Ashwell Street, as in later times. As Ashwell Street was still in use, the site of the later village of Fowlmere would have been on a Roman road junction.

Anglo-Saxon

Bran Ditch is the slightest of the four great Cambridgeshire dykes that were built to cut off east-west routes along the Icknield Way. Originally this Dyke consisted of a substantial bank and a ditch that was 6m wide and 1.8m deep near Black Peak. It has now been virtually levelled, surviving only as a low rise along field boundaries. One strange discovery on this Dyke was a cemetery of execution victims, either Late Saxon or medieval. The lords of the manor of Fowlmere had the right to hang thieves, and the area was known as Hangman's Pieces in the mid 19th century. With the skeletons were an iron knife, a belt clip and sherds of a handled pot. The site is marked by

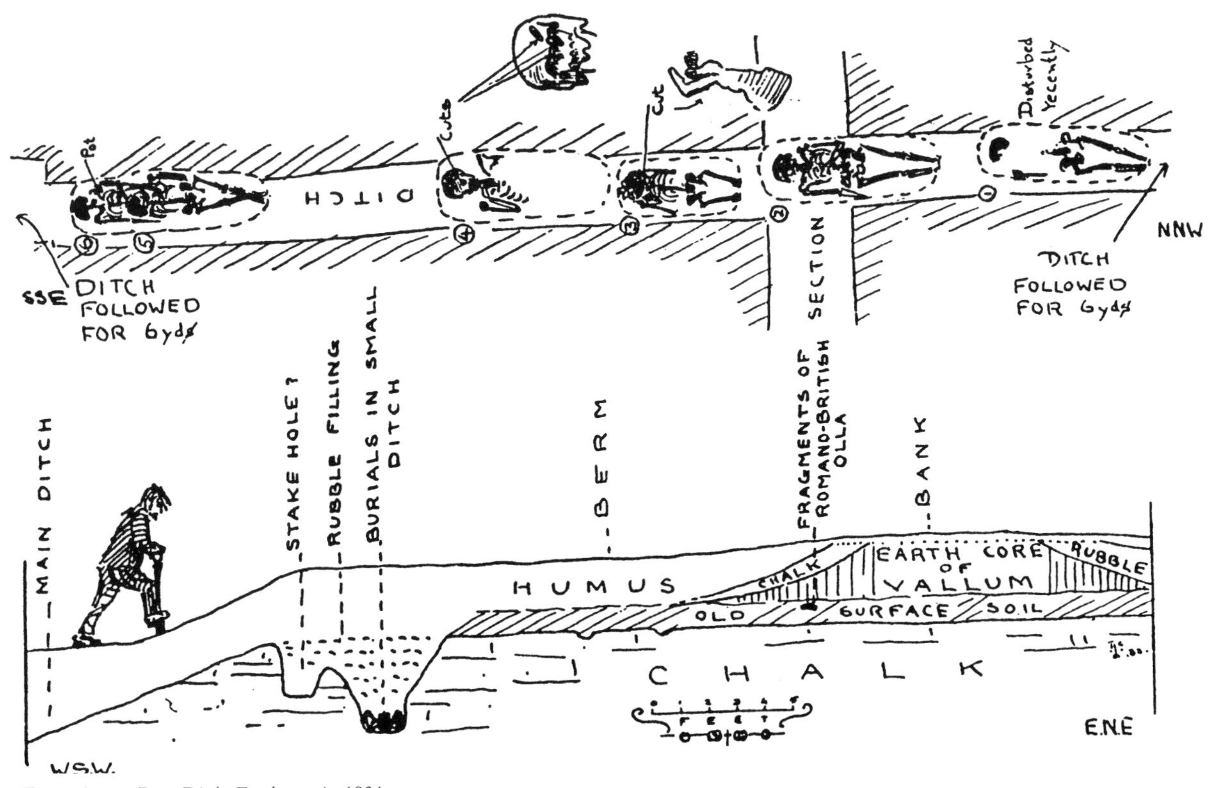

Excavations at Bran Ditch, Fowlmere, in 1931.

Bronze Age mounds and a group of converging tracks visible on aerial photographs.

Fowlmere Round Moat is in fact a large oval with a deep wide ditch. Its position on Ashwell Street, of which it forced a diversion, may be significant. Its resemblance to the round Iron Age hill-forts of Cambridgeshire has led to suggestions of an Iron Age date, and this has not been disproved. Blocking this tract of open chalk country was strategically important at various times in the past and it is also likely that there would be military advantages in commanding a stream crossing on this vital highway. Typologically, it is reminiscent of Late Saxon/early Norman ringworks. The ditch is steep-sided and flat-bottomed, like the Dykes, and the few examples of rounded as opposed to rectangular moats usually have Saxon connections, and so an origin as a Late Saxon manorial centre is suggested. However, it has a central position in the village, adjacent to the church, and medieval occupation is proven, and so it may be an unusually defensive version of a medieval moat. In the early 20th century 'British' pottery', horse-shoes and animal bones were found, and when trees were planted in the interior to celebrate Victoria's Jubilee a cobbled surface and a well were discovered.

Middle Ages

In addition to the Round Moat, Fowlmere has a square moat, Crow's Parlour, which has a substantial ditch, until recently water-filled but now usually dry. It is otherwise well preserved apart from recent in-filling with building rubble etc.

Fowlmere's main manor was part of the barony of Stansted Mountfichet, passing to the earls of Oxford in the 15th century. In 1600 it was bought by Edward Aldred, yeoman of Fowlmere and its first resident lord of the manor. The building known as 'The Old Manor', a late 16th or early 17th century timber-framed house that was extensively rebuilt in the 19th century, belongs to this period, probably on the site of a manor house that is recorded from the 14th century. By 1635 the estate was sold again and later owners were not resident here.

Village Development

As with other villages in South Cambridgeshire, Fowlmere's original form was the result of its growth along the numerous routes of the Icknield Way. The major route was Ashwell Street, which here was the High Street of Fowlmere, with the church set alongside it. The other track, south of the High Street and parallel to it, is the present Chapel Lane, which was also once a main through-street. Subsequent expansion, movement and contraction, as well as the existence of a fair which opened in 1207, led to the growth in importance of the cross-roads at Townhead. The widening of the road here may include the site of a market.

Later medieval growth of Fowlmere resulted from the development of the main London to Cambridge road which cut obliquely across the parish from Flint Cross to Newton and was channelled along the High Street. This route involved less steep gradients than a comparable one through Melbourn and increased in importance, especially in the 17th century. In the 18th century the road was a major stage-coach route and several inns survive from this period of prosperity.

Other remains of this time are the milestones along the road. These date from the early 18th century and are the oldest post-Roman milestones in England. They were paid for by investments of a bequest of 1552/3 by Dr. W Mowse, Master of Trinity Hall, who left money for highway improvements around Cambridge.

Fowlmere village is almost unique in Cambridgeshire in that its extreme east end is actually part of Thriplow parish, and thus legally and administratively a separate place. How this unusual situation came about is not known. Another example is Girton.

The present green lane known as Old Walden Way, which formed the County boundary before Heydon was transferred to Cambridgeshire, was a track of the Icknield Way. The present A505 was another. This was the main route from London to Norwich and was turnpiked in 1725.

At Domesday Fowlmere was well-established, with 36 villagers. The population grew to about a 100 households in 1279, perhaps 500 people in all, but fell to 31 tax-payers in 1327, and this figure stayed fairly constant before rising slightly in the 17th century. In 1801 there were 420 inhabitants, rising to 616 in 1841 but otherwise falling to the mid-1970s, after which new housing led to a population of 1170 in 1996.

Fowlmere was unusual in possessing large areas of common land available for the use of all villagers until 1845. Thriplow Heath was part of a tract of sheep-walks stretching from Royston to Newmarket, and many sheep are recorded in Fowlmere from 1086 until the 20th century. The Heath was used for royal hunting, most notably in the Stuart period, and there were artificial rabbit warrens there that upset royal hunters. It was also an area, still known as 'waste and wilderness' in the 19th century, that was renowned for semi-lawless activities such as the prize-fighting which attracted huge crowds, partly because it was easy to escape over the County border to another judicial area. It was on this Heath that 20,000 of the Parliamentarian army gathered in 1647.

Fowlmere's Great Moor was a stretch of marshy moorland, described at the beginning of the 20th century as 'the ancient glory of our village' and was home for abundant wildfowl which were a valuable source of food for villagers and were later hunted by sportsmen from Cambridge. It was also famous for a large, yellow-backed species of frog that was collected for food. Leech-gathering and reed-cutting, too, were lucrative pastimes before 1850. All villagers could pasture cattle freely on the Moor, and could gather dung and dig clay.

Foxton

Foxton is a small parish of 708 hectares, lying on chalk apart from gravel near the river and brook. Generally low-lying and level at about 15-25m above sea-level, the land rises to 30m on Chalk Hill and West Hill. There are marshy areas near the streams. The village itself was built along a brook, which is now filled in. The parish boundaries are the Rhee, Hoffer Brook, Shepreth Brook, and the old road to Fowlmere. Its open fields were enclosed following an Award made in 1830. In Domesday Book Foxton is *Foxetune,* or 'farm where foxes abound'.

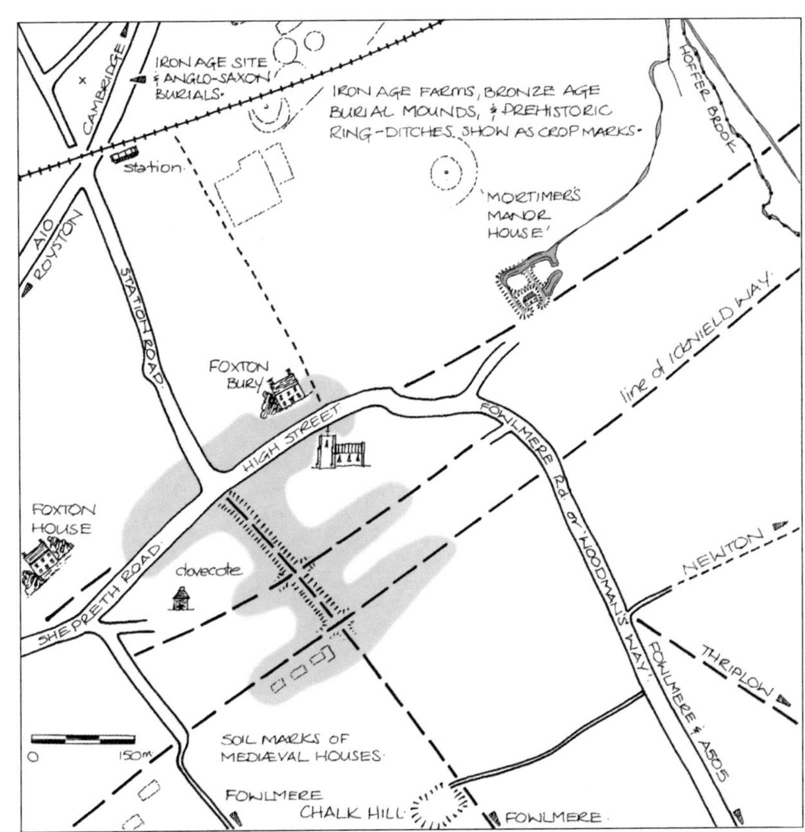

Prehistoric

A Palaeolithic hand-axe and a Neolithic polished axe and worked flints come from West Hill in the south of the parish, and a Neolithic axe and a Bronze Age axe-hammer were found near the station. Part of a bronze axe was discovered south of this and a complete axe is also known from Foxton. Excavations for a gas-pipe (below) found small pits, presumably part of a settlement of prehistoric date, including one with pottery, flint blades, scrapers and flakes, dated by radiocarbon to 2350-2175 BC. Ring-ditches are visible from the air in several areas. From their association with later enclosures it is likely that most are Iron Age huts, but in some cases a central pit is apparent or the ring-ditches are double, and these probably were Bronze Age burial mounds.

Foxton is remarkable for its extensive Iron Age sites, and the degree to which many of them developed into even more significant Roman settlements, with nearly half the parish containing crop marks of Iron Age farmsteads. Two distinctive areas have been investigated with quite different results. In the 1920s an area west of the station was found to contain evidence of dense settlement of the early 1st century AD with much wheel-turned Late Iron Age pottery. Layers of black soil were full of occupation debris (potsherds, animal-bones, pot-boilers, small pieces of iron and bronze), including two knives, a spindle-whorl and almost complete pots. South of this, on the Roman site, Iron Age enclosure ditches, a possible cremation within a shallow stone-lined pit, and pits with deliberately deposited pots within them were identified.

A very different area was examined in 1993. Crop marks covered about 50 hectares, of which only a very small part was trenched. Pottery evidence showed that the site was probably only in use during the 1st century BC-early 1st century AD with just a scatter of later Roman sherds. The well-made wares of the earlier site were absent. There was a small assemblage of animal bone, mainly cattle and sheep with some pig, horse, dog, hare and chicken. No structures were located although there were numerous ditches, a sub-circular enclosure, small pits and post-holes.

Roman

The above site presumably continued in agricultural use during the Roman period but its settlement moved elsewhere. In one field-ditch lay a crouched skeleton without grave-goods, thought to be Roman though it may have belonged to the original settlement. Roman sites are prolific in this river valley, usually with farmers living amongst their own fields and stock enclosures, and villas are also common. One villa is suggested by crop marks in the north of the parish, and there is another at Shepreth, on the border of Foxton. An area on the outskirts of the latter site, within Foxton parish, was excavated in 1994 with exceptional results.

A major feature was a cemetery with 23 skeletons dating to the 3rd-late 4th century. One male wearing a bronze buckle was in a lead-lined coffin with a Nene Valley dish and two black-burnished bowls (presumably heirlooms) and the bones of two geese and a chicken. Many of the graves had coffin nails and several burials were accompanied by chicken or goose bones. One woman aged

45+ was buried without her head, with a large bronze bracelet and a bone comb. Another headless woman was in a grave with two male skulls and a leg, with goose bones. One male had deep sword-cuts on his head. The cemetery was demarcated by a substantial ditch on two sides and the regular layout indicates that long-lived grave-markers were used.

North of the cemetery was a major building with a heating system, military-style ditches and an area of small-scale industry, perhaps smithying, all from the 1st century. Two pairs of side-ditches of a Roman road which leaves the A10 near Foxton Station and goes to the Shepreth villa were located. This is useful evidence that the A10, which was a medieval route known as 'Portway' at this point, was also close to a Roman road.

An almost square building with sides up to 7m long was possibly a small temple, and there were ditches and other features dating from the 2nd to the 5th century. The most interesting find of all on this site was a hoard of 4th century ironwork consisting of 113 items. This collection includes bucket-hoops, padlock-keys, a shackle, hinge, nails, knife-blades, a farrier's tool, smith's tools, pruning hook, coulter tip, scythe blade, hippo-sandal fragments, wheel parts, a steelyard set, various bindings, fittings, bars, etc. and a bell, all made of iron, plus an antler pendant, lead weights and a bronze box-fitting. The excavators thought that all the objects were in a sack placed in an open ditch that was then backfilled, quite possibly for religious reasons. Iron hoards are very rare in Roman Britain and this is one of the largest known.

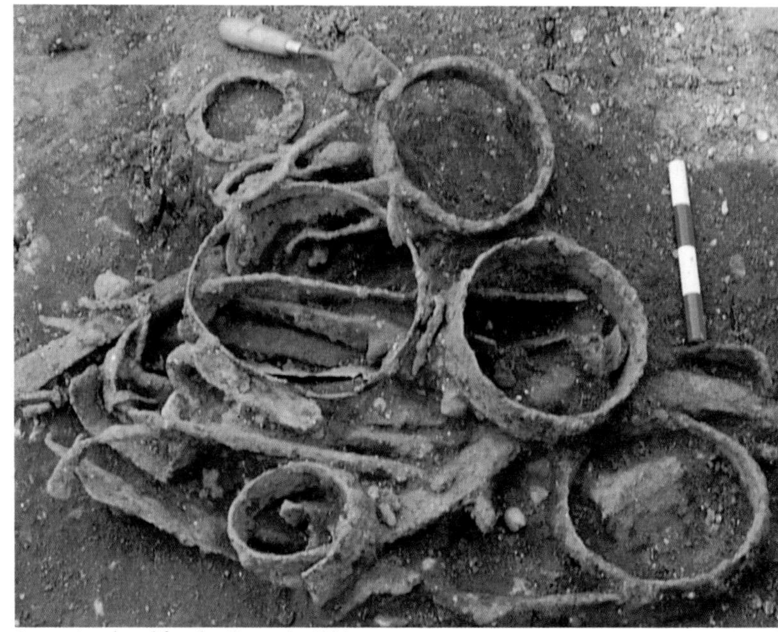

Roman iron hoard found at Foxton in 1994.

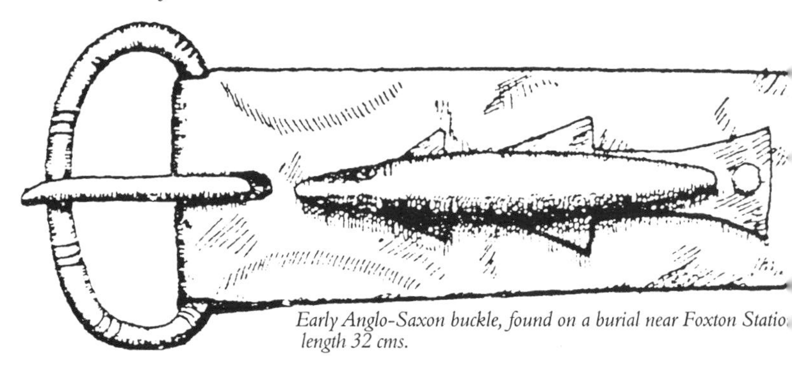

Early Anglo-Saxon buckle, found on a burial near Foxton Statio[n], length 32 cms.

Raising a lead coffin, 1994.

Anglo-Saxon

Skeletons were found on the site of the Iron Age settlement near Foxton Station. One was accompanied by a small spear, one by a knife and another had a unique bronze buckle decorated with an appliqué fish, two knives and a sandstone hone.

Middle Ages

The main manor house, Foxton Bury, is a fine building standing opposite the church. It was held by the nuns of Chatteris Abbey from before the Conquest to the Dissolution. It was very dilapidated in the 16th century, and was substantially rebuilt. Another manor house, Mortimer's, stood in a double ditched enclosure that is now mostly destroyed, at the east end of the village. The house that stood within the moat was rebuilt in 1548, and the present house is 19th century. There vas also a tithe barn here which was ismantled in 1968. Along the High street are many cottages that date back to the 15th, 16th and 17th enturies, one of which, The Cottage n the Green, was previously the ome of local historian Rowland Parker, and the subject of one of his books.

Village Development

As in Fowlmere, the medieval illage had two east-west streets of which the present High Street was once a route of the Icknield Way. There were also three north-south anes, forming a grid of streets where now only High Street and Fowlmere Road (previously Woodman's Way) urvive. The south arm of an old cross-road in the centre of the village s now a green hollow-way, the houses beside it surviving as earth-works. In the 16th century this hollow-way was known as 'the common lane leading from Foxton to Fulmayer'. The only building now left n the field is a dovecote built in 1706, once part of a farmstead that was demolished in 1825. The line of houses along the street parallel to the High Street have been recorded as soil marks. After Enclosure, land on both sides of the hollow-way was allotted to William Hurrell, the major land-owner in the parish, and o the road became a private farm-track. By 1887, the Hurrells had created parkland around Foxton House in the west of the village. Part of the park-bank with stumps of its trees survives in pasture.

Foxton, which had a high Domes-day population of 43, grew into a moderate-sized village through the Middle Ages with 68 tenants holding and in 1279. The population drop-ped in the 16th century, with 30 households recorded in 1563. It grew to 322 in 1801 and reached 450 in the 1840s. It fell after this, rising only in the late 20th century to 1140 in 1996.

Gamlingay

Gamlingay is now a very large parish of 1300 hectares, lying mostly on greensand, with patches of clay in the extreme north and south of the parish and to the east of the village. The land rises and falls between 25 and 75m above sea level. Very poor drainage in some places has created acidic bogs. It was previously considerably larger, but parts of the parish were transferred to Hatley in 1958 and to Bedfordshire in 1965. The areas that still remained as open fields were enclosed in 1822. Its place-name in Domesday Book is *Gamelinge*, or 'the low-lying land of the people of Gamela'.

Prehistoric

Gamlingay's sandy heaths were attractive to early inhabitants, who concentrated on hunting and gathering even in Neolithic and Bronze Age times after agriculture had been introduced elsewhere. There, where land was unsuitable for medieval agriculture, scatters of flint tools survived in good condition until 20th century ploughing led to their discovery. Palaeolithic borers, gravers and scrapers, the tools used for preparing meat and skins, working on wood and bone and many other tasks, have been found. Mesolithic microliths are common discoveries on the heath and near the brook in Dutter End, and there are also numerous tools of the Neolithic periods. Arrow-heads, knives, scrapers, blades, several hundred flint flakes, and two stone axes and one bronze axe have been found in these areas. Crop marks of pits, ditches, irregular enclosures and a 'pit-alignment' boundary are probably Iron Age, though no artefacts have been noted. These features suggest there was settlement in the extreme west end of the parish, adjacent to White Wood.

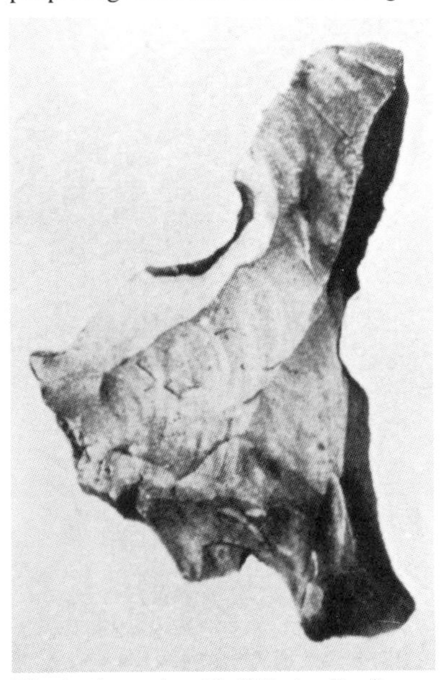

Flint implement from Neolithic site, Gamlingay.

Middle Ages

In 1268 Walter of Merton bought an estate that had been mortgaged by a rebellious baron and passed it to his house of scholars, which became Merton College, Oxford. Merton Manor Farm stood within a moated site of which two sides survived in 1968, although they had mostly been filled in by 1971. Features recorded here in the 13th century enclosed by a wall and the moat include a bailiff's and servants' houses, a kitchen, dairy, buttery, barn, two granaries, kiln, dovecote, sheep-fold, cattle-sheds and a vegetable garden. Parts of the building standing there are still structurally of 15th to 16th century date.

A manor house which belonged to the Avenel family is recorded from the 12th to the 14th century. It stood in a moated site at Dutter End which was levelled in 1983. In 1807 the house was described as ancient, built of timber, tiled and plastered, with a large thatched barn, stable, granary, cow-house and pigsties. It still stood, though in bad repair, in 1844. Pottery of the 11th to 14th century and a great many tiles have been noted during field-walking on the site. The Avenels also built a deer-park, from which the theft of a deer is recorded in 1289. The hedged bank of this oval deer-park, shown on a map of 1776, is still visible in places.

Gamlingay Wood, parts of which belonged to Merton College from 1268-1959, is one of the best documented woods in Britain. In it can still be seen remains of wood banks which divided it between two manors in the 12th century. One of its most enigmatic features is a circular ditched enclosure with an inner bank and wet ditch. It pre-dates the ancient wood banks, but its date and function are not yet understood.

Village Development

Gamlingay is a large and complicated village whose present form is the result of many changes and developments, not all of which are understood. Originally there were probably a group of separate hamlets lying at or around the place on the heathland where a series of routeways met. These hamlets are now apparent at Dutter End, Green End, Dennis Green and perhaps at the central cross-roads. At least one other hamlet, known as Newton-in-the-Heath, existed in the early 13th century but had apparently disappeared by 1279. Its name suggests it was a relatively late settlement on poor land.

Some of the hamlets were amalgamated, perhaps by expansion but more likely by the laying out of a regular planned village between Green and Dutter Ends and the present Church Street, with the church and rectory (now 'Emplins', a 15th century building), at the east end. A small rectangular open space at the cross-roads at the west end was probably used for the weekly market of Avenel's manor by 1279. The creation of this new village led to the alteration of the radial road system.

George Downing's Folly.

15th century rectory (now 'Emplins').

Gamlingay was always the largest village in its area and retained the craftsmen and traders expected in a small town even after the loss of its market which seems to have been caused by a widespread fire in 1600. Its population was 65 in 1086, and there were 219 poll-tax payers in 1377. Fifty families were assessed for tax in the 16th century, which must be a serious underestimate, given that 76 houses were destroyed in the fire of 1600. In the 17th century, 71 households were taxed. There were 847 inhabitants in 1801, rising to 2063 in 1871, but falling after that, down to 1408 in 1931. There were still good services and facilities in the village, and so new developments were encouraged after 1950, leading to a population of 3450 in 1996.

An area of heathland was given to Sawtry Abbey, who had a grange there. At the Dissolution the Cromwell family were given the grange and sold it to the Burgoynes 'who hath there the old grange and a park. There is now never a seate there, but only Woodbury hath a pritty gentlemanlike house there lately built upon it'. (John Layer, early in the 17th century.)

In 1712, Sir George Downing, grandson and heir of the George Downing who had made his fortune as a politician, managing to work for both Cromwell and Charles II and giving his name to Downing Street in London, bought Avenel's old deer park and used material from his manor house in East Hatley to build a mansion there. Around it he laid out formal gardens with ponds, a lake, woodland walks, classical statuary and a labyrinth, enclosed with a brick wall. The design of these gardens is shown on a plan of 1801 and can still be seen on the ground, where slight earthworks reveal one of the best preserved house and garden sites in East Anglia, though of the buildings only a fragment of its red brick folly is still standing. Sir George, himself an MP for Suffolk but never active in politics, left his fortune to his cousin on condition that, if he had no heir, it should be left to endow a new Cambridge college. The cousin's widow thought otherwise and spent many years and much of the fortune contesting the will before Downing College was at last founded in 1800. In the meantime she took revenge by pulling down the mansion only fifty years after it was built, and selling the materials.

Girton

Girton is quite a small parish of 720 hectares, lying on clay overlain in places with gravel. It is mostly flat and low-lying, only about 10-15m above sea level apart from a 'hill' 25m high south of the Roman road. Two brooks from the south meet just west of the village, in the once-marshy area known as Duck End, and then flow on to a tributary of the Cam. Girton's boundaries have been changed several times in the 20th century, but they never appear to have followed natural or historic features, and the parish is unusual in including land on both sides of the Roman road, rather than using it as a boundary. Its open fields were enclosed in 1814. In Domesday Book the place-name is *Greton,* meaning 'Gravel Farm'.

Prehistoric

A Palaeolithic hand-axe in fresh condition came from a gravel pit within the village, and a few prehistoric flint flakes have been found around the parish. The earliest settlement evidence is a small group of enclosures and circular huts of Iron Age date excavated between the village and Girton College before construction of Cambridge Northern By-Pass in 1976. Excavations on the Anglo-Saxon cemetery (below) uncovered part of a Bronze Age cremation urn, probably from a round barrow that marked the site as sacred and which later attracted further use as a cemetery in Roman and Anglo-Saxon times.

Roman

The Roman road from Cambridge to Godmanchester passed through this parish, well to the south of the village. It was marked in Girton by two milestones, inscribed with dedications to Constantine the Great which can be dated to 306-7 AD.

The Iron Age settlement site continued to be used for farming in Roman times, and the body of a young woman was buried in one of the ditches. The major site of Roman Girton was a cemetery, dating from

4th century Roman milestones found near Girton. Inscriptions (left) IMP[ERATORI] CAES[ARI] FLAVI[O] V[A]LE[RIO] CONSTANTINO PIO NOB[ILISSIMO] and (right) [NOB]ILISSIMUS CAESAR.

the 2nd to 4th century AD. It was found on the site of Girton College, adjacent to the Roman road, during excavations of the Anglo-Saxon cemetery. A rubbish pit contained massive carved stones, including the head of a lion devouring its prey, with pieces of its other limbs and a male torso wearing a belted tunic. There were also many stone blocks and hypocaust and roof tiles that could have come from a domestic site, but are more likely to be part of tombs or temples. A bronze statuette of a Celtic god came from the same area.

Roman burials had been disturbed by the later cemetery and construction works for the College. Excavators in the 1880s were only able to recover two 2nd century cremations, both in square wooden boxes with iron nails, one of which contained a wooden casket studded with eight bronze bosses in the form of boars' heads. This latter grave also contained cremated bone in a glass vessel, two stamped samian plates

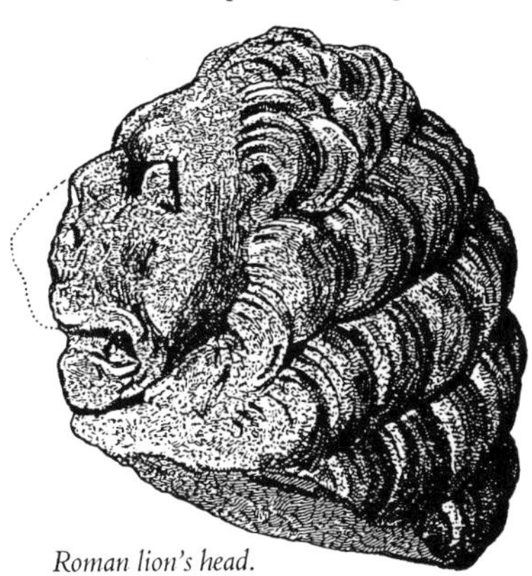

Roman lion's head.

Roman glass dish inscribed on the underside with a duck and Egyptian water-plants. Photograph © Cambridge University Museum of Archaeology and Anthropology.

and a cup, a cream-coloured jug, an extremely rare example of a glazed bowl, three more glass vessels, a glass dish inscribed with a duck and Egyptian water-plants, and an iron lamp. The second cremation was also in a glass vessel, with two stamped samian plates, two cream-coloured jugs, a dish, and an iron lamp. Another vessel suggested a further burial, and all three were in a line parallel to the Roman road. The style of these burials, with their extravagant feasting regalia, boxes and lamps are strongly reminiscent of the sort often found beneath mounds, and it is likely these graves were marked in this way. A short distance to the west a mound containing Roman coins beside the road was destroyed in the 18th century. Two later Roman inhumations in nailed coffins were also found, both with Nene Valley beakers, one of them with its head placed between its legs. At least three other burials with nails and without grave-goods were probably Roman.

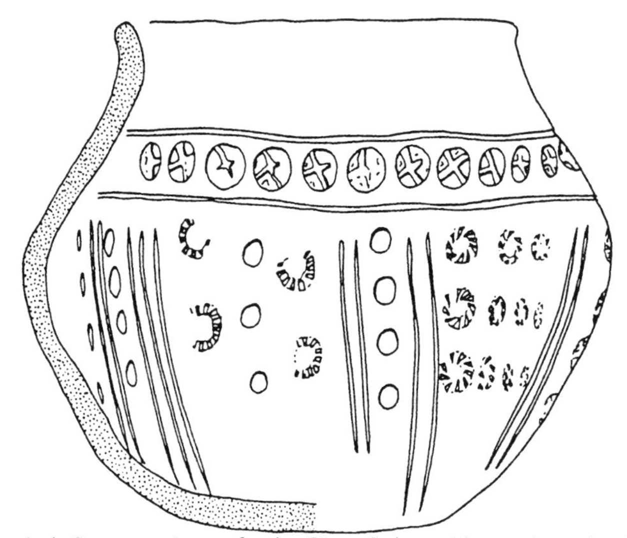

Anglo-Saxon cremation urn found at Girton. Scale: pot 1:2; stamp impressions 1:1. Illus. © Cambridge Antiquarian Society

Anglo-Saxon

The Anglo-Saxons re-used the Roman burial site for a large cemetery, beginning in the 5th century. Unlike the cemeteries further south in Cambridgeshire the majority of burials, 150, were cremations, with about 75 inhumations recorded, though many of both types were lost in the difficult circumstances of excavation. Grave-goods included many brooches, almost all of East Anglian types, knives, several pairs of tweezers and wrist-clasps, bone combs and a comb-case, buckets, finger-rings, necklaces of glass and amber, pierced Roman coins and an axe, but only four spears and no shield bosses. Most cremations were in urns, some of them decorated, and some of these also had grave-goods, mainly brooches, tweezers, combs, and shears. Some artefacts, such a pair of tweezers and shears, were miniatures. Both inhumations and cremations had occasional objects of Roman date, and in one grave a woman wore a Roman brooch as well as an Anglo-Saxon one.

Roman influence on this Anglo-Saxon cemetery was great. The well-marked Roman site was deliberately re-used about a century later, and common use of grave-goods such as combs, tweezers, finger-rings and even a shale bracelet is typical of Roman tradition. The number of weapon burials is exceptionally low. On the other hand, the cremations are distinctly East Anglian, and none of the inhumations individually are really out of place in an Anglo-Saxon context. The cemetery mainly dates to the late 5th and early 6th centuries, earlier than others in South Cambridgeshire though it overlaps with these.

Village Development

The village of Girton originated near the church, and Middle and Late Saxon pottery, pits and ditches were found in excavations just to the north of this, outside the present village framework. Occupation on this site seems to have stopped abruptly in the 12th century, for there are no finds after this date until the 19th century. It is not known how it acquired its present lay-out. It may have developed from a group of separate hamlets, including Duck End and the area around the church, but then became little more than a long single street, High Street. Though there is no obvious indication that the village had a planned, regular original form, its almost complete dislocation from the surrounding pattern of roads and tracks, which have to turn abruptly to enter Girton, suggests a deliberately conceived arrangement. One unusual feature of Girton is the fact that Manor Farm, at the northern end of the High Street, was until 1934 actually in the parish of Histon. The reason for this is unclear, though Manor Farm may have been the centre of a nucleated estate recorded as early as 1086.

In medieval times there was a small hamlet, Howes, situated at the extreme south-east corner of the parish alongside the Roman road. This hamlet extended into the adjacent parishes of Chesterton and Impington, as well as Cambridge. Though recorded in the 13th century, with its own chapel, little is known of its history. Its cross-parish situation implies that it was a comparatively late settlement, perhaps connected with the growth of traffic on the former Roman road.

The population at Domesday was 34, growing to 90 landholders in 1279, and then falling to 196 poll-tax payers in 1377. After the Middle Ages the population was smaller, about 35-40 houses in the 16th and 17th centuries, and only 25 recorded in the 18th century. Modest growth led to total populations of 232 in

1801 and 470 in the 1860s, and the village was described as 'small, but has lately been much improved by Miss A M Cotton, who has built several neat cottages and a handsome school-house in it'. A later fall in the population of the village was compensated by the foundation of Girton College. The village has grown considerably since the 1950s, and in 1996 there were 3770 people within the parish.

In the late 10th and early 11th centuries much land in Girton was given to Ramsey Abbey, which held the largest estate in the parish until the Dissolution and used the profits from it to buy clothing for the monks. There seems to have been no manor house, but in the 12th century the wife of 'Robert de Gretton' was given land in exchange for building a house where the Abbot could stay when he visited. In the 16th century the Crown sold the estate to the Hindes of Madingley. This family, and their successors, the Cottons, bought up two smaller manors in Girton, and most of the land held by smallholders. At Enclosure the Cottons owned nearly all the parish, and only 12 acres were allowed to villagers in compensation for common rights.

Ramsey Abbey had a small flock of sheep from the early 12th century, and in 1653 every villager with common rights could pasture a cow and 30 sheep. Large flocks were recorded in the late 18th century. Otherwise, apart from a few craftsmen, the economy depended on agriculture until the 1870s, when Girton College, Cambridge's first women' s college, was founded.

Grantchester

Grantchester, a small parish of 490 hectares, lies on gravel and alluvial soils near the river, with bands of chalk, gravel and clay elsewhere. It is generally flat and low-lying, rising to about 20m above sea-level in the south but with the village situated only a little higher than the Cam. Its boundaries include two important watercourses, the Cam on the east and the Bourn Brook on the south. Its border on the north with Coton was not fixed until Enclosure in 1803, when it followed Bin Brook and the road to Cambridge, and the area of Newnham Croft formerly in Grantchester was detached to become part of Cambridge in 1912. At Domesday it was *Granteseta,* or 'the settlers on the Granta', the alternative name for the Cam.

Prehistoric

Prehistoric finds include scatters of worked flints and one Palaeolithic, two Neolithic and one Bronze Age axe. By the Iron Age there were substantial areas of settlement within the parish. Important collections of Iron Age pottery, some dating as early as 500 BC, were rescued from coprolite mines to the south and west of the village, and an iron spear, an unusual item for this date, was found. The river-crossing to Trumpington, where similar material has been found, was presumably in use by this time, and the river provided communications to settlements at Haslingfield, Hauxton, Harston and further afield.

Roman

During coprolite mining in the south of the parish, near the medieval Tartars Well, a Roman villa was discovered. Finds included a carved stone column, large quantities of bricks, roof and flue tiles, Roman concrete, painted wall-plaster and stone wall-foundations. Stray coins and sherds of pottery have been noted in many areas around the village, and the church has Roman flue and roof tiles built into its fabric. The Roman road from Cambridge to Arrington Bridge passes along the north-west of the parish, probably with a branch to the ford as in later times. The route that ran to Barton, later called Deadmans Way, and then, as Lot Way, on to Comberton, Toft, Caldecote and possibly Bourn and Eltisley, was probably also in use by this time.

Anglo-Saxon

A sunken-floored hut dated to approximately 500 AD provides rare evidence for a settlement which continued into medieval times. The hut was excavated at Fiddler's Close, now the site of school playing-fields in the north-east corner of the village. It was sub-rectangular, had a post at either end to support the roof, and the soil within it contained sherds of decorated pottery and a brooch. More pottery, animal bones and fragments of bone combs were found nearby. Later in the Saxon period defensive ditches and fences surrounded a settlement area, and there was a road to the ford. Nearby, in a gravel pit on the opposite side of the cross-road, spears and knives were found in the 1880s, presumably from a small cemetery used by Early Anglo-Saxon inhabitants of the first

Saxon carved stones, set in the walls of Grantchester church.

settlement. A decorated urn found somewhere in Grantchester probably also came from a grave.

When the south wall of the nave of Grantchester church was demolished in the 1870s many carved stone fragments were found in its rubble. Five of them proved to be portions of grave-slabs with plait-work decoration on them, and there was also a small round-headed window. All were of the early 11th century, and they can now be seen in the rebuilt fabric of the church. The grave-slabs are thought to have been manufactured in Cambridge, using stone from Barnack.

Village Development

Grantchester, like Duxford, grew up at the place where two adjacent and parallel tracks running east from Barton, Comberton and Toft crossed the Cam at fords. The northern road to Coton, now the wide road which was at one stage used as a green, led down to the ford. A hollow-way, the successor to the Saxon road, still runs across the fields behind the Rupert Brooke public house, and the closes and paddocks, also still visible as low banks and ditches, continued in use until the 14th century.

Only a small fragment of the southern track is now a road, the village street west of the Old Vicarage, though its east-west continuations are still footpaths, eastwards to the river and a ford across both the Mill Stream and the Cam, and west towards Barton. The church lay between the two tracks, on a raised area, perhaps an older religious site. Subsequent expansion and growth of the village led to the development of a north-south routeway which dog-legged its way around former rectangular fields, past the church, thus linking the two older tracks. This north-south route was also extended south to the watermill, recorded in 1086, where it could cross the mill-stream on a bridge, as it still does.

Newnham, now Newnham Croft, within Cambridge, to the north of Grantchester parish, was formerly within it. Until recent development, it was a tiny hamlet, presumably, as its name implies, founded as an offshoot from Grantchester.

The manor that was known as Jaks in the 14th century was a group of properties acquired by the Grantchesters, a successful yeoman family that took its name from the village. The Grantchesters' early manor house stood in a square moated site in the south of the village, near to the church, where three sides of the moat and a later extension survive. In the early 15th century it was sold to the Chancellor of the Exchequer, Henry Somer, who had already inherited the other Grantchester manor of Laceys. He then bought the land of several Grantchester smallholders, and so owned a large part of the parish, and he built a new house for himself just to the north of the moat. He bequeathed all this estate to King's College later in the 15th century, and his house was used as an out-of-town retreat for fellows and as a farmhouse. It was altered in the 17th century and later years, but the building survives as Manor Farm.

The combined parishes of Grantchester and Coton had a large population of 76 in 1086, most of them in Grantchester, and this grew to about 100 tenants, perhaps 500 people, in the 13th century, though only 177 adults paid the poll-tax in 1377. In the 16th century, when Coton's population was counted separately, as few as 16 families were recorded, rising slowly through the 17th and 18th centuries to a modest total of 294 in 1801. This rose to about 625 in 1871 before falling in the late 19th century. In the 20th century, when it was still mostly owned by King's College, its attractive character and pleasant associations for the University meant that little development was allowed, and later planning policies have continued this pattern. The population has therefore only risen to 560 in 1996.

In the 15th century, when King's College used their Grantchester estate for their own food supply, agriculture in Grantchester included flocks of sheep, a dovecote (the largest in South Cambridgeshire, now converted to cottages) that produced more than 1500 pigeons in one year, swans, saffron and cherries in addition to crops in the open fields. Eels were caught prolifically at the weir. In 1086 the lord of the manor was owed 1000 eels from here, and an eel-trap was used until 1928. A woman in the early 20th century claimed her grandfather sold enough eels to buy a grand piano, and presumably there were similar catches in the years in between.

King's College dovecote

Graveley

Graveley is a small parish of 640 hectares, lying entirely on clay. A brook flowing from a spring known as Nill Well forms most of the eastern boundary, and another brook in the east of the parish joins it. From the valley of these brooks the land rises gently to a plateau about 40m above sea level, on which the village lies. The open fields were enclosed in 1805. In Domesday Book it is named *Gravelei,* probably 'a clearing in a grove', perhaps an indication of the wooded landscape at this time.

Roman

Two Roman coins, one dated to the late 2nd century AD, were found in allotments near the north-west parish boundary, and pieces of Roman pottery were dug up in a garden in the village.

Village Development

The village, which belonged to Ramsey Abbey from the 10th to the 16th century, was perhaps planned around a loose grid of lanes, some of them now lost, with the church in the centre of the northern side. The main street runs east-west, with a small green where a road goes north to the church. Church Lane, parallel to the main street, also widened into a green, just north of the church. The grid was never fully built up and habitation was always rather scattered. There is also a small hamlet of Duck End, north-west of the village. A manor house, which in 1250 had a hall and chamber, with a kitchen and chapel added by 1300, probably stood just east of the church, where Jesus College built a large farmhouse (now demolished) in the 17th century. Areas of waste land around the village were being built upon in the 17th and 18th century, for which there were fines but no serious attempts to stop the practice.

At Domesday the population was only 20, rising 45 tenants in the 13th century and then falling to 94 poll-tax payers in 1377, and to about 23 householders in the 16th century. There were fluctuations after the Middle Ages, with a maximum total population of around 150 in the 17th and 18th centuries. In 1801 there were 156 people, and the population reached 334 in 1851, after which it declined to about 175 in the 1900s. In 1996 it had only risen again to 250.

In the later 16th century the village was sold by the Crown to Jesus College, and it was leased out at favourable rents until the 19th century. Owners of one piece of land were the Pepys family, who lived nearby at Brampton. Samuel Pepys hoped to inherit this, but he recounts in his Diary how his case was dismissed in a court held in the village by a jury made up of 'a simple meeting of country rogues'.

Agriculture was always the basis of the economy, and an interesting list of provisions with which the village was expected to supply the Abbey included cheese, bacon, honey, geese, lambs, salt-pork, sheep, eggs and cake, all payable every November and May. Considerable numbers of sheep were kept, especially in the later Middle Ages, though there were often problems in finding sufficient pasture for all those with common rights. There were also problems when tenants enclosed plots of land in the 17th century, which was presumably illegal, although it was their neighbours who broke down the fences who ended up in the stocks.

Graveley church is on a high point in the north of the village away from later settlement, apart from very modern houses surrounding a new green. The two roads leading to it are now cul de sacs, though they both continue as footpaths, running north towards Godmanchester and east towards Papworth St. Agnes.

Great Shelford

Great Shelford, a medium-sized parish, now covers 838 hectares, having lost 80 hectares to Cambridge in 1934. Much of the parish is on fairly low-lying land, especially near the River Cam which forms its southern border, where land was liable to flood. The village itself is about 23m above sea level and contains very low ground near an extinct tributary of the Cam, an area which was used for meadow in the Middle Ages. Apart from gravel and alluvial soils by the river and streams the parish lies on chalk, and one of its important features is the site of Nine Wells. Here, pure springs feed Hobsons Brook, the source of Cambridge's water supply from the 17th to 20th centuries. In the north of the parish the foothills of the Gog Magogs begin, and chalk hills rise to over 50m. Before the northern parish boundary was changed in the 20th century it ran along Worts Causeway, a Roman and possibly pre-Roman route that was rebuilt as a road to Wandlebury in 1709. Other boundaries are mostly field edges and were fixed at a late date, for fields were shared with Stapleford, Trumpington and Hauxton until Enclosure in 1835. In

Domesday Book Shelford is *Scelde-forde*, a suitable description meaning 'a ford through a shallow place'. There was no distinction between Great and Little Shelford until the 13th century.

Prehistoric

Areas where chalk soils were watered by streams provided favourable environments for very early settlement, and the density of Neolithic flint tools and waste flakes left from tool manufacture in areas north of the village and on the slopes near Wandlebury indicate far more than casual use of the land here. Three Neolithic axes have also been found within the village. There are also flint tools of Bronze Age date, and it can be assumed that many areas within the parish were farmed at this time.

In the Iron Age there was a major centre of settlement that is clearly visible on aerial photographs, adjacent to the north bank of the river where it is now crossed by the M11. Excavations here before the motorway was built revealed an oval enclosure containing one large round hut, hearths, gravel-covered yards and about sixty storage pits, one of which still had part of its wicker lining. There are also crop marks of other enclosures, track ways, field ditches, and a line of pits that was superseded by a ditched track, both leading down to the river. Features on this site must have been repaired and re-planned several times within the Iron Age. The settlement spread for over a mile along the river bank, extending to Hauxton Mill where important burials were found during coprolite digging. These have been described under **Hauxton**, but may have come from the Shelford side of the river. In any case, traces of occupation on both sides of the river were similar in this area, for the river was easy to cross at this point and did not act as a barrier.

Roman

The extensive Iron Age site was also used from the 1st to the 4th century AD, judging from pottery found on the field surface. In addition, there was a comparable farming settlement on the chalk slopes near Nine Wells. Crop marks here indicate that there were ditched track ways, rectangular buildings and more neatly shaped fields than the earlier site. Pottery found here also dates to the 1st to the 4th centuries.

Middle Ages

There are two moated manor house sites in Great Shelford, one at either end of the village. Granham's Manor, at the north end, still has the remains of a rectangular moat and a large rectangular enclosure that is surrounded by a low bank. The manor belonged to a succession of significant figures, including Nicholas le Moyne, sheriff of Cambridgeshire in the 13th century, the Earl of Pembroke in the 14th century and the de Vaux family in the 15th century, before being sold to John Hinde of Madingley in the 16th century. None of these were resident in Great Shelford. However, the le Moynes are known to have had a manor house here in the 13th century which is also recorded in later centuries. In 1392, when some buildings were described as ruinous, a hall with a kitchen and other rooms, chapel and farm buildings, all stood within the moated enclosure. The house was replaced with a larger building which destroyed part of the moat's ditch in the 19th century.

The other manor, which had a manor house south of the church at the southern end of the village, was given to Ely in the late 10th century. It was held by the bishops until 1600, when it was taken over by the Crown and later sold to Gonville and Caius College. Its medieval fishponds can still be seen near the river. The moated manor house near the church was recorded from the 14th century, when it had a hall, kitchen and other rooms which were rebuilt when they had become ruinous. It was repaired throughout the 15th century and then rebuilt, probably in the 16th century. It was sold separately from most of its land in the 17th century and became a private residence known as the Grange. In the 18th century, when it was set within a small deer park, it was visited by the antiquarian William Cole.

Village Development

The medieval village was built around two centres based on the manor houses described above, of which the earliest settlement was perhaps the southern part, close to the church and a river crossing to Little Shelford, itself probably an earlier and more significant centre at this time. It consisted of a single street following the northernmost line of the Icknield Way. The other

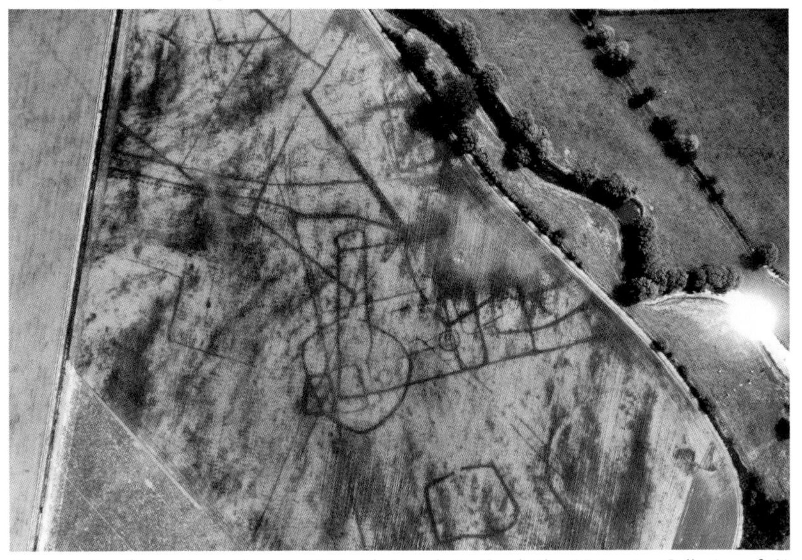

Crop marks of Iron Age settlement, 1969. Photograph © Cambridge University Collection of Air Photographs

centre, around Granhams Manor, was three-quarters of a mile to the north and was separated by an area watered by a small stream, with damp meadows and pasture that was valuable for grazing. Later in the Middle Ages houses were built around the edge of 'High Green', as this area became known, but it was only after Enclosure that this green was used for housing and the village started to take on its present form.

In Domesday Book 38 people are recorded in both Shelfords, and in Great Shelford there were 90 tenants in 1279. Great Shelford seems to have escaped the first outbreaks of plague, but suffered badly in the late 14th century when there were complaints that no crops had been harvested through lack of people. Growth followed the Middle Ages, and there were between 60 and 80 households in the 16th and 17th centuries. This figure continued to increase, to 570 people in 1801, and it then accelerated to over 1000 in 1851. This population level was sustained and was even able to grow steadily in the late 19th century, to 1466 in 1911, largely thanks to the railway. Its station, opened in 1845, was only one stop from Cambridge and, apart from easy commuting for the middle classes, it was of benefit to industries, haulage yards etc. A particularly large brewery and coal store, for example, opened next to the station. Subsequent growth, too, was led by residents who commuted to Cambridge, London and other centres. By 1931 the population was 1864, and unrestricted ribbon development almost linked Great Shelford to Cambridge. Despite planning restrictions which limited this type of development, the village still grew substantially, reaching a total of 4080 inhabitants by 1996.

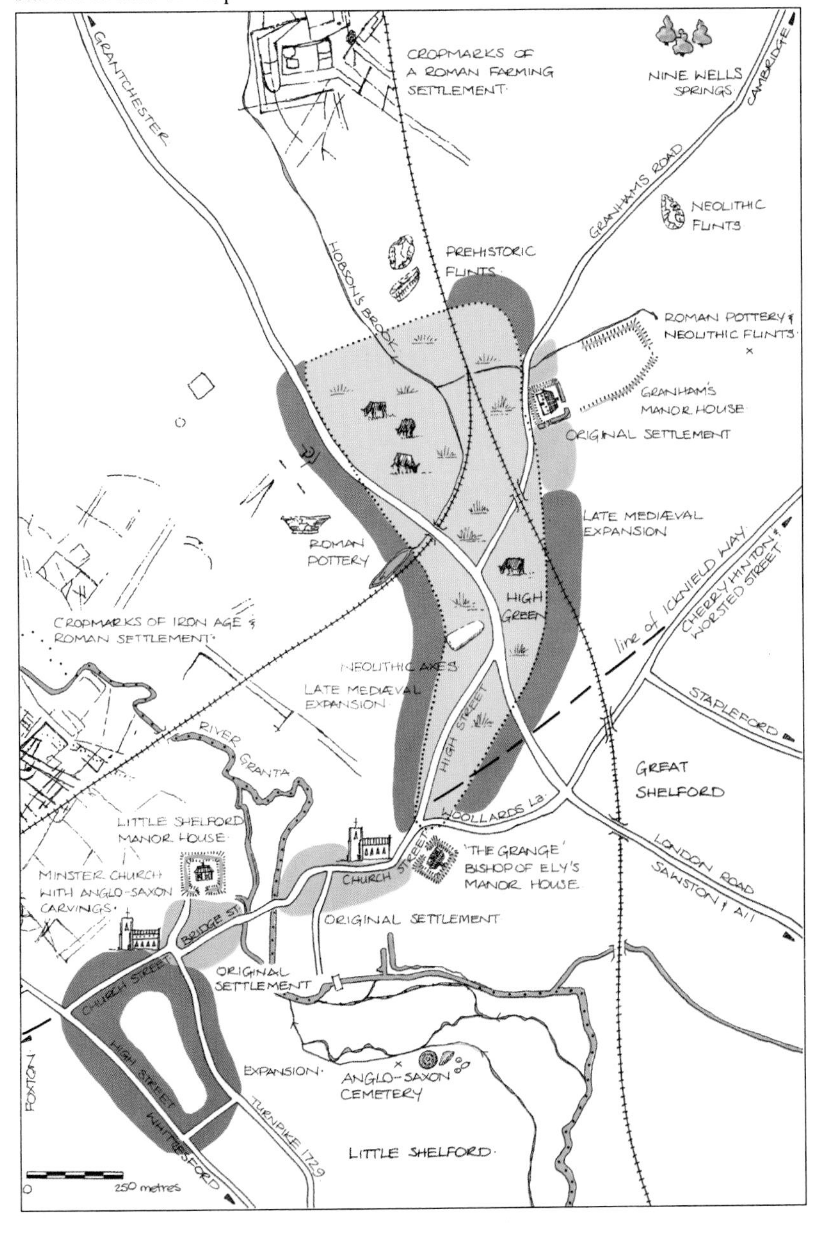

Apart from grazing land on High Green, Great Shelford had extensive areas of common moor in the north of the parish, one moor being shared with Trumpington and another lying near the Gog Magog hills. Land near the river and along streams running through the parish provided further grazing, and land was being enclosed from arable fields for use as pasture in the later Middle Ages. Animals, particularly sheep, were important in the economy from late Saxon times until the 19th century, and the parish was unusual in having goats included in its Domesday account.

Guilden Morden

Guilden Morden is a medium sized parish of 1052 hectares, on low-lying clay with marshy ground near the Rhee, its northern border, but rising to 40m above sea level in the village and to 75m at Odsey Grange on the chalk uplands along the A505, a major line of the Icknield Way and the County's southern border. Its western boundary, a tributary of the Rhee, is also the County boundary. In Domesday book, where it is not separated from Steeple Morden, its place-name is *Mortuna* or 'Marsh-hill'. The open fields were enclosed in 1804. From the 13th century 'Guilden', meaning golden or rich and productive, was added.

Prehistoric

Two Neolithic polished flint axes found on the western County boundary and a scatter of prehistoric flint flakes at the north end of the village are the earliest finds. The earliest monuments are Bronze Age burial mounds, surviving as ring-ditches in two clusters near the A505. One of these ring-ditches, though ploughed, still surrounds a mound nearly 1m high, and the dark fill of its two concentric ditches is visible in winter.

Roman vase painted with the words VTERE FELIX - "Have a good life".

Five cremations found in the Roman cemetery (below) dated from the Late Iron Age, 0-50 AD, one being in an urn with a brooch, another with just a brooch, and three without grave-goods. The Shire Balk could just possibly be an Iron Age boundary. Today it is a distinctive bank in use as a green lane, dividing Cambridgeshire and Hertfordshire as it has since at least medieval times. A machine cut revealed it was built up of tips of orange silt to a height of 1.6m, and the only finds were 12th-14th century pottery from later deposits.

Roman

The southern part of the parish is crossed by Ashwell Street, close to which is a villa and the cemetery connected with it. The villa, known from aerial photography, was a rectangular house and courtyard within an enclosure, with an aisled barn that was built over an enclosure ditch. The cemetery is exceptional for its origins in the Iron Age and also for the mixture of funerary rites it displays.

One inhumation of mid 1st century date was accompanied by three imported Roman pots and four mutton cutlets. Another burial of this date was a cremation in an urn together with hobnails, two bronze bangles and a small iron chain. Another cremation with three pots also had an iron lamp. Pots were the most common grave goods, and there were occasional bracelets and glass perfume bottles. The rite of cremation continued well into the 3rd century, long after most Roman cemeteries had adopted inhumation. Of the later inhumations, many were in coffins and grave goods are less common. One child had a coin in its mouth in the traditional manner and another had a bronze bell on its wrist. Two women and a man were decapitated, perhaps for witchcraft (or just bad tempers, as one at least suffered from rheumatoid arthritis). Bracelets of bronze, shale and bone, occasional brooches and fragments of what may have been a sceptre with bronze phallic pendant attached were founds. In all 286 burials (139 cremations, 147 inhumations) were recorded and many others are said to have been found here. When a gas pipeline was laid in 1991, six more inhumations without grave goods and a cremation with two 1st century AD pots were excavated.

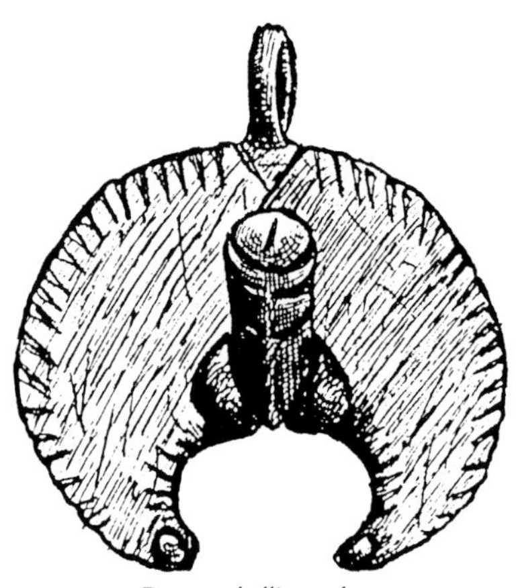

Roman phallic pendant.

Anglo-Saxon

The pipeline also revealed two sunken-floored buildings approximately 4.5m long and 5m deep, just east of Shire Balk near the road to Ashwell in the south of the parish. Pottery dating to the mid-late Saxon period, including Thetford, St. Neots and Stamford ware was found in these. Also found in Guilden Morden was the bronze figurine of a boar, originally the crest of a helmet, said to be found in a grave with glass and amber beads during coprolite digging.

Middle Ages

Bondesbury Manor house, fragments of whose moat survive near the Black Swan in the north-west of the village, was given to Thomas Haselden, the steward of John of Gaunt's estate in Bassingbourn. Haselden was unpopular in Bassingbourn, the seat of much unrest during the Peasants' Revolt, and rebels made a particular point of destroying his house in Guilden Morden and stealing £100 worth of goods from it. The house he rebuilt on a new site to the east of the village therefore was within an imposing moat, still 10m wide and water-filled, with an outer enclosure. The house

Guilden Morden Hall and Moat, 1985.

itself contains 15th century timbers, perhaps from Haselden's rebuilding, and the moat is one of the finest examples in Cambridgeshire.

Village Development

Guilden Morden lies on a north-south track that runs from the old Cambridge-Oxford routes through Tadlow to the routes of the Icknield Way, and it probably always has been a rather scattered village strung out along this track. It is made up of a series of distinct hamlets which may not all date from the same period, for Guilden Morden was a village that saw some dramatic rises and falls in population, notably in the 13th and 19th centuries. These hamlets included Church Street running south-west from the church, the Fox Hill/Trap Road area, Little Green, Great Green, Pound End and Town End. In addition, there was once a small hamlet at Ruddery End, known as Redreth, mentioned by 1100 and last recorded in the 1340s, which lay to the south of the village, on or near Ashwell Street. It had a chapel, where a hermit remained after the settlement had gone, and it is probably to this chapel that Barnwell Priory was appointing hermits in the 1520s.

At Odsey, between Ashwell Street and Icknield Way, land was given to Warden Abbey in Bedfordshire and a grange was built. The monastic buildings were allowed to decay after 1500. Later buildings were for a 'Gentlemen's residence' for the Duke of Devonshire including stables for racing horses, a sporting lodge, and jockey house for the race-course on Odsey Heath.

Guilden Morden was a substantial village throughout the Middle Ages, with a population of 51 at Domesday, about 130 tenants or 650 people in 1279, and 222 poll-tax payers in 1377. There were over 80 households at times in the 17th century, when John Layer describes it as 'a great towne' with six manors, and a population of 428 in 1801. It then went up to a peak of 1059 in 1871, but fell to half this in the early 20th century, before rising again to 900 in 1996, mostly from the 1970s onwards.

Medieval agriculture concentrated on barley production, and large flocks of sheep were kept in the Middle Ages and in later years (1200 in 1800, for example). There was extensive common pasture, including marshy areas near the Rhee and in the north of the parish, although much of the chalk heath in the south was taken over by Odsey Grange. Cattle were also important, and some commons were reserved for them in the Middle Ages. Certain peasants prospered between the 15th and 18th century, and much land near the village was enclosed by them before the official Enclosure of 1805. Craftsmen mentioned in the Middle Ages include weavers and a chandler, and later there was a brickworks and the usual rural crafts and trades, especially in the thriving 19th century. Straw-plaiting and hat-making by women raised family incomes, and in the late 19th century coprolite mining brought brief prosperity.

Hardwick

Hardwick is a small parish of 600 hectares, lying on clay on fairly level ground that rises gently from about 50m above sea level in the south to 70m on the ridgeway of the Cambridge-St. Neots Road, its northern border. Its southern boundary with Toft was not fixed until 1815 when common land that they shared was divided. The open fields were enclosed in 1837, and the straight east and west boundaries were both routeways at that time. Its Domesday place-name is *Herdwich,* meaning 'sheep farm'.

Prehistoric and Roman

No definite sites have yet been found on Hardwick's heavy clays, notorious for being waterlogged and impassable in wet conditions, but aerial photographs suggest two small settlements that may be Iron Age or Roman in date. In addition to the probable Roman road of the northern boundary, it is likely that the route from this road through the village to Toft, the Bourn Brook and beyond was also in use well before the medieval period.

Middle Ages

A moated site to the south of the village was trenched in 1974-5 before it was finally filled in, revealing cobbled areas and much 13th century pottery, including sherds of East Anglian red ware with painted decoration. Other finds included a loom weight, iron knives, nails, a buckle, horseshoe, animal bones and oyster shells. This was presumably the site of the manor house of the bishops of Ely when a detailed account of their holdings was made in 1251.

Another important part of the bishop's estate was Hardwick Wood, which, as *Bradeleh Wood*, is described in the Ely Coucher Book of 1251 and is also recorded in later medieval documents. This ancient wood, now managed by the Wildlife Trust, contains earthwork remains of ridge and furrow ploughing, indicating that it was encroached upon, probably illegally, in the Middle Ages. Some

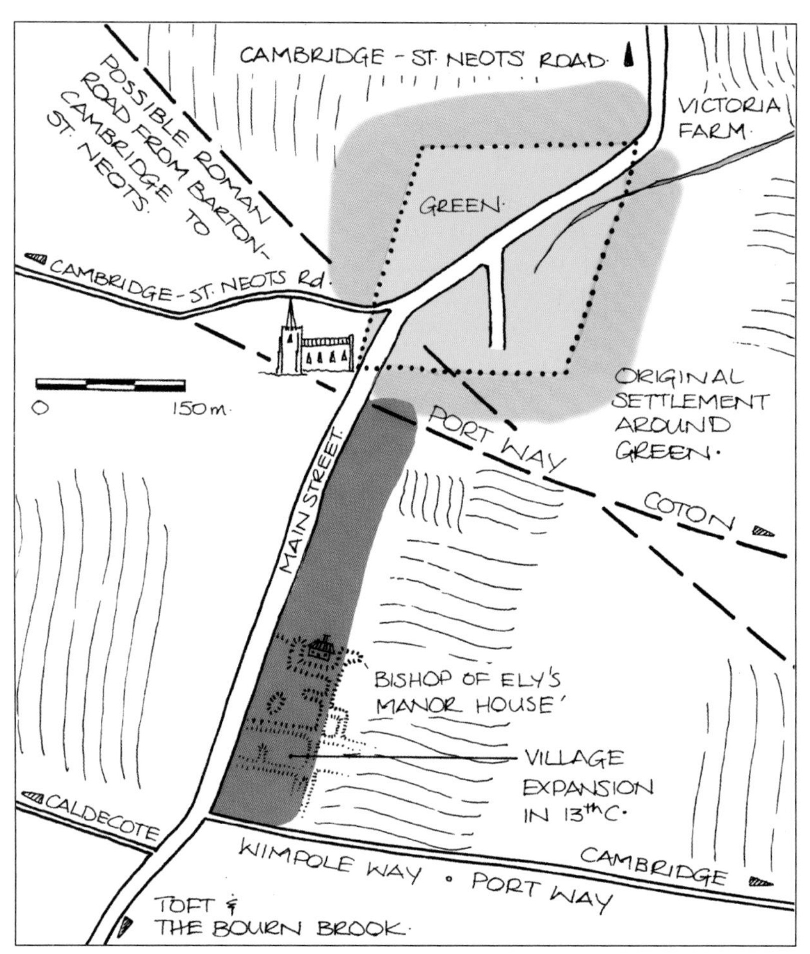

villagers were allowed wood for fencing from Hardwick Wood, and one villager was responsible for guarding the trees. A few fragments of ridge and furrow can also be seen still in the south end of the village, where areas had been enclosed during the Middle Ages.

Village Development

Most of Hardwick belonged to the Abbey of Ely from 991, when Brihtnoth willed an estate at *Herduic* before he was killed by the Danes, until the 16th century. At Domesday the population was small, and it is clear from the configuration of the parish boundary that the settlement was originally a hamlet set up as an outpost from Toft. The village lay where the north-south through-route crossed two separate branches of the Portway, here running east-west from Coton to Bourn. The church stands at the junction of the north-south route with the northernmost of the Portway routes, at the south-west corner of a former green. This green was largely enclosed in 1806, though there had already been earlier encroachments on it. Originally it was trapezoidal in shape, with houses arranged around all four sides. Its regular form suggests that this green was deliberately planned for a relatively small number of families.

The increase in the population of Hardwick during the early Middle Ages led to the extension of the village southwards along the road to Toft, as far as the second line of Portway. This development included the moated site noted above and closes around it. As the population declined from the 14th century much of this extension was abandoned, leaving the earthwork remains of former houses and gardens. These were destroyed in the 1970s.

As at Caldecote, the adjacent parish to the west, the 20th century has seen the appearance of what is a new settlement in the north of the parish along the Cambridge-St. Neots road. This began to be developed in the 1930s, and when Hardwick was designated a growth village in the 1970s there was considerable ribbon development here. The village was also expanded by a new estate, The Limes.

The small population of 11 at Domesday grew through the early Middle Ages to 43 tenants in 1279, falling to 81 poll-tax payers in 1377 and to 14 families in the 16th century. There was a total population of 158 in 1801, reaching 248 in 1871 but falling to 112 in 1901. After 1930 there was extensive development, and the village was chosen for growth in the 1970s, expanding to 2490 in 1996.

Hardwick continued to be held by Ely until it was forcibly given up to the Crown in 1600, after which it was sold to successive private landowners. In the later 17th century the manor was donated in order to provide funds to support Matthew Wren, Bishop of Ely, who had been imprisoned by Cromwell. After the Restoration, Wren gave it to Pembroke College to help build a new chapel. Another significant estate, based on Victoria Farm, was owned by the Bishop of Peterborough in the early 17th century, and in the 18th century by 'Capability' Brown, though there are no signs he undertook any landscape gardening on his own behalf.

Harlton

Harlton is a small parish of 508 hectares, sloping gently from low-lying gravel and alluvial soils by the Bourn Brook, its northern boundary, to about 30m above sea level where the village lies on a spring-line at the foot of a chalk ridge. This then rises steeply to 70m along Mare Way, the southern boundary. Other boundaries are either Roman roads or field boundaries with Orwell and Little Eversden. Its open fields were enclosed in 1810. In Domesday Book Harlton is known as *Herletune,* 'the farm of Herula'.

Harlton Church.

Roman

The Roman road from Cambridge to Arrington Bridge forms part of the western parish boundary, the remainder being a minor road that crosses the Bourn Brook at Fox's Bridge and runs through Comberton to meet the Cambridge-St. Neots road. Mare Way itself was used both in Roman and in prehistoric times. Just to the west of the village is an area of Roman occupation, revealed by cobbles, tile and pottery, perhaps the location of a villa which is noted in museum records.

Middle Ages

The principal medieval manor house was probably at the moated site north of the church. It was held by the Huntingfield family from the 12th to the 14th century, although the land was confiscated twice, for fighting once against King John and once against Henry III, for both of which rebellions they were pardoned. In 1376 William Bateman acquired the manor. He was a sufficiently prominent and unpopular figure to attract rebel action during the Peasants Revolt. John Hanchach attacked his manor at Harlton, stealing goods worth £40 and burning down his houses. Bateman was later one of the justices to try the rebels, apparently not vindictively as a Harlton man, John Prat, was pardoned and his goods restored to him. The Prats went on to become a successful Harlton family. Bateman's son Ralph was another controversial figure, contesting law-suits with his neighbours and being outlawed for incitement to murder.

Another more complex site, comprising two moats, a small moated island and some ponds further to the north, may be either a replacement for the principal manor house or the site of a second manor. Most of the extant features seem to relate to its use as a garden, perhaps in the 16th or 17th centuries. The manor house was said to be deserted in 1587 when a new farmhouse was built (soon after which the owner temporarily lost his lands for helping Catholic priests), but finds of tile and pottery show that the site was used after this. In the late 17th century the manor was given to Christ's Hospital, to endow the teaching of mathematics and navigation. A former embanked pond in Butler's Spinney may also be medieval.

On a chalk ridge in the extreme south-west of the parish, at a point with extensive views in all directions, close to the junction of five parishes and where the Mare Way crosses the principal Roman road, is an area of former intercommoned land. This is thought to have been the Moot or Meeting Place for Wetherley Hundred. A low mound once existed here. A maypole on it was still used through 19th century and is commemorated in the name of Maypole Farm. Earlier the site was known as Beacon Green. Fragments of medieval pottery have been found there.

Village Development

Until recent infilling Harlton was little more than a line of scattered dwellings centred on the church and the remnants of a small green, south of Manor Farm. In Domesday Book its population was 20, and it remained a small village, rising to 57 tenants in the 13th century but falling to 21 families in 1563. After this it rose extremely slowly to a total of 156 in 1801, shot up to 335 in 1871 due to coprolite mining then suffered a considerable fall, and in 1996 had a population of 290.

A quarry was used for stone for Cambridge Castle in 1295 and was still in use in 1906, continuing after that as a source of marl. A clay pit known as Lady Quarry, and a gravel pit near Bourn Brook, are known from 1484 and were still in use when they were allotted for road repairs at Enclosure in 1810.

Harston

Harston is a medium-sized parish of 709 hectares, lying on gravel and alluvial soils near the Rhee and the Hoffer Brook which form parish boundaries on its western and southern sides. Chalk hills rise to 30m at St. Margaret's Mount in the east and to 45m at Rowley's Hill in the south. The eastern boundary was fixed at Enclosure, which followed an Award made in 1802, when common land shared with Hauxton and Newton was exchanged. It is known in Domesday Book as *Herlestuna*, 'the farm of Herel'.

Prehistoric

Burial mounds were built on the chalk uplands of Rowley's Hill and on the gravel soils of river valleys such the Hoffer Brook, where they may have been close to habitation. Excavations near the Brook at Manor Farm in 1991 showed that ring-ditches there were definitely Bronze Age burial sites. One of them surrounded two cremations that had been burnt on site, dated by radiocarbon to about 2510 BC. Both contained circles of stakes that were contemporary with the mounds. A burial with a polished flint knife has also been found at Manor Farm.

Iron Age farming complexes that continued in use in Roman times occur in the extreme north of Harston and at Manor Farm, where excavations showed they originated just before the Roman Conquest, and in the south there are individual rectangular enclosures which may be the remains of settlement. There are also four lines of closely-spaced pits, probably marking Iron Age boundaries, although one on St. Margaret's Mount is in association with Roman pottery kilns.

Roman

The Manor Farm settlement continued until the early 2nd century, was then apparently abandoned and came back into occupation in the 4th century. Its buildings, presumably of timber, had tiled roofs which suggests a degree of Romanisation and above average standard of living, but luxury imports were rare and even the pottery seems to be mostly from local sources and made in Iron Age styles during the first phase of use. The settlement was crossed by a trackway with side-ditches which had small rectilinear enclosures surrounding paddocks ranged along it. This track, which runs from Hoffer Bridge to Newton, continued in use in later periods and is marked on the 1836 Ordnance Survey map.

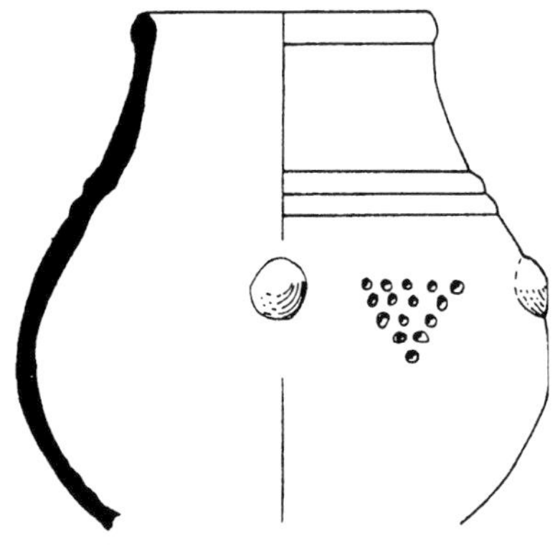

Pottery from Obelisk kilns, Harston.

When the M11 was built, timber buildings and three pottery kilns of the 4th century were found near the Obelisk on St. Margaret's Mount. The pottery was identical to wares being made on a much larger scale in Oxfordshire at that time, and the kilns are thought to be the work of an itinerant potter. The majority are colour-coated wares, usually bowls, some of it imitating earlier imported samian ware.

Anglo-Saxon

Two small sunken huts were among the features excavated at Manor Farm, one of them being constructed in the centre of an earlier prehistoric ring-ditch. Spindle-whorls and loom-weight fragments were found in the huts. Some of the enclosures, boundary ditches and post-holes are also thought to be Saxon, which would make this a large settlement. Not far from Manor Farm, on the site of ring-ditches on Rowley's Hill, a 6th century bronze disc decorated with garnets and green glass was found. An item of this kind almost certainly relates to a burial, perhaps a secondary Saxon burial re-using an upstanding prehistoric mound. Another Anglo-Saxon burial site may have existed at Button End, north of the church, where numerous skeletons and a small spear have been found.

Middle Ages

The main manor house was in the area of Harston Hall. In the late 13th century the Crown sold it to Sir Robert Tiptoft, a minister of Edward I, whose successors, many of whom were also ministers of the Crown, held it until after 1600. In 1279 it is recorded as a 3-acre close, and in about 1390 it had a chapel, chamber and kitchen. In the grounds of the present hall is a small round moat. However, the ditch is only just over 3m wide and 1m deep and the site is

Anglo-Saxon spindle whorls, bone comb, and pot and loom weight fragments excavated at Manor Farm 1991.

more likely to be a later garden feature than a manorial moat. Two fishponds in the grounds, however, may be medieval.

The present Old Manor House may be approximately on the site of another medieval manor house known as Shadworth's, which in 1310 had included a hall and solar, lord's chamber and great wardrobe. This had gone by 1435. Later the site was occupied by a dovecote and orchard.

Village Development

Harston was probably originally situated at the crossing place of the river, near the church and manor house, on the road from Newton to Haslingfield. However, the road from Royston to Cambridge also passes through the village and this latter road became much more important during the Middle Ages with the establishment of Royston as a new town and the growth of Cambridge. The road was also a main route from London to Cambridge. By this time the lay-out of the village had been fixed, and so the road had to make dog-leg turns to negotiate a north-south route. A village green, recorded from the late 13th century, was the Moor which extended for half a mile along the Cambridge Road, in the north-east of the village. There are also small greens at the two places where the main road bends. Cottages set in long narrow closes probably formed by enclosing open field strips lie along the west side of the Moor. They are recorded from the 14th century and may be the result of encroachment there.

The population of the village grew through the Middle Ages from 29 at Domesday to about 65 tenants in 1279, dropping to 38 families by 1563. During the 15th century many tenements were regularly said to be ruinous. The population rose slowly to a total of 160 people in 1728, then more steeply to 412 in 1811 and 860 at its peak in 1871. After that it fell, but Harston was chosen as a growth village in the Town Plan of 1957, and in 1996 the population reached 1580.

In addition to the usual village craftspeople, weavers are recorded in Harston from the early 14th to the 16th century, and one of their specially designed cottages survives. There was also a tailor and fuller in the 15th century. The road to Cambridge was always busy. Several inns were built to cater for passing trade, and ale-wives in the Middle Ages were fined for selling ale to strangers. After the Middle Ages, the road continued to attract travellers to an increasing number of inns, and tradespeople and craftspeople also multiplied. Tailors, coopers, tinkers, shoemakers (of whom there were ten in 1841), and wheelwrights were in addition to all the usual shopkeepers. There were two brickfields in Harston, and extensive coprolite digging especially on the Harston/Hauxton border, in the late 19th century. Clunch was quarried and lime burnt on St. Margaret's Mount. Enclosure, proposed in 1796, was strongly and even violently opposed. Labourers rioted and used scythes and pitchforks to beat off a yeoman detachment that was sent to arrest the ring-leaders.

Excavation of sunken-floored Anglo-Saxon hut, 1991.

Haslingfield

Haslingfield is a large parish of 1228 hectares, including 156 hectares which were added from Trumpington in 1934. It has gravel and alluvial soils near the Rhee and the Bourn Brook, which form its eastern and northern boundaries, and chalk and clay elsewhere. The village itself is near the river, on low-lying ground at the foot of White Hill, which rises sharply to 70m above sea level in the south of the parish. Lingey Fen is a particularly low and marshy area in the angle where the Rhee and the Bourn Brook meet. The open fields were enclosed following an Award made in 1820. Haslingfield is known as *Haslingefelde* in Domesday, 'the people of Haesel'.

Prehistoric

Burial mounds were built along the ridge followed by Mare Way, and the river valleys were suited to early settlement. The earliest known finds are Mesolithic axes, cores, scrapers, blades and other tools from Cantelupe Farm, and there are also records of scatters of worked flints including Neolithic and Bronze Age arrow-heads from Iron Age settlements that have been investigated. One site near the Rhee, for example, is notable for producing two Mesolithic axes, a hundred cores and 700 other flint tools including microliths, scrapers and borers. A fine Early Bronze Age flint dagger was found in Haslingfield and an arrow-head of the same date was found in the churchyard. Neolithic flints occur on Chapel Hill, where there was also a group of nine Bronze Age burial mounds. They are now all ploughed flat, even the significantly named Money Hill itself being barely discernible. Two timber causeways of the Late Bronze Age, radiocarbon dated to 1000-900 BC, have been excavated at Lingey Fen. One, of oak, ash and hazel, consisted of series of horizontal posts and brushwood-packing, lying between two gravel terraces before peat was formed. The other also spanned a low-lying area and consisted of large timbers notched at each end, held in position by stakes.

Stray finds of Iron Age date include a harness trapping, a decorated bone weaving comb, bone cheek-pieces from a bridle bit, two large bronze pins, a coin of Cunobelin and an imported 'tazza' or drinking vessel, all from various places around the village, discoveries that are reminiscent of sites in adjacent parishes such as Lord's Bridge, Barton. Two Iron Age settlements investigated belong to more humble farming people. Both consisted of ditched enclosures and were used late in the Iron Age for mixed farming, of which there was evidence for horse, cattle, sheep and weeds resulting from cultivation. The sites grew larger in the Roman period (below). An Iron Age and Roman site of over 50 hectares shows as crop marks at Cantalupe Farm, where the M11 crosses the Bourn Brook. There are numerous enclosures, pits, straight ditches, and a 'pit-alignment' that marks a boundary at right angles to the river.

Mare Way loses its distinctive route in Haslingfield, where it splits into minor trackways that use crossing places such as Hoffers Bridge (Harston), and Burnt Mills (off River Lane). Crossing places of the Bourn Brook gave access to areas of Barton and Grantchester, as in the Middle Ages.

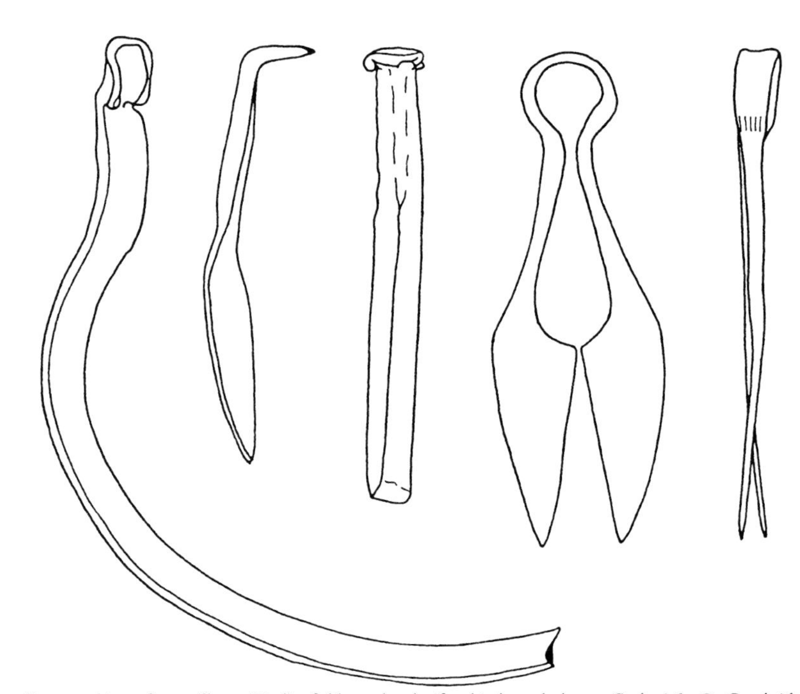

Roman objects from villa at Haslingfield: scythe, knife, chisel, and shears, Scale 1:3. © Cambrid Antiquarian Society.

Roman

The three Iron Age settlements noted above were used in Roman times, probably without a break. The one at Cantelupe Farm in particular has produced tiles and tesserae in addition to pottery and coins, and some of its crop marks could indicate small buildings. One excavated site included a villa with at least five rooms and a verandah of the 2nd century, surrounded by a ditched and fenced enclosure. Finds from excavations here included brooches, pins, bracelets, a scythe, chisel and fragments of three pots representing female faces.

Anglo-Saxon

An Anglo-Saxon cemetery was destroyed during coprolite digging in chaotic circumstances, antiquarians from Cambridge, Oxford and London competing to purchase objects from workmen for many years with no attempt to record graves. It was one of South Cambridgeshire's large and rich cemeteries, and had both cremations and inhumations though the majority seem to have been inhumations. They dated to the 5th to 6th centuric AD, slightly earlier but substantially overlapping the cemeteries at Barrington. Finds include much women's jewellery, with at least 55 bronze brooches, many wrist-clasps and glass and amber beads. Men's weapons included two swords and a axe in addition to spears and shields. Unusual finds were cowrie shells, iron pincers, fragments of a work-bo and draughtsmen made from horses teeth. Sets of toilet implements and a bracelet suggest some Roman influence.

Middle Ages

The Scales were the major local family from the 13th to late 15th century, when the last lord was executed by Richard III. They were important landowners who fought fc the Crown during the Hundred Yea War with France, and one of them is

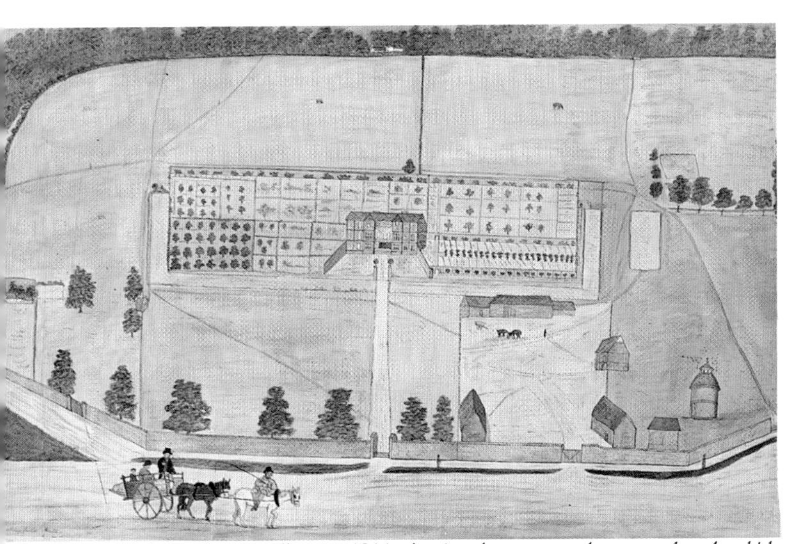

Iaslingfield Hall, drawn by R. Relhan in 1814, showing the ornamental moat and park which ırrounded the Hall. © Cambridge Antiquarian Society.

ıentioned in the summons Joan of ʌrc sent to Henry VI. He was a •articularly unpopular figure in ɉorfolk, even the Duke of Norfolk omplaining about 'riotts orryble ʏrongs done in these partyes by the aid Lord Scales...' During the ɩiddle Ages the Scales obtained icences to have their own oratory in heir manor house at Haslingfield. n the 16th century their land in Iaslingfield was bought by Sir 'homas Wendy, physician to Henry 'III and a favourite courtier. Wendy •ought most of Haslingfield and built Iaslingfield Hall, possibly on the site •f the original Scales manor. The Vendys were a wealthy and powerful amily with royal and University onnections, and Haslingfield, as heir home, became an important ocial and cultural centre. Another 'homas Wendy in the 17th century •equeathed his library of over 2000 •ooks to Balliol College, Oxford.

Part of the first Thomas Wendy's Iall, whose three-sided garden moat urvives in good condition, was set in ı large park of 21 acres in the centre •f Haslingfield. The mansion was re-•nodelled and cased in brick in the 7th century and garden features vere added. It became ruinous in the arly 18th century when it was owned or forty years by a widow who was •fficially a lunatic. In the 19th entury Earl de la Warr removed finer parts of it to Bourn Hall and demolished much of the rest. 16th and 17th century barns and materials from the Hall were re-used at Cantelupe Farm. Its 16th century garden walls and 17th century dove-cote, granary and well-house survive.

One unusual site in Haslingfield was the chapel on White Hill, in the same prominent position as the pre-historic burial mounds. The shrine was set up by William Sterne in 1343 and was reached by Mare Way. It became a well-known centre for pil-grimage, and John Layer tells us that:

'...in the chappell was placed the image of the said Lady of Whitehill, adorned with costly ornaments to the admiration of the people who flocked thither from all quarters out of a religious devotion, to offer presents and oblations, none came empty handed, wch enriched the priest and yielded benefit to the inhabitants, for every year at the least, at the feast of Easter, the whole town was scarce able to receive the pilgrims'.

The chapel was eventually sold to Thomas Wendy.

Village Development

Because of the ovoid arrange-ment of its streets it has been sugg-ested that Haslingfield grew up around a large green similar to that at Barrington. There are references to a 'Great Green' from the 14th to the 18th centuries which support this idea. However, it is likely that Has-lingfield was originally more compli-cated, growing along a routeway running east from Harlton which divided into three roughly parallel tracks. One, now New Road, goes to the River Lane crossing, after which it splits to go to Hauxton and Hars-ton. Another, High Street (west), School Lane and Back Lane turned south-east to the river crossing at Harston, while the third, High Street (east) in the middle of the village crossed the river at a ford beyond River Farm. The small triangular green on the central High Street (east) was once much larger, perhaps extending north to the Hall, with the church on its south-west corner. This

5th century Anglo-Saxon silver wrist-clasp found at Haslingfield, size 95 x 50mm. © Cambridge Museum of Archaeology and Anthropology

The quiet village of Haslingfield, drawn in the early 19th century by R. Relhan.
© Cambridge Antiquarian Society.

green may have been the centre of the main village, which was only one of several linked hamlets, including Frog End to the north and three settlements near the river, one at River Lane, another at the eastern extremity of the High Street and another at Back Lane. Here, before recent developments, there were remains of medieval house-platforms and paddocks. In addition, large quantities of medieval pottery, dating from the 11th century onwards, have been collected from fields between Back Lane and the river. The 16th century Hall and its park occupied the northern half of the village, apart from minor encroachments along the High Street, until the 19th century.

Medieval Haslingfield was the largest village in the area. From a very high Domesday population of 81 it grew to 140 tenants, as much as 700 people, in 1279. This was down to 271 adults in 1377, dropping to 53 families in 1563. The hearth tax of 1664 gives 70 houses, yet by 1801 there were only 65 houses with 90 families crowded into them, a total of 387 people, less than the Domesday population, which would have totalled about 405. The population and housing stock grew during the 19th century, with 762 people in 150 houses by 1861. Coprolite mining brought a temporary increase to 871 in 1871, but the population fell below 600 by the end of the century. Each family now had a house, and some were standing empty. Numbers began rising in the 1920s, especially in the 1960s, and in 1996 there were 1500 inhabitants.

Hatley

The two medieval parishes of East Hatley and Hatley St. George together make the modern parish of 962 hectares, lying on clay in fairly level upland countryside, over 60m above sea level. The boundary with Gamlingay follows old routes known as the Bar and Procession Ways, other boundaries being re-organised in 1957. Both parishes are still well-wooded, with much ancient woodland. In Domesday Book Hatley is *Hatelaie*, incorporating 'ley', meaning woodland clearing. Hatley St. George, previously 'Hungry Hatley' because of its poverty, was named after the family who were the principal landowners from the 13th to 17th centuries. Its fields were enclosed without an official act at an early date, probably starting in the 15th century. The two parishes were united in 1957.

Middle Ages

The moated site of Manor Farm to the west of East Hatley village green was a complete enclosure on a map of 1750, and was the manor house of the Castell family, who held the manor from about 1490 until it was sold to the Downings in 1661. The Castell's house was described as an ancient timber building in 1660 and was demolished in 1712, materials being used for a new house in Gamlingay Park, although Manor Farm still contains early woodwork that perhaps was salvaged. An adjacent moat is the site of Hatley parsonage. This was a substantial house with four hearths in 1660 but was dilapidated though still inhabited through the 18th century. It was described as a miserable cottage in 1807, and was not rebuilt after it burnt down in 1821. A nearby building known as The Palace was used by members of Downing College when they were inspecting their estate here.

West of the village is Buff Wood, an ancient wood which belonged to Cambridge University for many years and was therefore well studied. The present wood covers the same area as in 1650 and includes a nucleus of primary woodland that is listed in the Hundred Rolls of 1279. The secondary woodland covers areas containing ridge and furrow and also a large, possibly double, moat with a wet ditch where test excavations suggested there may have been a wattle and daub building. This is thought to be the site of Quy manor house which can be traced back to ownership by Picot, sheriff of Cambridge, in 1086.

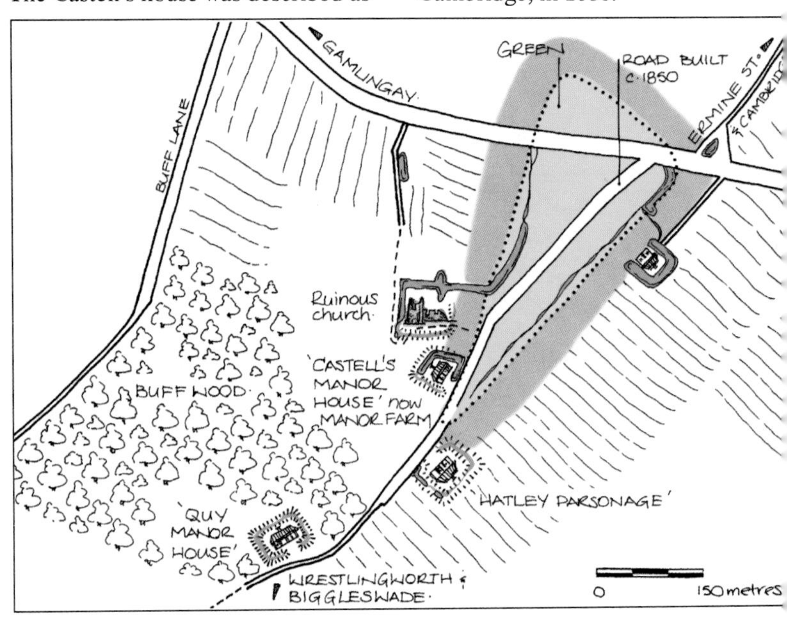

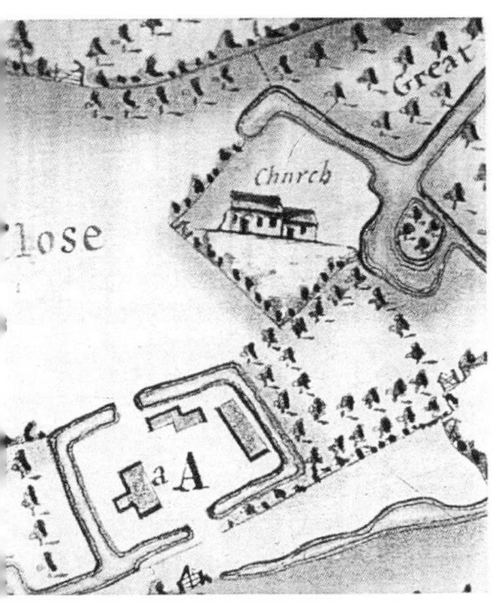

East Hatley Church and Manor, on the estate map drawn in 1750.

Even the church in East Hatley is surrounded by a ditch on three sides. This church has suffered the very rare fate in Cambridgeshire of desertion in the mid 20th century in favour of a hall in the village. It was a humble building, consisting of a 14th century nave and Victorian chancel, which has become ruinous and is now valued as a natural history site.

Village Development

The medieval village of East Hatley was arranged around a triangular village green, with its moated church, manor and parsonage in the southern corner. It was virtually deserted in the 18th century, leaving a parsonage at one end of the green and a farmhouse at the other. From the 1850s houses began to be built on the green itself, with main street moved to run through the centre of it. The south-east side of the medieval green is still defined by ditched platforms and moats of medieval houses and other buildings, although they are being increasingly disturbed by modern developments. To the north-west of the green there are irregular scarps up to 30cms high, indicating further house sites. The road that ran through the middle of the medieval village, now a cul-de-sac, was once part of an important route from Cambridge to Oxford, through Biggleswade.

The whereabouts of the medieval village of Hatley St. George is not known. It may have been near the church or possibly on Bar Lane which runs along the western parish boundary, near to Park Farm, the probable manor house of the St. George family. Alternatively, the small number of parishioners could have been in scattered farmsteads around the parish. Nowadays, Hatley St. George consists of Hatley mansion and its park, which covers about half the parish, and a straggle of 19th century estate cottages and 20th century houses along the Gamlingay-Croydon road. The Park, which was arable until the 17th century, contains earthwork remains of ridge and furrow and also 19th century garden features.

East Hatley had a population of 24 in Domesday Book, and 19 tax-payers in 1327. It declined in the late Middle Ages, and was down to 9 households in 1563, in houses that were scattered around the fields. In 1801 there were still only about 100 people in all, less than in 1086. Eventually the population rose to a peak of 155 in 1871. Decline after this was reversed after the 1950s, and in 1996 240 people lived in the combined parishes. There were 17 families living in Hatley St. George in 1086, and 69 poll-tax payers in 1377. In 1563 only four families lived here, and there was little growth until the late 18th century. In 1801 there were 101 inhabitants. The population rose to a peak of 164 in 1861, though it subsequently declined well below 100, and has not recovered.

Hatley St. George was the chief seat of the St. George family from the 13th century until John St. George was fined for supporting Charles I. His son sold the estate to the wealthy Cotton family, who held it until the 18th century. John Layer, writing while the St. George's lived here in the early 17th century, said 'The auncient seate is decaied, a fair sight of an old house and a pritty gentlemanlike seate now there built' which sounds as if the original Park Farm manor had already been rebuilt on a new site. This rebuilding was probably by Sir Henry St. George, Garter Knight of Arms, and it was in a grand new classical style. After its sale the house continued to be the principal residence for families of wealth and was therefore constantly enlarged, altered and refitted in succeeding centuries. In 1851 it is described as 'the seat of Thomas St. Quinton Esq... a fine

East Hatley Church c. 1910 and (above) in 1996.

mansion surrounded by rich plantations, gardens and fish-ponds', a description which still applies.

Enclosure of fields in East Hatley by the Castell family began in the 15th century. By the mid 17th century, when they owned virtually all the parish, it was complete, and most of the land was pasture. Hatley St. George was mainly arable until the 17th century. Land was gradually enclosed before the late 18th century, but outside the Park it was still mostly used for arable farming. In both parishes early enclosures have left fields of rectangular shape but with the curved sides which are characteristic of medieval furlongs and strips.

Roman flask and jug in colourless glass found at Hauxton.
© Cambridge University Museum of Archaeology and Anthropology.

Hauxton

Hauxton is a small parish of 207 hectares, mostly lying on gravel and alluvial soils near the River Cam, which forms its long northern border. It is flat and low-lying, only about 15m above sea level. At Hauxton Mill, at the east end of the village, is a ford that has always been important for travellers approaching Cambridge from the south. Apart from the river, its boundaries are 19th century, mostly following roads and the railway. The open fields were enclosed by an Award made in 1802. Its name in Domesday Book is *Hauextona,* or 'Heafoc's farm'.

Prehistoric

The gravel soils along this stretch of the Cam valley were some of the most densely settled areas in Cambridgeshire in Iron Age and Roman times. Crop marks include numerous trackways, circular huts, rectangular enclosures and two 'pit-alignments', one at least 350m long, apparently dividing up territory near the river. None of these sites have been excavated.

An area near Hauxton Mill was dug for coprolites in the 19th century, along with workings in Haslingfield and the Shelfords. This led to the discovery of many artefacts which were labelled 'Hauxton Mill', some of which would have come from this parish, but others no doubt were found elsewhere. There was, in any case, no attempt to record how they were grouped. Early finds in this category include Neolithic and Bronze Age axes, Early Iron Age pottery and a Late Iron Age cemetery that contained urns, a brooch, weaving comb and shears.

Roman

A Roman cemetery, apparently in the area of Hauxton Mill used in the Iron Age, contained 33 skulls, cremations, regularly spaced graves and a number of Roman objects, including pottery, coins, glass and bronze vessels and an iron lamp. Some of these artefacts are in the Cambridge Museum of Archaeology and Anthropology, where the finest are on display. Some seem to have belonged to high status burials, reminiscent of those at Bartlow, particularly in light of their feasting regalia and lamps. They include two glass bowls, a jug and a flask of a unique form, all of colourless glass and imported between 150 and 250 AD, three ornate bronze jugs with handle terminals in the form of human masks, birds heads and human feet, two clay lamps and one of iron, and several pots, including Nene Valley beakers with hunt scenes and vine scroll decoration. Judging by the remains and the scanty reports, it seems that Hauxton is another example of a Late Iron Age cemetery continuing through into the Roman period, distinctive for the importance of its extravagant feasting wares and its lamps. It is very unfortunate that objects were not recorded in their original contexts, and that lesser object, such as boxes and their nails, were inevitably ignored.

Anglo-Saxon

A small Anglo-Saxon cemetery is also reported at the ford, though the recording of finds makes it difficult to be confident even that artefacts have been assigned to the right parish. An Early Anglo-Saxon bowl, knife and latch-lifter, several brooches and fragments of a shield boss are described as coming from Hauxton Mill, and a skeleton was excavated with a 2-horned axe, knives, key and hilt-plate, which we can at least be confident was actually found on this site. Later in the Saxon period most of Hauxton belonged to the abbey of Ely.

Village Development

The village developed as a linear settlement along the road to Little Shelford with a short extension south along the road which formerly ran to Newton, and there is a small rectangular green in this area. There is also a small hamlet at Mill End. Its manorial site was in Newton, which may have been colonised from Hauxton, but in the 12th century the Prior of Ely created a separate manor and granted it to a Hauxton man, who built a substantial house. In 1261 this house was attacked by clerks from Cambridge but they were

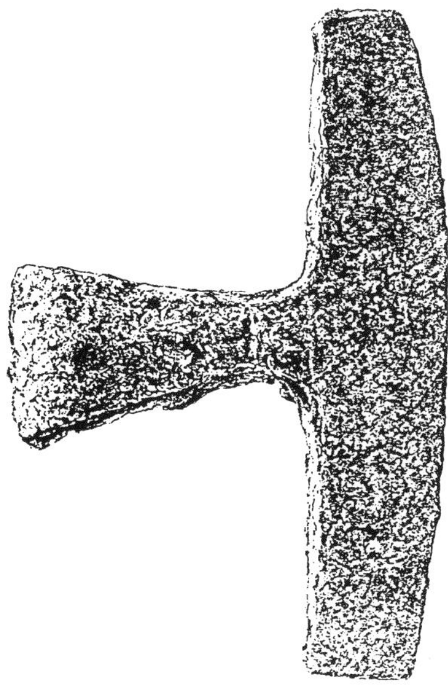

Anglo-Saxon axe head found at Hauxton.
© Cambridge Antiquarian Society.

beaten off and beheaded by the villagers. In the 15th century the estate was held by the Earls of Oxford and in the 17th century it was sold to the Wendys of Haslingfield. After Enclosure, much land was bought by the Hurrells of Newton, re-uniting the old manor.

Hauxton, paired with Newton for many purposes until about 1600, shared a population of 27 at Domesday, and 37 people paid tax in Hauxton in 1327. This figure fell to 16 households in the 16th century, rising very slowly to a total population of 144 by 1801. It reached a peak of 270 in the 1890s before falling and then growing to 710 in 1996.

There was considerable common land, mostly shared with other parishes, and sheep were numerous. In the late 14th century Hauxton had a shepherd looking after about 300 sheep, and the Abbot of Ely had kept 400 swine here in Late Saxon times. Horses, cattle and sheep were noted on the Abbot's land in 1300. Fields close to the village were enclosed well before Hauxton's Enclosure Act of 1798, probably by yeoman farmers who were buying land here from the 16th century.

Hauxton Mill, which appears in Chaucer's *Canterbury Tales* was a well-known land-mark from the Middle Ages onwards, grinding corn that was brought from Cambridge. It expanded, with an oil-mill to make animal feed in the late 18th century, and for trading in other products over a wide area. It declined in importance by the mid 19th century, but ground corn until 1975 and it is still a very fine example of a 19th century watermill.

Heydon

Heydon, a medium sized parish of 866 hectares, lies on clay except for a tongue of chalk stretching towards the village. It is on high and hilly ground which rises from about 55m above sea level on the Old Walden Way, one of the tracks of the Icknield Way, to 135m in the village, the church (which was bombed in 1940) being on one of the highest points. Bran Ditch forms most of the western boundary. The Old Walden Way, which was the County boundary until 1895 when Heydon first became part of Cambridgeshire, is part of the northern boundary. Enclosure began in the 18th century and was officially completed in 1831. Heydon's name in Domesday Book is *Haiendena,* perhaps 'Hay Valley'.

Prehistoric

Apart from the Old Walden Way another long-lived route of the Icknield Way forks to the south-east of Heydon Grange, one route running towards Newmarket, the other towards Ickleton. Several areas with scatters of Neolithic worked flints were found during recent field-walking on the site of the golf-course near Heydon Grange, sufficient to suggest there may have been some short-lived habitation here. Crop marks of ring-ditches indicate at least four Bronze Age barrows near Bran Ditch, and a bronze axe was found just south of the village. Iron Age pottery and a quern were found in a chalk-pit to the north.

Excavation sketch by R.C. Neville of the possible Roman temple on Anthony Hill.

Roman

A structure was discovered in the 19th century near the south end of Bran Ditch, just below the summit of Anthony Hill. It had walls of clunch forming a small rectangle, and contained artefacts such as a bronze bracelet and bell, a coin of the 4th century AD, instruments of iron and many bullock horns. This solid building may have been a corn-drying kiln but the finds suggest it is more likely that it was a small temple.

Anglo-Saxon

Bran Ditch, one of the four Anglo-Saxon dykes of Cambridgeshire, is now flattened but it survived as an earthwork until the mid 19th century, when its overall width (bank and ditch) was estimated at about 80ft. Where it was excavated in Heydon the ditch was nearly 7m wide and 2m deep. In addition to a trench cut in the 1860s, there have been excavations in the 20th century which showed the original flat-bottomed, steep-sided shape of the dyke was similar to the other three dykes, though not quite as large as Fleam and Devils Dyke. This dyke terminates just north of the village, where chalk meets boulder clay.

Middle Ages

A roughly square moated site about 100m north of the church was the site of a manor house for the principal manor of Heydonbury. It has now been virtually levelled by ploughing, and flints and red brick have been noticed in the plough-soil. The manor, previously held by a Saxon thegn, was taken over by Picot, sheriff of Cambridge at the Conquest and passed to a junior branch of his family. In the 13th century one of their descendants, Thomas de Hedon, was the first lord of the manor to live here and it was probably he who built the moated house, in about 1230. His successor was given hunting rights in Heydon.

The moated manor house was replaced in the 17th century by a mansion built for Sir Peter Soame, Lord Mayor of London, on the site of the present Heydon House. This mansion stood within a three-sided moat which later was made part of a lake, and there were fishponds in the grounds. It was a famous landmark for many years, its position making it visible for miles around. In the early 19th century it was replaced by a more modest house.

A small and short-lived manor known as Earles was in existence in the 15th and 16th century, and its title deeds refer to a 'site or manor-plot' next to the churchyard, opposite Heydon House. It consisted of fifteen fields of about 20 hectares and was sold to the Soame family in 1616.

Impressive strip-lynchets, the result of medieval ploughing in strips along the contours, similar to those at Great Chishill, survived in Heydon until the mid 20th century. Where they lay in ploughed fields they were bull-dozed and can no longer be seen, but in adjacent woodland their banks can still be found.

Village Development

The village of Heydon grew up at the crossing of four minor roads, to Elmdon, Great Chishill, the Icknield Way and Chrishall. There is still a small triangular green, with the

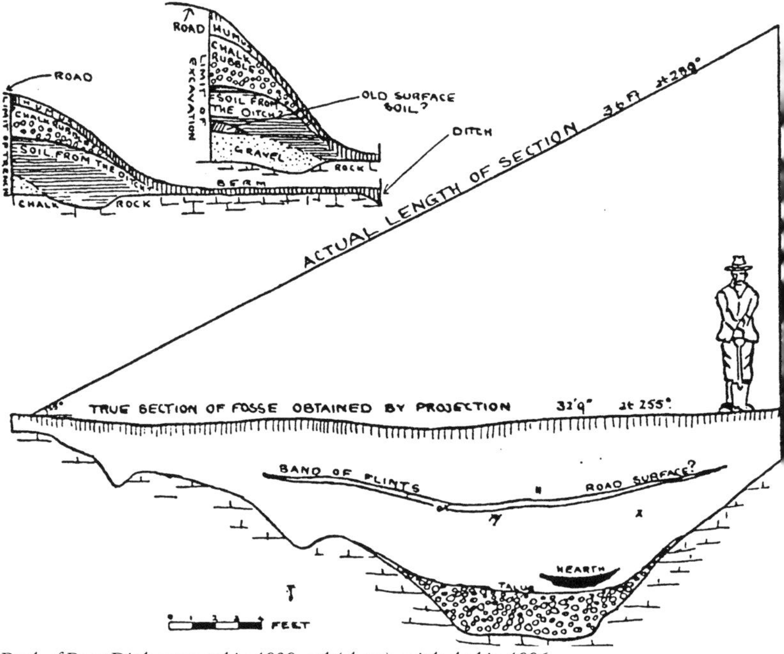

Bank of Bran Ditch, excavated in 1939 and (above) as it looked in 1996.

This line of Icknield Way is now part of a long-distance footpath.

church on one side and the site of the moated manor house, later Heydon House, on the other. Heydonbury, in contrast, is a double-row settlement, with many small plots which looks as if it may have been a planned settlement for lower-status people. This pattern has not changed since the early 17th century, and probably not since medieval times, except that the road to Chrishall, which does not appear on a map of 1777, is now only a footpath.

At Domesday the population was given as 30, and there were 21 taxpayers in 1327. In the 16th century 30 households were recorded. By 1801 the population reached 246, after which it grew to a peak of 368 in 1851, but had declined to 191 in 1901. In 1996 there were still only 200 people living here.

Apart from small areas owned by estates outside Heydon, almost all the parish belonged to the resident Soame family from the 17th to 19th century, the last baronet holding the manor for 89 years. In the 18th and 19th centuries, particularly under the Braybrookes, the parish was best known for its hunting and shooting, probably the last bustards in England being shot here, for example, and this tradition carries on. Otherwise, agriculture was the only employment.

Ickleton

Ickleton, a medium sized parish of 1080 hectares, lies mainly on chalk but with clay and alluvial soils near the Cam, which is its eastern border, and along a stream that flows west to east across the centre of the parish, joining the Cam just north of the village. The south, west and most of the east borders are County boundaries, and the one to the west is also part of a route from Cambridge to Elmdon which passes through Thriplow. Low-lying land near the Cam and the stream rises to the northern and southern parish boundaries, which are both mainly on crests at about 100m. The open fields were enclosed following an Award made in 1814. Ickleton's name in Domesday Book is *Inchelintone,* meaning 'Ikel's Farm', and it is not thought to refer to the Icknield Way, the tracks of which cross the parish and converge to ford the river and have strongly influenced land-use in this parish from prehistoric to late medieval times.

Prehistoric

Abundant Neolithic worked flints have been found, particularly in the south-east of the parish by Coploe Hill and the line of the M11, where detailed field-walking has been carried out, and a Neolithic axe was found during Roman villa excavations. The chalk hill-crest along the southern border was the site of some of the burial mounds which marked much of the route of the Icknield Way. One still stands as a tree-covered mound. It is over a metre high, and has a typical position on a

A Bronze Age burial mound, still standing on a 'false-crest' of the chalk hills, 1985.

'false-crest', ie from below, where it is intended it should be viewed, it seems to be on top of a hill and so is very prominent when seen from the valley. A cluster of mounds is now ploughed flat and they are only visible as ring-ditches. A Bronze Age spear-head from the village is the only artefact of this period known so far, and a stray discovery of a gold torc, probably deliberately buried for some reason, is the only Iron Age object recorded.

Roman

Ickleton is close to the Roman fort and town of Great Chesterford and it is not surprising that its chalk downlands were used for a villa of considerable luxury south of the village, and for a another large building to the north. The villa, which was excavated in the 1880s, was built in the early 2nd century. It measured about 30m by 20m, and had at least seventeen rooms, some of them with underfloor heating. Adjacent buildings included a timber aisled barn with stone roof-tiles. Walls of many rooms in the villa were decorated with painted plaster in designs that included scarlet fleur de lis, a wild rose and a dancing nymph. Six infant burials were discovered in the foundations.

The other large site has not been investigated. Brick, tile, stone and much pottery of the 2nd to 4th century occurred on the surface, and a hoard of metal objects nearby included pewter dishes and chalice, and iron objects such as a spade-edge, hammer, nails and fittings. Other Roman artefacts have been found to the west of the village. Roman brick and tiles have been used in the fabric of Ickleton church, and it is possible that even the monolithic pillars of the church arcades came from a Roman building, perhaps in the town at Great Chesterford.

Middle Ages

A small nunnery was founded in the mid 12th century at the west end of the village. It was a major landowner and important influence on the parish until 1536 when it was

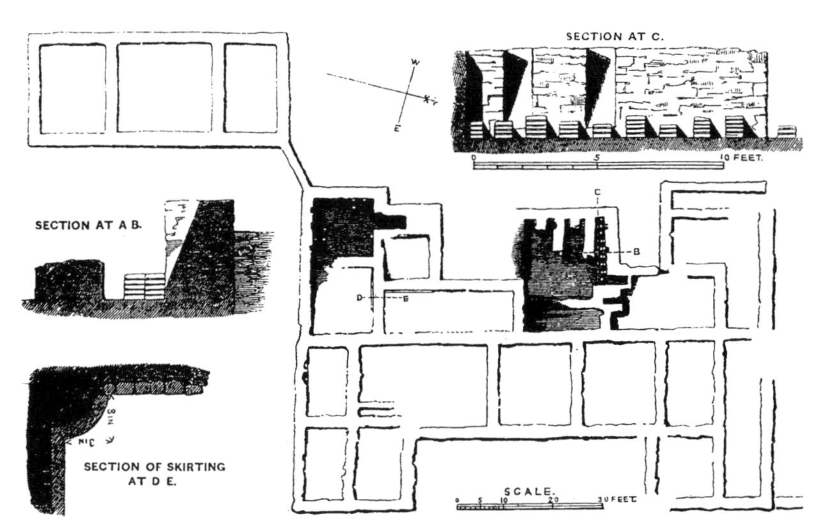

Plan of Roman villa in "Church Field", Ickleton

dissolved. There were about 9 to 12 nuns housed here, and they augmented their income by taking in lodgers, sometimes getting into trouble with authorities for housing married women. Some income also derived from administration of justice. One of their privileges was the right to hang thieves, and the gallows stood near the road to Duxford. They always claimed to be too poor to be taxed but evidently roused enough enmity to be attacked during the Peasants' Revolt, when a man from the village entered their close and burnt the court rolls and other documents. The present Abbey Farm house, which dates to the 17th century, includes a medieval doorway and other stone work. There is also a barn which displays 13th or 14th century carpentry. A sub-rectangular enclosure south-east of Abbey Farm was surrounded by a slight double bank and ditch which were levelled in the 1940s. There are fishponds nearby, and stone coffins from the nuns graveyard were excavated, of which only one broken example now survives at Abbey Farm, although in the 1930s several coffins here were used as cattle troughs. The nunnery church was described in the 16th century as 'a pretty building with a steeple and three bells'. Artefacts found north of Abbey Farm include coins and other items lost at the fairs and markets held there. A highly ornate bone comb also comes from this area.

Ickleton's parish church is an exceptionally interesting building. Most of it seems to have been built in about 1100, with later additions, using some Roman materials as described above. After an arson attack in 1979 restoration work uncovered early wall-paintings dated to the 12th century, showing the Passion of Christ and martyrdoms of saints. There is also a 14th century wall-painting of Doomsday over the chancel arch. Strip-lynchets at Coploe Hill illustrate the way medieval farmers cultivated steep slopes when population pressures made it necessary to provide more food.

Village Development

In medieval times the village consisted of one main street, Abbey Street, on the line of one of the Icknield Way tracks, running east from the Abbey to a large green, and then on to a ford. When a north-south road became important in the Middle Ages there were already houses on its direct route and so it made the awkward right-angled

Medieval comb from the nunnery at Ickleton.

bends which are still part of the character of the village. Quarter of a mile north of this street and parallel to it was another settlement, Brookhampton, recorded in documents from the 14th and 17th centuries, which has now disappeared. This too was on a track of Icknield Way that crossed the Cam by a ford before reaching Hinxton. There is still a remnant of the original green south of the church, and an area north of the church was the Camping Close, or sports field, in the Middle Ages.

Ickleton was a large village, with a population of 46 at Domesday, rising to 115 who were taxed in 1279. There were still 68 tax-payers in the 16th century, and this stayed stable until there was some growth in the 18th century, to a total population of 493 in 1801. At its peak in 1851 there were 813 people living here, falling to 543 in 1921 and only rising slightly to 640 by 1996.

A weekly market and annual fair were granted to the nunnery in the early 13th century, and the fair was still being held on a site near the Priory in the late 19th century, when it was well known for its sale of horses and of quantities of cheese brought from places such as Cottenham and Swavesey. The village was on the edge of the cloth-producing area of North Essex, and it seems to have benefited from extra wealth this provided, especially in 15th, 16th and 17th centuries when many other villages were shrinking. There were two fulling mills in the village and cloth could also be finished nearby at Great Chesterford's fulling mill. Sheep were kept in large numbers from the 15th century onwards, both for wool and for meat for the London market, though there was serious pressure on land for grazing, particularly after waste land was enclosed at Ickleton Old Grange by Sir John Wood in the early 17th century. Several important houses date to these centuries of prosperity, for example Hovells, Frog Hall and Mowbrays are 15th century, Durhams is 16th century, and Limburys, Abbey Farm and Brookhampton Hall are 17th century, though all have later alterations and additions.

Hovells, one of Ickleton's 15th century houses.

Kingston

Kingston is a medium sized parish of 795 hectares, lying on clay with patches of gravel, notably around the church. The village is on a sloping clay plateau which rises from 25m above sea level by the Bourn Brook, its northern boundary, to 80m on Mare Way, the southern boundary. Porter's Way and Armshold Lane ran along the western and eastern edges. The open fields were enclosed in 1815. Its Domesday place-name is *Chingstune*, or 'King's farm', indicating ownership of most of the parish by Saxon monarchs.

Prehistoric, Roman and Anglo-Saxon

Apart from a Mesolithic 'macehead' early finds in Kingston are a few sherds of Roman pottery and bone and bronze pins found in the garden of the Old Rectory, which is on the small area of gravel near the church. Adjacent to this garden, in the churchyard, a complete Late Iron Age urn was found, perhaps indicating a burial site there.

Middle Ages

After the Conquest William I still held an estate here, but other royal land was taken over by Norman lords, in particular Sheriff Picot. Much of Picot's estate here was held from him by the Banks, then the Mortimers. Their manor house was probably Kingston Wood Farm, a moated site carved out of ancient woodland on the western edge of the

Devil/demon wall painting in Kingston Church.

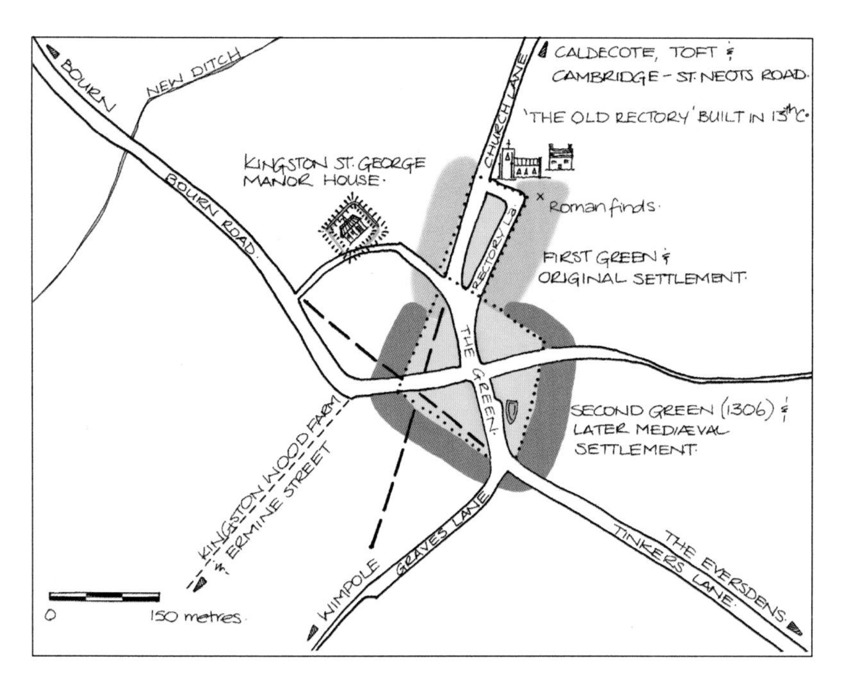

parish, an unusual place for the village's main manor. It was therefore perhaps once secondary to Kingston St. George. A chapel is recorded here from 1280, of which remains were noted in the 18th century. The moat is still a substantial water-filled feature with fishponds and an outer enclosure, but has been much altered by gardening in later years. It surrounds an early 16th century house, built by Ralph Chamberlain with wealth made in part from enclosure of common land. In the 18th century the manor became part of the Wimpole estate.

The other manor of Kingston, Kingston St. George, also derived from land Picot took over from the king. This seems to have been taken over at a slightly later date, after 1086, and may have previously been the kings' main manor, as the site of its manor house lies within the village. Part was given to nuns at Clerkenwell but otherwise it stayed with the St. George family from the 12th to the 16th century. Their manor house was at Moat House Farm where the rectangular moated site has also been much damaged by gardening although the house, dating to about 1500, is well preserved.

Village Development

Kingston was originally a 'green' village, with the church on a high point on the north-east side of a small green. In 1306 Constantine Mortimer of Kingston Wood Manor was given a charter to hold a market and fair, and it was probably he who laid out a large rectangular green at the cross-roads to accommodate these. However, the village declined from the 14th century and the market never flourished. The original green was eventually built over, but the later green survived until Enclosure in 1818 when it was divided up and houses were built upon it.

The village, which had a Domesday population of 21, in 1340 claimed to be unable to pay taxes because it was so oppressed by royal taxation and because land was uncultivated even before the Plague struck. In 1377 there were 111 poll-tax payers but by the early 17th century the population fell by 53%, to 25 houses in 1666, a record even for the claylands of west Cambridgeshire. The population rose to 225 in 1801, and was 322 at its peak in 1871. It declined considerably after this, and even with new building it was only 240 in 1996.

Villagers complained about enclosure of common land in the early 16th century by Ralph Chamberlain of Kingston Wood Manor. His family bought most of the rest of the parish, including St. George's manor, whose owners were also accused of enclosing common land. The small hedged fields of this 'old enclosure' are still a distinctive feature of Kingston, and about half the parish had been enclosed before its official Act. After that Act, most of the land was given to the Earl of Hardwicke, the rector and Queens College.

Kingston church, which is mostly 14th century, was repaired after extensive fire damage in the 15th

Kingston Wood Manor and moat.

The 16th century doorway of Kingston Wood Manor, where William Cole stopped for refreshment in his way from Cambridge to Oxford in the 18th century.

Kingston Old Rectory, dating from the 13th century.

century and has outstanding wall-paintings. The Old Rectory is also notable as a rare survival of a medieval house. It originally had an open hall dating to the 13th or 14th century, mostly built of timber but with stone and clunch used on some walls. Changes were made to it in the 14th, 16th, 17th and later centuries.

Knapwell

Knapwell is a small parish of 500 hectares, lying on clay, with a stream which flows down one side of its triangular shape and forms its east boundary. The land rises gently from 30m in the north to about 60m along the Cambridge-St. Neots ridge-way, its southern boundary. It was once part of the parish of Elsworth, and the boundary with that parish follows field-edges. There is still some ancient woodland in the south, and very old pollarded trees could be seen until recent years within the village. Knapwell was the first Cambridgeshire village to have its open fields enclosed by an official Award, which was made in 1775. Its name in Domesday Book is *Chenepewelle*, the well perhaps referring to an unusual iron-rich spring later known as The Red Well, in Overhall Grove.

Roman

A surprising amount of evidence for Roman occupation has been found considering the heavy clay soil of Knapwell. Aerial photography in 1995 revealed three groups of crop marks that may be Roman settlements, at least two coin hoards were found in the 19th century, and several bronze objects have been discovered in the village.

Anglo-Saxon

A fragment of an Early Anglo-Saxon brooch and a 9th century bronze strap-end provide some slight evidence that, if land was cleared by the Romans, it was not allowed to go back to waste. By the late 10th century estates in Knapwell were mentioned in wills, and in the early 11th century considerable land was given to Ramsey Abbey. Ramsey already owned most of Elsworth and Graveley, and it organised the life

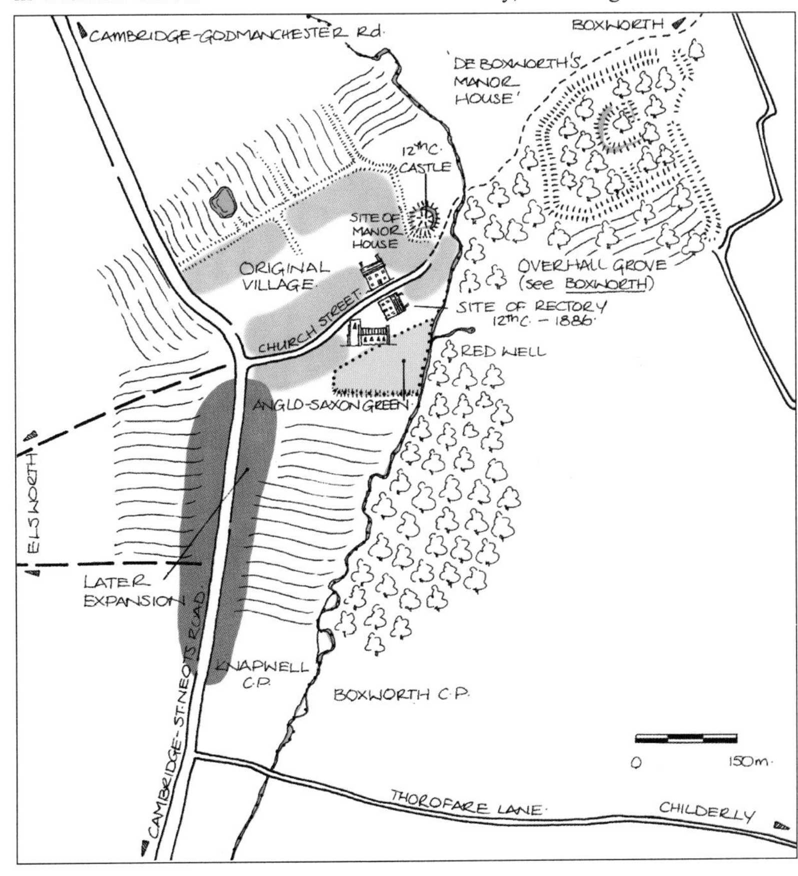

Knapwell from the air in 1956, showing the castle, the back lane to the village, ridge and furrow, house-sites on the track to the stream, and an old brick pit.
© Crown Copyright - Ministry of Defence.

and farming of the three villages closely together, with Elsworth as the centre. It was probably this institution which planned the grid of streets on which the early village was based, but it seems that their regular design may have had to incorporate a triangular green to the south which was already in existence.

Middle Ages

A small motte near Overhall Grove consists of a ditched mound about 25m in diameter and only 2m high. St. Neots ware of the 11th or 12th century has been found within it. Though it seems to be in an unlikely place for any defensive purposes, it is in fact close to a point where an east-west route through the village crossed the stream and was in a good position to protect the manor house and church. The records of Ramsey Abbey show that the Abbot ordered his villagers to build defences during the Anarchy period of the mid 12th century, and presumably this was their response.

Village Development

The village was laid out, presumably by Ramsey Abbey, as a grid between two almost parallel streets in an east-westerly direction at right angles to the stream. The church was built in the centre of the southern side, encroaching on the earlier green, and the manor house was on the opposite side of the same street, now Church Street. A rectory was later built east of the church. Communications that were important to the village in the Middle Ages were the routes west to the parent-village of Elsworth and east to Overhall Grove and Boxworth. In addition, the village seems to be on an older and longer east-west route that may go back to Roman times.

At the Dissolution in the 16th century Ramsey lost its property, and its villages were sold off separately. Overhall Grove was deserted at about this time, and Boxworth had shrunk to a few households. A route that linked Knapwell to the Cambridge-St. Neots road in the south and Cambridge-Godmanchester road in the north was now more used, and at Enclosure money was allocated to re-surface this road. The village therefore changed its lay-out to use this route, a move that had probably begun in the Middle Ages, and it became a linear north-south settlement. When the Enclosure map was drawn in 1775 a few houses, including the manor house, still stood on Church Street, and vestiges of the road parallel to it were still visible, but the village otherwise followed the pattern we see today.

While Knapwell belonged to Ramsey it continued to be organised as a dependent of Elsworth. Its harvests were largely stored in Elsworth and in the 15th century, for example, the Elsworth bailiff and rent-collector controlled Knapwell's agriculture. Even when it was owned as a separate estate in the 17th century the village was sometimes known as 'Little Elsworth'.

The church, too, was united with Elsworth, but it had its own rector, who lived in a rectory which Ramsey provided in the field to the east of the church in the 12th century. This medieval rectory, which always belonged to a poor living, was largely rebuilt in 1730, but in the mid 19th century the rector was described as living 'in a vulgar manner in the tumble-down Rectory and was addicted to card-playing and heavy drinking'. It was demolished before 1886. The church itself had mostly fallen down in the late 18th century, but in 1860 Henry Brown, an energetic curate who walked from Cambridge every Sunday to hold two services in a barn, raised the money to rebuild it. Later in the century it was neglected once more, and extensive repairs were needed after 1900.

Knapwell had a population of 24 in 1086, and there were 50 tenants in 1279. In the 16th and 17th centuries there seem to have been about 30 families, and in 1801 the total population was down to 97, less than in Domesday Book. This figure rose to a peak of 188 in 1881, but then declined. By 1996 it had risen again slightly to 110.

Litlington

Litlington is a medium sized parish of 865 hectares, lying on chalk in gently rolling countryside. The land rises from a stream that forms part of the north-western parish boundary, where it is about 30m above sea level, to over 70m along the A505, the parish and County boundary and also one of the lines of the Icknield Way. Limlow Hill, south of the village, is nearly 60m high. Litlington's open fields were enclosed following an Award made in 1830. Its name in Domesday Book is *Litelingetone,* or 'The farm of the people of Lytel'.

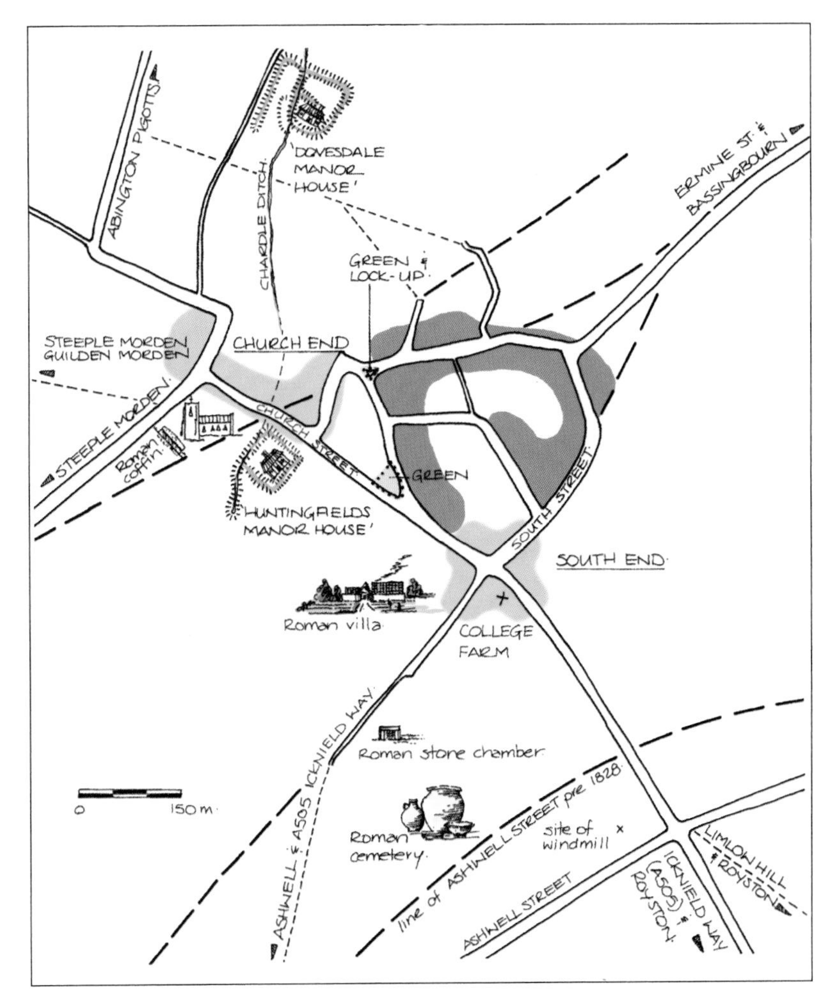

Prehistoric

The earliest finds are Mesolithic worked flints and a 'macehead' from near Sheen Farm, and three axes of the same date are known from the village. Ashwell Street and another of the routes of the Icknield Way cross the parish, and Bronze Age sites include numerous burial mounds now only visible as ring-ditches, which occur along the southern route of the Icknield Way in particular. Sixteen have been recorded so far from aerial photography, including a triple-ringed example in the south of the parish. An early Bronze Age dagger was found in Litlington, and a later axe together with lumps from an ingot, indicating bronze working, came from Limlow Hill.

There was an Iron Age settlement at Litlington which precedes wealthy Roman sites, but its nature is unclear. Late Iron Age features and pottery, including an amphora sherd indicating close contacts with the Roman world before the conquest of Britain were found in 1995 adjacent to a Roman villa. On Hill Farm, just north of Ashwell Street, small almost square enclosures, still showing as very slight banks and depressions in the field, may belong to this period. Mile Ditches (see **Bassingbourn**) also ran through the eastern edge of Litlington. However, a supposed hill fort, apparently indicated by triple ditches around Limlow Hill on aerial photographs, was shown to be to be due to natural soil slippage when excavations in 1935 showed they were shallow, although there were occasional sherds of both Early and Late Iron Age pottery in a Roman ditch there.

Roman vessel of green glass found in Roman cemetery at Litlington in 1821.

Roman

Cambridgeshire's most outstanding Roman cemetery was found in Litlington, just north of Ashwell Street, during gravel digging in 1821. The vicar's wife, Mrs Webb, made 'accurate and tasteful drawings' of many of the objects, usually in the groups in which they were found, and these, with a letter by A J Kempe published in 1836, give a reasonable impression of what was found. The cemetery was surrounded by a flint and brick wall, said to measure 38 by

Stone coffin found in the Roman cemetery and now located outside the west end of the church.

27 yards. At least 80 cremations were recovered, lying neatly in rows about 1m apart, parallel to Ashwell Street, which suggests there must have been grave-markers. Some urns were in wooden boxes, of which iron nails and bronze lock-plates survived. Others were in graves lined with flints or tile or covered by a roof tile. As well as cremation urns many burials were accompanied by other grave goods, usually vessels needed for a feast. Typically, groups of grave-goods consisted of a handled flagon, storage jar and a samian cup or dish. There were also about 250 inhumations, some in wooden coffins. Interesting objects that were probably found with inhumations include a perforated incense burner, small iron tongs and shovel (also for incense?), a pottery feeding bottle, bronze bracelets, glass beads, numerous coins, brooches, bone pins, needles, and several vessels of blue, brown, amber, green, white and yellow glass. A short distance from the enclosure was a stone chamber containing a stone coffin which can now be seen outside the west end of the church.

A villa near this cemetery was excavated in 1829 and 1881, and was probably the finest villa in Cambridgeshire, but unfortunately records of its excavation are lost. All we know is that it is said to have contained 30 rooms, hypocausts, a bath and at least one mosaic pavement, and measured about 100 by 120m.

Later in the 19th century a burial mound on Limlow Hill was destroyed, presumably with great difficulty for it was said to stand 6m high. Beneath was a rectangular pit filled with flints. Skeletons and several 1st and 2nd century coins had been reported in 1833 either on or near this site. The mound was set within a large rectangular enclosure which was trenched in 1936 and proved to be a substantial flat bottomed ditch up to 8m wide, over 2m deep, containing Roman pottery and tile.

Middle Ages

Dovesdale manor house stood in the moated site at Bury Farm. It consisted of a rectangular enclosure with a partial outer enclosure containing fishponds and was fed by the Chardle Ditch. Much of this moat has been levelled in recent years and can only be seen as dry depressions in the field and dry ditches of adjacent woodland. This site was purchased by John of Uvedale in 1305 and was held by his family for the next century. In 1428 it passed to the Pigotts of Abington Pigotts, and in the early 17th century Layer said that there 'may be seene the scite moted and ruines of many decaied houses...'

Another manor was Huntingfields, which acquired its name when its heiress married Roger of Huntingfield, lord of the Boxworth manor, in the mid 13th century. The manor house itself is first recorded in 1337. An estate map of 1804 shows three sides of one moat and two sides of another surviving south-east of the church, but the moat around the present house, which dates to the 16th century, only survives as a widening of the stream, other ditches being infilled in the 20th century. This manor held two windmills in 1291, one being destroyed by lightning and then rebuilt in 1318. One mill recorded in 1350 stood in Mill Field where the Bassingbourn road crosses the parish boundary.

Green and lock-up at Church End.

Village Development

The village may have grown up near a junction where one of the lines of the Icknield Way, running parallel and a little to the north of Ashwell Street, met another route running east from Steeple Morden. However, these routes seem to have had little influence on the detailed form of the village, which seems to have originally been made up of two quite distinct parts, one around and east of the church and the other a little to the south-east at a former cross-road, now a T-junction, near College Farm. The church lies on the east-west track in a prominent and now almost lonely position in the north-west corner of the village, with the Huntingfields manor house close by to the south and Dovesdale manor house to the east. These two settlements seem to be the Church End and South End recorded in 1378. Church End has a small green with at least five lanes leading into it. The green may once have been much larger, extending south as far as another small green which still remains north-west of South End. This green could have served to funnel animals from grazing lands to the north of the village.

The Domesday population was high at 43, and there were 235 poll-tax payers in 1377. There were 36 households counted in 1563 and about 50 in 1728. In 1801 the population was 350, rising to 790 in 1851. It fell to only 396 in 1930, but extensive new housing helped restore it to 790 in 1996.

Little Gransden

A cottage near the church, the oldest part of Little Gransden.

Little Gransden, a medium sized parish of 800 hectares, lies on clay except for a strip of greensand by its stream. The countryside is very gently rolling, between 50 and 90m above sea level, and it is cut by the steep sides of Gransden Brook. Its parish boundaries include Deadwomen's Way, (a disused road between Great Gransden and Longstowe), Gransden Wood, Waresley Wood and Hayley Lane. This road through the extended village was part of a route from Oxford to Cambridge and was marked by crosses at the Gamlingay border. Little Gransden's open fields were enclosed after an Award made in 1826. In Domesday Book its place-name is *Gratenden*, or 'Granta's valley'.

Village development

Little Gransden belonged to Ely from the 10th to the 16th century, and the original village was virtually an extension of its holdings in Great Gransden. There was a small settlement around the church, which stands on a high point almost in Great Gransden, and an adjacent manor house for the bishops of Ely's estate at Berry Close, where a hall, chamber, kitchen, dovecote and farm-buildings were ruinous by 1356. The nucleus of the village originally consisted of two linked loop-roads, similar to but less complex than Great Gransden. Part of the south-west loop has been abandoned. However, what made, and still makes Little Gransden a remarkable village is the extraordinary long extension for nearly one mile along a road which followed and sometimes lay within the bed of the stream. The large closes within which houses stood appear to have originally been remarkably regular in width, indicating that the whole extension was planned, but by whom, when and why? The purpose was presumably to accommodate the rapidly expanding population of Little Gransden in the 12th and 13th centuries. The instigator may have been the monastery of Ely if it occurred before 1100, or the Bishop if after. Alternatively, the extended settlement could have been created by the peasants themselves, (see **Longstowe**). The subsequent decline of the population of this parish led to the abandonment of this extension, especially at its south-east extremity. However, four dwellings still stood at Crow's End at the far end in the mid 19th century.

The Domesday population was tiny, only 11, but this grew to 75 tenants, about 375 people in 1279, and there were still 126 tax-payers in 1377. In the 17th century it was flourishing, with 46 houses counted, but the population then stayed fairly stable or even declined somewhat, to 232 in 1801. Its 19th century growth was modest, to a peak of 305 in 1871. After this it declined to 168 in 1931, and had only grown to 220 by 1996.

The heavy soils of Little Gransden were mostly used for arable farming, from which extensive ridge and furrow remains, but they were also comparatively well wooded. Woodland for 60 pigs was recorded in Domesday Book, one area of wood was not cleared until 1670, and Hayley Wood was economically important for the timber it produced, especially in the Middle Ages. Hayley Wood, owned by Cambridgeshire Wildlife Trust since 1962, is recorded in the Ely Coucher Book of 1251. 'The wood. There is one wood which is called Heyle which contains 4 score acres....' and, together with the rest of the village, it belonged to the bishops of Ely. It is an ash-maple-hazel wood with oaks as timber and was regularly coppiced from before the 13th century until the early 20th century, a practice which has now been revived. Its wood banks are still alongside an adjacent wood, the Triangle, which has grown up in the 20th century. 17th century ridge and furrow belonging to old enclosure can be seen beneath the trees of the Triangle.

In 1600 Elizabeth I insisted on taking over the estate and sold it to help a bankrupt courtier. Late in the 17th century it passed to the Cotton family of Hatley St. George, and was then bought and sold by non-resident landlords through the 18th and 19th centuries, sometimes being in the same possession as Hatley Park, until its sale in 1918.

Little Shelford

Little Shelford is a small parish of 484 hectares, lying mostly on chalk apart from a strip of alluvium and gravel along the Cam, which forms its eastern border. Its boundaries with Whittlesford, Hauxton, Harston and Newton were not fixed until Enclosure in 1815. The parish is generally very low-lying, but Cockle Hill rises to 30m in the extreme south-east. Like Great Shelford, from which it was not separated, its name in Domesday Book is just *Sceldeforde.*

Prehistoric

A Bronze Age axe was found near the river, and the gravel soils were widely used for settlement in Iron Age times, crop marks showing settlements similar to those in the adjacent parishes.

Anglo-Saxon

A cemetery, with an unknown but apparently small number of burials was found very close to the river. The only artefacts in the Museum of Archaeology and Anthropology from this site are two gilded brooches, six amber and two glass beads, a cowrie shell, buckle and a knife, which could all have been in one grave.

Anglo-Saxon grave slab set in the porch of Little Shelford church

In the Late Saxon period it seems that Little Shelford was a place of some importance. Its church, which belonged to Ely, was one of only three in Cambridgeshire to be mentioned in Domesday Book, and was a minster, from which a group of priests served a wide area. A stone church was built here, of which fragments exist in the present building. Some of the burials here, probably those of priests, were covered with slabs of Barnack stone that have been carved with ornate plait work decoration, and these too can be seen in the church fabric where they were placed during late 19th century restoration work.

Middle Ages

The main manor of Little Shelford belonged to Hardwin de Scalers, one of William's principal followers, in 1086, and his son moved his main residence and the administrative centre of his part of the estate to Shelford from Caxton. In the 13th century his descendant and heiress married into the de Freville family who held this manor with their many other estates until the late 16th century, though a 16th century description of the house, with a hall, two parlours and two chambers hardly suggests a house of any importance by this time. The manor house was bought by Tobias Palavacino, who built a much larger house in brick with classical colonnades on the site. His house too was rebuilt in the late 18th century by William Finch, and this, with some alterations, still survives, as does a small landscaped park.

Village Development

As in Great Shelford, the earliest part of the village was very close to the bridging point of the river, only about a quarter of a mile from its twin settlement. It grew up on a crossing place on a route from Foxton to Worsted Street, principally along the short stretch between the church and the river, where the manor house also stood. Later, the settlement spread further west along Church Street and south along High Street from where these two roads met near the church. The houses along the road down to the river ma have been moved as the land arounc the manor house was expanded to form the park. In 1729 there were extensive improvements to the road from Whittlesford, part of a turnpik route, and this involved building a new road to the west of the village, effectively acting as a bypass to the original village but also attracting a new line of housing.

Little Shelford's population is nc given separately in Domesday Book, but it was probably over half of the 38 inhabitants that it shared with Great Shelford. It later declined in relation with Great Shelford. There were 60 tenants in 1279, 36 tax-payers in 1327 and between 30 and 40 households were recorded from the 16th to the 18th century. In 1801 the population was 220, and this rose to 580 in 1851 despite the small size of the parish. Later there were slight falls, but since the 1960s there was a steady rise in population to 810 in 1996.

The Shelford's river crossing, so important to the origins of both villages, had a wooden bridge and a causeway in the 14th century, with a hermitage that acted as a toll-booth. A stone bridge stood here in the 17t century and was rebuilt in 1782.

Lolworth

Lolworth is a very small parish o 450 hectares, lying on clay and risin only gently from about 30m above sea level along the Roman road fror Cambridge to Godmanchester, its northern border, to 40m on its sout ern border with Childerley, which was once part of it. Open fields that had not been enclosed by the Cutts or other land-owners were officially enclosed by an Award made in 1848 In Domesday Book it is *Lolesuuorde* 'Loll's Enclosure'.

Prehistoric

A long Mesolithic axe was found near the church.

.olworth church, drawn by R. Relhan in the ırly 19th century.
) Cambridge Antiquarian Society.

Middle Ages

A moated site at Lolworth ǀrange still had four sides in 1841, hough now only one arm which has een enlarged to serve as a drain urvives. 13th century pottery has een found within the moated area. This was the site of the manor house or Lolworth Manor, an estate which ad been given to a follower of Picot fter the Conquest. Medieval owners of the manor probably all lived outide the village, and in the 16th centry it was acquired by John Cutts of Childerley, whose successors used it s a farmhouse at the time when nost of the parish was in their ownership.

Village Development

The village of Lolworth today etains little of its medieval origins part from its church, but its shrinkge has meant that the sites of earlier uildings have remained as slight earthworks and as crop marks. These suggest that the church was once approximately in the centre of he western edge of the village, with settlement areas extending north and east of the present row of houses, giving a roughly rectangular lay-out. A triangular green in the south of the village, stretching along the road to Childerley, is mentioned in 1615 and survived into the 19th century. Only one of Lolworth's existing houses was uilt before the 19th century, a hatched 17th century house north of he green. Otherwise it is essentially Victorian settlement based on the crossing of roads which at that time still ran to Childerley, Boxworth, the Cambridge-Godmanchester road and towards Dry Drayton. It now primarily consists of just one street leading north to the church.

For its size, Lolworth had a reasonably high population in the Middle Ages, with 16 people in 1086, 50 tenants in 1279 and 154 tax-payers in 1377. After the 14th century the population declined, to 17 householders recorded in the 16th century and only 14 at one stage in the 17th century. By 1801 there were 98 inhabitants, rising to 170 in 1871, and then declining. There was short-lived increase in the early 20th century, and several new buildings since the 1950s. In 1996 there were 150 people living here.

The Late Saxon village that had populated secondary settlements at Great and Little Childerley and was consolidated in one manor by 1086, still had several rent-paying freeholders in the Middle Ages. After about 1300 their land was being bought up by the lords of the manor, and peasants were able to acquire land that was easier to work in more favourable areas. Depopulation might have increased after many houses were destroyed by fire in 1393, though this alone should not have had lasting impact. The process of consolidation in one ownership was largely completed by the Cutts of Childerley in the 16th century. There were a few substantial rent-paying farmers living in the village at that time but the labouring population was very low. After the Cutts sold the village in the late 17th century, Lolworth was held by outside landowners until it passed to the Daintrees, who built Lolworth Grange in the mid 19th century.

Longstowe Hall, drawn by R. Relhan in 1833.
© Cambridge Antiquarian Society.

Longstowe

Longstowe is a small parish of 643 hectares, lying on clay in gently rolling country between 70 and 85m above sea level, and is bounded on the east by Ermine Street. It is poorly supplied with water, apart from ponds. Gradual enclosure of fields in Longstowe started in the late 15th century and was linked with depopulation, with about half the parish enclosed before the official Act was made in 1799. In Domesday Book it is simply known as *'Stou'* or 'Place', probably meaning 'Holy Place', but had acquired 'Long' by 1268.

Middle Ages

The manor house of Longstowe belonged to Ramsey Abbey throughout the Middle Ages, but was leased out until the Dissolution, when it was taken over by the Cromwell family. John Layer, writing in the early 17th century, states that Sir John Cage, who acquired Longstowe in 1571, had 'a fair lordship house there, with park, coney warren and fair demesne'. The Cages replaced the medieval manor house with Longstowe Hall. This Elizabethan manor house can still be recognised in the present Hall, despite drastic alterations in the 19th and early 20th centuries. It contains high quality imported woodwork re-used from 15th and 16th century buildings. In the grounds is a rectangular moated site, of interest because, although it appears to be medieval, it was actually constructed in the early 19th century as a garden feature.

A square medieval moat stood near Ermine Street, just south of the cross-roads. This was the site of the Hospital of St. Mary of Stowe, founded before 1250 by Walter the Chaplain, Longstowe's vicar, and staffed by a Master and sisters. Its lands were taken by the rector towards the end of the 14th century and it passed to the Crown, although an 18th century map shows a parsonage within it. One arm of the moat survives as a wet ditch, the rest being covered by a bungalow.

Village Development

The village itself may possibly have developed as a small nucleus near the church and Hall, but there is no trace of it there now. Instead it stretches south, with many gaps, for about a mile along a minor road that rather indirectly links Bourn and the Gransdens, totally ignoring Ermine Street, apart from houses built after the railway opened in 1862. Its plan thus mirrors that of Little Gransden, which lies immediately to the west and was also held by a monastic house throughout the Middle Ages, and it may have developed in the same way. It is also similar to Little Gransden in the way its long extension was subsequently abandoned. The village is an excellent example of the decay and contraction from late medieval times onwards that small villages on heavy clay soils commonly suffered, especially when in the single ownership of great houses. Its comparative success in the Middle Ages is demonstrated by the house-plots that can be recognised as low platforms or, where ploughed, as pottery scatters dating between the 14th and 18th century which fill the many gaps between houses. One particular concentration of pot sherds, dating back at least to the 12th century, with other occupation debris such as cobbles and oyster shells, occurs at the extreme south end of the village, near where the B1046 diverges from the old road.

Though small at Domesday, with 17 villagers, and complaining in 1341 that they could not pay taxes because much of the village was fallow, many house plots were empty and they had already paid too many taxes, including supporting the king's horses, there were still 97 tax-payers in 1377. There were 24 households recorded in the 16th and 17th centuries, but then only slow growth to 175 inhabitants in 1801. The population rose to 296 in 1891, after which it fell again to a 1996 population of 210.

Madingley

Madingley is now a medium size parish of 840 hectares, after adjustments to its boundary with Girton followed construction of the Cambridge bypass. It lies on clay except for a strip of chalk marl in the present village, but in places underlying chalk is close to the surface. The land is more hilly than most of this part of Cambridgeshire, and rises from less than 20m above sea level in the north to 65m on the Cambridge-St. Neots ridgeway, its southern border. The village, which is at the foot of the ridge, is at about 25m. There are good water supplies, including a spring near Moor Barns Farm, and the parish has always been well wooded, with some ancient woodland surviving. In Domesday Book it is *Madingelei*, 'The wood or clearing of the people of Mada'.

Prehistoric and Roman

Occasional Roman coins and sherds of pottery have been found in the parish, particularly in the south, near the probable Roman road from Cambridge. Within and outside Madingley Wood, a high point with wide views, are low banks of rectangular enclosures which, when cut by a pipe-trench, revealed pottery of the 1st century AD, belonging to the Late Iron Age or early Roman period.

Anglo-Saxon

Excavations close to Madingley Hall, at the top of a slope used for medieval settlement, uncovered ditches containing pottery of Middle to Late Saxon date, approximately 800-1100 AD, showing that this part of the village was settled by this time.

Middle Ages

A double moat near Moor Barns Farm, close to the Cambridge-St. Neots road, was probably the site of a grange owned by Barnwell Priory from the 12th to the 16th century. This manor had previously been part of Burdeleys Manor, which covered the whole parish and originally belonged to Sheriff Picot. Later it was bought by the Hindes of Madingley Hall, who were restoring much of the parish to one ownership again in the 16th century. Another significant manor that was subdivided from Burdeleys estate in the early 13th century and augmented with land

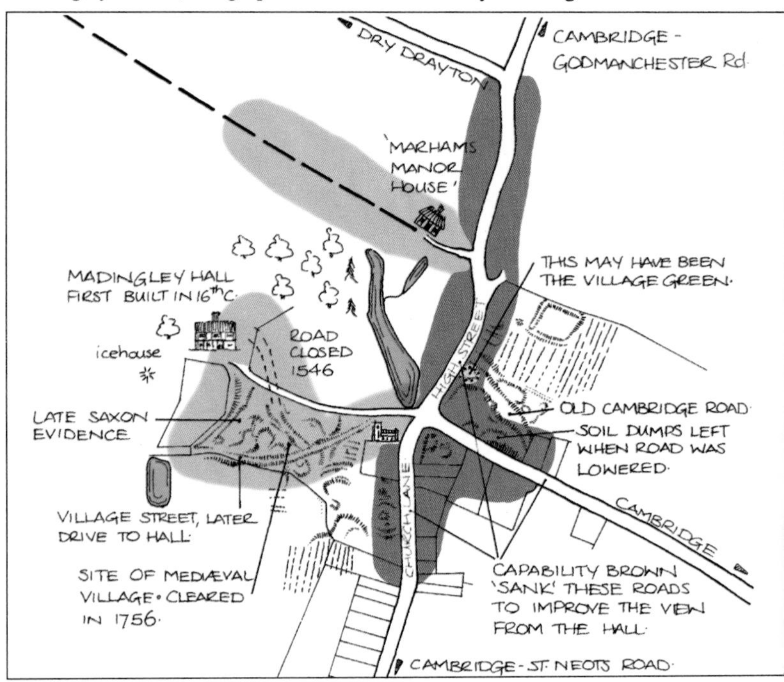

bought from villagers was Marhams Manor, whose centre was the present Manor House, a timber-framed and plastered medieval building that is set back from the west side of the High Street.

Village Development

Judging from the earthworks that survive around the village of Madingley and in the grounds of the Hall and from an engraving of the Hall made in 1705 it seems that the medieval village was more extensive than is now apparent, covering a roughly T-shaped area that included the Hall, Madingley Manor, the school and an area south and west of the church. Former streets, now hollow-ways within the parkland, are edged by the earthwork remains of former houses and gardens, indicating there was once a green north-east of the church.

In the early 16th century John Hinde, a sergeant-at-law, acquired the manor of Burdeleys which had become the Shire Manor, providing all expenses for the Members of Parliament for Cambridge, and bought other parcels of land in the parish. By the mid 16th century, when he owned most of the parish and had been made a knight and a Justice of the Common Pleas, he began building the present Madingley Hall, on a high point on the west side of the medieval village. Part of his red-brick building, with a private family hall above a medieval-style hall used for public functions, survives. One feature incorporated in this Tudor building was a 15th century hammer-beam roof which was probably brought from Anglesey Abbey, another of John Hinde's acquisitions. He and his son Francis continued to acquire land and develop the Hall and its grounds in the 16th century, stopping at least one of the village streets but not changing the settlement significantly. One of Francis' contributions was a long gallery which included fragments from a medieval church in Histon, whose demolition won him much unpopularity. It was probably Francis' son Edward who contributed lively wall-paintings of hunting scenes to the Hall, being fond of all blood sports and even keeping his own bulls for baiting.

16th century wall-painting in Madingley Hall depicting a hunting scene.

Madingley Hall.

In the 17th century the estate descended by marriage to the Cotton family of Landwade, but the family seat was Madingley, and the Hinde-Cottons continued to expand and aggrandise the Hall. One of their additions was a fine stone arch displaying arms of various benefactors to Cambridge University Library, from where it was moved in 1755. The major impact of the Hall on the village came in the 18th century, when 'Capability' Brown was employed to replace formal gardens with a 'natural' landscape, which involved destruction of much of the village around the church and the sinking of both new and surviving roads into cuttings which acted as ha-has, making traffic invisible from the Hall and thus giving uninterrupted views across an enlarged park to Cambridge.

The population of Madingley in 1086 was 31, and there were 90 tenants, perhaps 450 people, in the 13th century, but this was down to 123 poll-tax-payers in 1377. This figure was remarkably stable, at about 28 householders, 150 people, in the 16th, 17th, and 18th centuries. Growth of the village had not been encouraged by the presence of a great house, but even clearance of houses had not significantly depressed population figures. In 1801 there were 190 inhabitants, rising to a peak of 280 in the middle of the century, before falling again and then rising slowly. Very little new development has been allowed, and in 1996 the population was 220.

The last baronet at Madingley gambled away the family money in the 19th century and had to earn his own living driving a stage-coach. The Hall was neglected and, though it was leased for a time to Queen Victoria when the Prince of Wales was a student at Cambridge, it gradually became semi-ruinous, and part of it had to be demolished and rebuilt in the early 20th century. Later it was sold to the University, and in 1975 became the head-quarters of the Board of Extra-Mural Studies, now the Board of Continuing Education.

Another prominent feature in Madingley is the windmill which stands by the Cambridge-St. Neots road. A post-mill had been built here in the late 18th century, but it fell

Madingley's restored post-mill.

down in 1909. In the 1930s it was replaced with another post-mill, parts of which date from the 16th century, that had already been moved from the Huntingdonshire village of Easton to Ellington, and it was brought to Madingley as a decorative landscape feature. It decayed and lost its sails in the 1970s and '80s, but is now repaired.

The American Cemetery is also an important landmark. Land given by the Madingley estate in 1943 was made into a commemorative landscaped garden where nearly 4000 American servicemen who died in World War II were buried.

Melbourn

Melbourn is a very large parish of 1760 hectares, lying on chalk, within which is a narrow band of harder chalk known as Melbourn Rock. The land rises gently from a former marshy area about 20m above sea level in the north to nearly 60m along the A505 and the green lane known as Walden Way, both lying on courses of the Icknield Way and forming the southern parish boundary. There are high points which rise to 80m at Goffers Knoll and nearly 100m at Heath Farm. The village is on the lower ground, at about 30m. Other parish boundaries are Bran Ditch, the Mill Stream which flows from a spring at Melbourn Bury, and a route of Ashwell Street. The boundary with Meldreth was changed in 1820, when intercommonable land was divided between the parishes, and that with Royston in 1896 and again in 1988 when a village bypass was built. Enclosure of the parish's open fields was made by an Award in 1842. In Domesday Book it is named *Meldeburna,* but its derivation is not known.

Prehistoric

A major Neolithic monument, dated to about 3000-2500 BC, has been discovered by aerial photography near to the Icknield Way in the south of the parish. About 120m in diameter it consists of a discontinuous ditch with a wide entrance flanked by two ring ditches. Sometimes described as 'causewayed camps' or 'interrupted ditch systems' only about sixty examples of this sort of monument are known in Britain, and they are our earliest known enclosures, preceding the better known 'henges'. Their function is

Neolithic causewayed camp on the Icknield Way. © Cambridge University Collection of Air Photographs, 1971.

A Bronze Age cremation urn from a barrow excavated in the 19th century.

unknown, but clearly not defence, farming or settlement and so communal activities such as ceremony, religion, exchange and land-division are more likely. Elsewhere on the Icknield Way two Neolithic axes were found, and a sherd of pottery of similar date was found in the ditch of a circular soil mark. Settlement evidence for Late Neolithic or Early Bronze Age occupation was excavated on the route of the bypass, near to Grinnel Hill. About forty sherds of pottery, mostly decorated, and many worked flints, were found in a shallow hollow.

Like most parishes along the Icknield Way, Melbourn once had numerous Bronze Age burial mounds, of which at least fifty can still be traced as ring-ditches. Because some of the land in the south of the parish was unploughed grassland until Enclosure in 1839 several of them survived to be recorded as 'tumuli' on Ordnance Survey maps, or to be excavated in the 19th century. Two of them survive today. The one known as Grinnel Hill, just south-west of village, is approximately 3m high, 18m in diameter and is on top of a slight rise. The other, Goffers Knoll, about a mile south-east of village is 1.5m high, 25m in diameter, and still makes an impressive mound on top of a commanding hill with wide views. These two mounds give some impression of the innumerable examples which we have now lost. A group of five were excavated in 1847. The largest contained 'cinerary vases' and a very small pot that could have been an incense cup. The report also refers to a double bronze buckle in this mound, and an iron pike and six skeletons in another. These were probably Anglo-Saxon burials that re-used the prominent historic features. More recent examination of a barrow circle revealed by deep ploughing uncovered a crouched skeleton, with a secondary burial surviving only as fragments of bone and pottery. At least seven more cremations in Late Bronze Age urns were found, mostly outside the barrow-ditch. Finally from the Bronze Age, we have a 19th century record of an important bronze hoard containing an axe, fragments of a sword blade, gouge and blade, and the tip of a scabbard. These broken pieces must have been the collection of a smith, intended for recycling.

Roman

Scatters of Roman pottery have often been found on sites of other periods, and the Melbourn Bypass produced some minor occupation evidence, including ditches, tiles, nails and pottery. There are 19th century references to a Roman cemetery containing urns near Black Peak, and a small hoard of 1st and 2nd century coins has been found in a pot somewhere in the parish.

Anglo-Saxon

A cemetery of early 7th century date was excavated in 1952 after being discovered in the quarry of Melbourn Whiting Company. Six of the seven women found had rich and unusual grave-goods. They wore necklaces made up of silver rings, coloured glass beads, amethysts and silver pendants and were accompanied by bronze-bound wooden boxes and buckets. One women had small iron shears and another a spindle-whorl, probably originally in boxes. There were thirteen men of whom

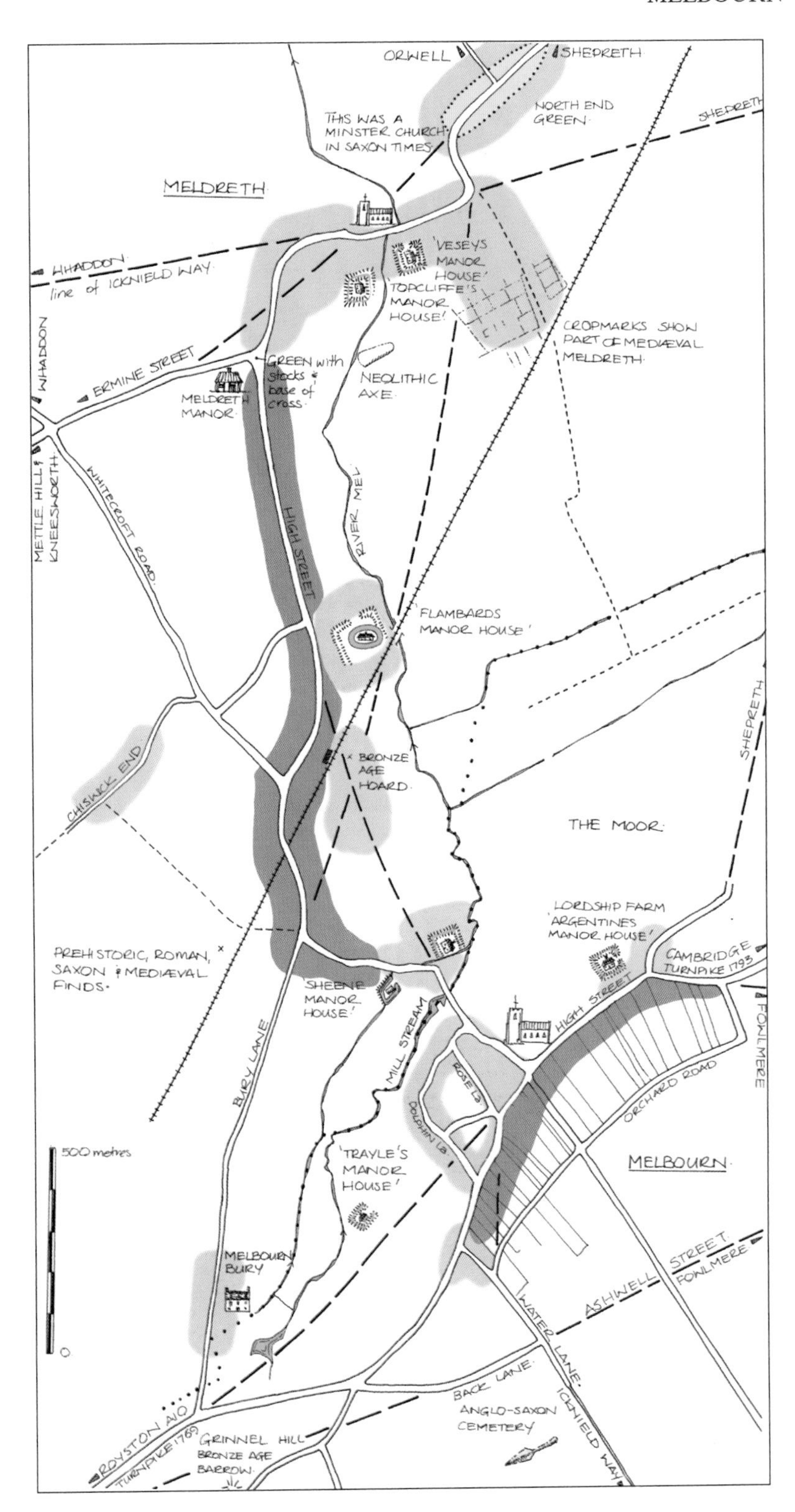

only two had spears and one a shield. Seven had knives. Of the six children and infants, two had knives and two wore buckles. Two women and one child wore pins to fasten their head-dresses. The cemetery has parallels with sites at Shudy Camps and Burwell and to the latest graves at Barrington, but is different to 6th century cemeteries where many women wear brooches, spears and shields are normal with adult males and amber is the favourite substance for beads.

Middle Ages

Melbourn Bury, a royal estate, was given to Ely in 970. It was the property of the Abbey until the Dissolution when it passed to the Dean and Chapter. It was leased out from the 16th century and in 1864 was sold to the Fordham family who still (1996) reside there, in a house which retains 17th century features, although nothing earlier than the 19th century is visible. The manor house of Argentines, another major Melbourn land-holder, stood at Lordship Farm, where there is still part of a damaged moated enclosure. The house within it contains timbers of the early 14th century, and its accounts for 1317/8 record a hall, thatched chamber, chapel, kitchen, granary and brew-house, all surrounded by a deep moat on which swans were kept and which was crossed by two bridges. Reginald de Argentine, sheriff of several counties, fought against King John, and his seal is on Magna Carta. Later rebellious lords of this manor fought against kings at Evesham, Bannock-burn, and Bosworth.

A moated area off Dolphin Lane was the site of Trayles manor house and chapel in 1395. The manor had been given to the French priory of St. Valèry in the late 11th century, being acquired from them for New College, Oxford in 1392. It was leased to the de Travilly Family from the early 12th to mid 15th century, and was bought by the Abingtons of Argent-ine manor in 1530.

Village Development

Melbourn now lies at the junction of an old north-south route, and the east-west Ashwell Street, here sur-viving as two routes, High Street and Back Street, with remnants of a third. However, originally Melbourn, like so many other South Cambridgeshire villages, was made up of a group of separate hamlets. One is likely to have been around the still isolated Melbourn Bury, another centred on Lordship Farm, where the old road left Ashwell Street and once ran north-east to Shepreth, while a third lies between High Street and the Mill Stream. Here is likely to have been the main part of the original village, for not only does the church stand on the north-east side, but there is still an irregular grid of lanes. A fourth hamlet may have occupied the area around the Water Lane-High Street junction. The process by which the separate hamlets were transformed into a long linear village along High Street with a small green in the centre by the church may be the result of the development of the road between Royston and Cambridge, perhaps after the town of Royston was founded in the 12th century. Certainly the main road runs north-east from Royston, joins the northern line of Ashwell Street just south-west of Melbourn, passes along High Street, and then swings away from the ancient line, heading north-east towards Cambridge beyond the village. The extraordinary long closes of the houses on the south side of the High Street, perhaps reflect this late development.

Melbourn was usually one of South Cambridgeshire's largest villages. In 1086 there was a population of between 50 and 60, and there were 323 poll-tax payers in 1377. 80 households were recorded in the 16th century, and in the 17th century it was known as 'a great towne' and had 125 houses. There was particularly rapid growth in the 18th century, to a total of 819 inhabitants crowded into 130 houses in 1801. By 1851 there were 1931 people, and poverty and overcrowd-ing were dreadful. All but 30 of its 200 homes were shared by more than one family and the Morning Chronicle of 1850 mentions 13 families in one house. Though families were large, few had more than two rooms. In spite of incoming coprolite diggers the population later fell. In 1965 Melbourn was selected as a village where growth should be encouraged because of its high level of services and good communicat-ions, and the population rose to a total of 4220 in 1996.

Sheep were an important part of Melbourn's economy from the Middle Ages until the 19th century. In 1826, shortly before Enclosure restricted commons and when the south of the parish contained at least

The cross-road by the church, in the centre of Melbourn.

210 hectares of grassland, 1960 sheep were kept, regulated by parish sheep masters. In the late 16th century orchards were becoming common, and new crops included saffron in the 17th and hops in the 18th century. Good road and, later, rail communications helped Melbourn's growth and the development of crafts and light industries, although, presumably because it was close to Royston, it had no market.

Meldreth

Anglo-Saxon bangle, and a Roman brooch, spoon and armour-hinge.

Meldreth is a medium sized parish of 976 hectares, lying on chalk, on fairly flat and low-lying ground that rises from about 15m near the Rhee, its northern border, to 40m on Ashwell Street which forms part of the southern border. Its Enclosure Award was made in 1820. In Domesday Book its name is *Melrede,* the meaning of which is not known.

Prehistoric

A Neolithic axe, worked flints and pottery have been found within the village and there are two ring-ditches in the valley of the Rhee. The original mounds were built of gravel, and so would never have stood as high as the barrows along the Icknield Way. Near the station was found an important Late Bronze Age smith's hoard of broken bronze objects. This included 27 axes, a gouge, chisel, knife, 9 swords, 3 spear heads, a cauldron ring and 15 lumps of bronze. Sherds of Iron Age pottery were found on two sites along the Melbourn bypass.

Roman

While digging into a natural hillock at Mettle Hill, now an old chalk pit on the Kneesworth road, in 1816 a lead coffin was found, which was said to have contained 5 perfume bottles, a bronze armlet, bone pin and a coin of Cunobelin. There is also a 19th century reference to several stone coffins being found here in a hill, and one of these can be seen outside the west end of the church. Another Roman site was found during field work in advance of construction of a golf course in the north of the parish. Pottery of 1st to the 4th century was collected and also artefacts of bronze including a brooch, spoon, enamelled handle and seal box lid, and a hinge from armour plating.

Middle Ages

A complex of moats was the site of successive manor houses for Sheene, a manor which was given to the French abbey of St Evroul after the Conquest, and then to Sheen Priory in Surrey in 1415. The present house still has part of a moat, and a dovecote previously stood in another small moated enclosure.

The site of Topcliffe's manor house, also once part of St. Evroul's estate, was in a moat to the south of the church, now changed by landscaping and a septic tank. The manor house appears in texts from the 1290s, and sales of surplus apples and cherries are recorded from 13th century. In 1380 there was a thatched house and gatehouse, and in 1404 the house had a chamber, kitchen, hall, and bakehouse. In the 16th century the manor was granted to St. Thomas' Hospital, London. During the Peasants' Revolt John Topcliffe was appointed to help deal with the rebels. He was forced to leave his house in Meldreth due to the rebels threats, and robberies and burning of houses were reported.

Veseys Manor stood in a moated site close to Topcliffe's, also in a private garden where flower beds contain tile, oyster shell and animal bone. It is dry now and it too has been changed by landscaping. In the 13th century a licence was given to build a chapel here and in 1503 there was a 2-storey house with kitchen, hall, chapel and several chambers around a courtyard. A house stood within the moat in 1820.

Yet another moat was that of Flambards Manor, just north of the station, now obliterated by a housing estate. It was a particularly interesting site because of its oval shape and because trial excavations by TC Lethbridge uncovered occupation layers of 11th to 13th century date. Two latrine pits and several pebble and cobble floors were found. The manor had belonged to Ely Abbey and passed to Hugh de Scalers after the Conquest.

Village Development

The village is made up of at least six groups of houses which can be seen as distinctive clusters on the Enclosure map of 1820 though they have now tended to grow together. These groups are mostly spread for nearly two miles along the winding

The minster church of Meldreth.

road from Shepreth to Melbourn, and the settlement is continuous with Melbourn. Judging from the position of moated sites and earthwork remains of house-sites this pattern is similar to the medieval lay-out, although some areas have been deserted.

Two of these hamlets lie on a twisting south-west to north-east road which is a branch of the Icknield Way, running from Bassingbourn via Kneesworth to Shepreth and beyond. The westernmost hamlet includes the church and two manorial sites as well as a small green where the village stocks, whipping post and the base of a medieval cross remain. The easternmost hamlet once had an elongated green, traces of which are still visible, known as North End Green. The remaining hamlets lay on routes running north from Melbourn. The Sheene manorial complex is the southernmost, and there is another a little to the north. Two more are Chiswick End and one that is associated with the Flambards manorial site.

Like Melbourn, Meldreth was a large village in the Middle Ages. There were about 50 people recorded in 1086, and 253 poll-tax payers in 1377. 47 households in the 16th grew to 70 during the 17th century, but then there was only slow growth to 444 inhabitants in 1801. The maximum 19th century population was 776 in 1851. This fell until 1921, and since then has risen, especially since the 1950s, to 1790 in 1996.

The moot, or meeting place, for Armingford hundred was held in Meldreth on Mettle Hill, known as *'Motloweyhil'* in 1319, on the road to Kneesworth, probably on the high point that the Romans had used for a burial site. Meldreth church was particularly important in Late Saxon times. It was what was known as a minster and existed before most of the surrounding villages had acquired their churches. From it five priests served the adjacent parishes. It is one of the few churches to be mentioned in the Domesday Book for Cambridgeshire. Later in the Middle Ages a chantry was founded by a local man, for which a chapel and probably a priest's house stood in the churchyard.

Stocks on the village green at Meldreth

Newton

Newton, a very small parish of 420 hectares, lies on chalk which slopes gently from 30m above sea level near Harston down to Hoffer Brook, a tributary of the Rhee which rises within the original village and forms short sections of the parish boundary. Most of the other boundaries are furlong edges, and were agreed at a late date, and the open fields were enclosed in 1854. Its name means 'New Farm', indicating that it was a late creation, and it is not mentioned separately in Domesday Book

Prehistoric and Roman

The earliest finds are two Late Bronze Age axes and a spear-head, and the earliest known site is a large Iron Age and Roman settlement showing on aerial photographs, with trackways, an aisled building and rectangular enclosures, close to Hoffer Brook in the east of the parish. There is a single enclosure with small buildings likely to be Roman in date near Rowley's Hill in the west. Newton shares a group of enclosures and an Iron Age 'pit-alignment' that runs to the Brook with the parish of Harston.

Middle Ages

The manor house, owned by the Abbot of Ely, was in a moated site known as Newton Bury, adjacent to the church, where it was recorded before 1300. It was fed by the spring which flows into Hoffer Brook. By the 16th century it was leased out to lay land-holders. In 1650 it was described as a tiled, timber-framed house with a hall, parlour, kitchen and several chambers. It had a brew-house, dairy, malt-house, stable, great barn and dovecote. The 1669 lease mentions water 'stocked with fish that is to say the cisterne pond, the moat and the malthouse pond and the breeding carp pond within the great yard'. The fish in the carp breeding pond had been excluded from earlier leases, being kept for the monks of Ely for their own use. When the manor house burnt down in the 19th century it was rebuilt on the same site. An interesting feature of the later park is an 18th century ice-house.

Village Development

Newton, probably once part of the parish of Harston, was normally paired with Hauxton, with whom it was jointly owned by Ely, a gift of King Edgar. It grew up as a linear village on one of the tracks of the Icknield Way, which ran from Foxton and crossed the Cam at Durnford in the parish of Sawston. In the 18th century the main Ely manor was purchased by the Hurrell family whose descendants acquired the rest of the parish in the 19th century. It was the Hurrells who removed all of the houses on the south side of the village street and created a small landscaped park there. Subsequently, estate cottages were erected at the north-east end of the village at a point where the village street crosses what became the main road between London and Cambridge in the 17th century. Later expansion has been concentrated in this area.

Newton, counted with Hauxton in Domesday Book, was evidently quite small, and stayed this way. In the 16th century there were 20 households. This barely rose at all, with a total population of 114 in 1801, rising to a maximum of 220 by 1880, before the usual fall and slow recovery, with two housing estates built in the 1970s. In 1996 there were 370 inhabitants.

The common moorland that separated Newton and Hauxton was shared by those two parishes and also by Little Shelford and Harston, and boundaries between them were not set down before 1800. Newton's church counted as a chapel that was dependent on Hauxton's church for much of the Middle Ages. There was considerable common land and also rights of grazing after harvest, so many animals were kept. Large flocks of sheep are recorded, notably when they strayed into Harston, and there was a professional shepherd in the village. Saffron was grown in small enclosed fields, but otherwise traditional open field agriculture continued until the 1850s.

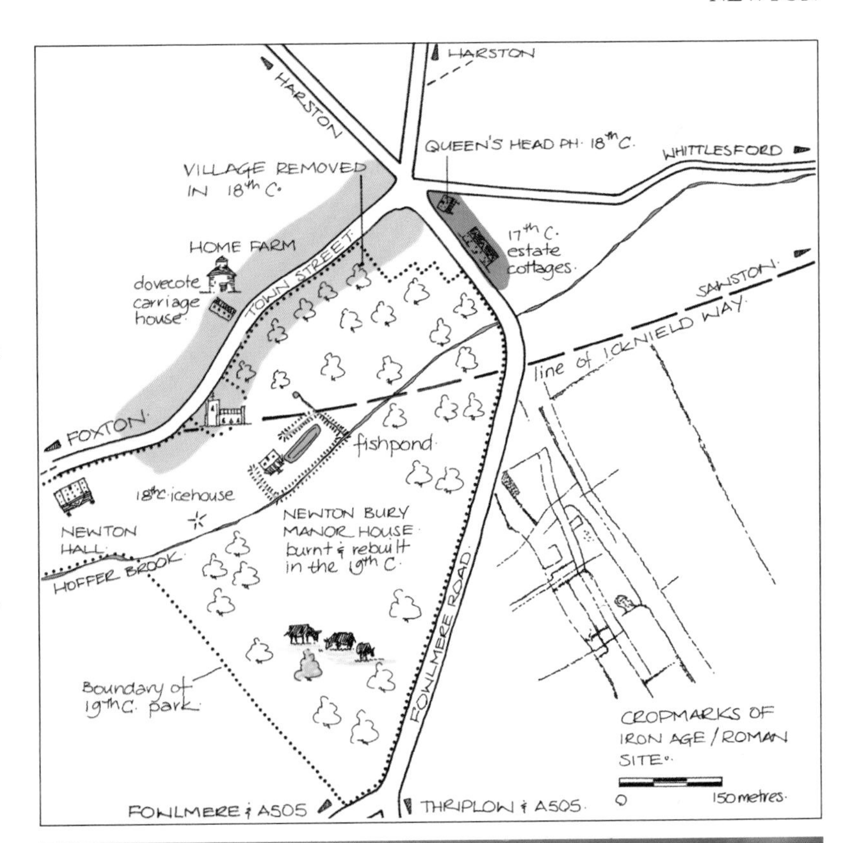

Dovecote at Home Fram, Newton. Photograph by Beth Davis, 1987.

18th century milestone at Newton.

Newton has a circular clunch-built dovecote at Home Farm, perhaps the most interesting of South Cambridgeshire's large number of dovecotes. It is lined with nesting boxes and has a conical roof with louvred entry to a flight platform and chute, and it housed 500 doves until 1930. Other interesting estate buildings on the north side of the old village street include the Hurrell's coach buildings. Although the village grew around a crossing-place on the main London to Cambridge road, it was not noted for its inns. Even the Queen's Head, at the junction of five ways, only dates back to the early 18th century. However, because of the main road, Newton has two of the Trinity Hall painted iron milestones, erected in 1730, the earliest in England after the Romans.

Orwell

Orwell is a moderate sized parish of 850 hectares, lying on clay except for a chalk ridge followed by Mare Way, its northern boundary, which reaches a height of 90m above sea level. Otherwise the parish is fairly level, dropping to about 20m near the Rhee, its southern boundary. The open fields were enclosed by an Award made in 1836. There is a spring in the village from which it derives its Domesday place-name of *Oreuuelle,* and several streams and ponds.

Prehistoric

Areas close to the river have been used at many times from Neolithic times onwards. Scatters of Neolithic and Bronze Age flint tools and waste-flakes and a fragment of a bronze axe have been found here, with a concentration near the ford, and a Neolithic axe is known from the parish. Sherds of Iron Age pottery were collected before the golf-course was built, and much Iron Age and Roman pottery and building debris were discovered between Field Barn and the river, where it is likely that a Roman (and probably earlier) track led to a crossing place. A distinctive Iron Age weaving comb comes from Malton Farm, and Iron Age coins occur near the river. Mare Way was a major prehistoric trackway across the north of the parish.

Roman

Artefacts found on both sides of the river during dredging include Nene Valley and Samian wares, a bronze javelin head, coins and three brooches. Excavation of sites on and just south of the High Street and in Chapel Orchard has also revealed Roman pottery. The A603 was a Roman road and it is likely that some of the medieval tracks leading to it from the river were used in Roman times.

Anglo-Saxon

Other finds reported from river dredging at Malton are Late Saxon, including a Viking spear, key, spindle-whorls and axe-heads.

Middle Ages

The parish of Orwell included what is now Malton Farm, which was a hamlet with its own church and parish between the 13th and 17th century. Malton, which has an early place-name and evidence for Saxon settlement, is on the ford, bridged in the 19th century, which crosses the Rhee. It was part of the estate of the Tyrells of Shepreth, from whom it was acquired by Lady Margaret Beaufort and given to Christ's

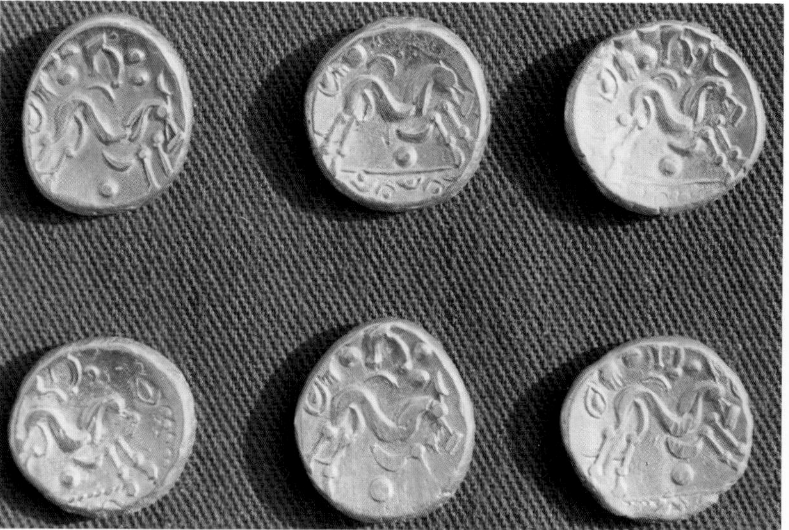
Iron Age coins from Malton.

College in 1505-7, principally as a retreat for fellows in times of plague in Cambridge. Malton was already described as depopulated by 1428, and enclosure of its fields began in the 15th century. A rectangular moat with outer enclosure, one arm being formed by the river, fell out of use early on, for a mid 15th century house is partially built over it, indicating it had been deserted for some time. Most of the church was pulled down in the 16th century. John Layer writes 'we know of no church that is demolished except the chapel at Malton... but now the chappell is ruinous and used they know not how. About 37 years since it was used for cows and afterwards used for a chappell agen about 18 years since'. The last traces of the church were obliterated in the late 20th century. The scholars built a separate house and let the old manor. The college retreat, 'consisting of such a quantity of Rooms as might receive the Master and Fellows to retire into in the time of any Visitation and other necessary houses for their servants, officers and scholars' contained a Long Gallery often mentioned in College accounts. Perhaps thanks to improvements to drainage Layer could describe Malton as 'now but one house, a pretty seat, a chapel for divine service, but belongs to Orwell. The river watereth it pleasantly and a great store of good pasture ground'

There is no recognised manorial site in Orwell itself. However, a map of 1680 shows an area known as 'Lordship' with what appears to be a large mound on it, possibly a castle. This was levelled for a school in 1883 and when redeveloped there were no indications on the site of any such structure, which would in any case have been in a poor defensive position at the bottom of a hill.

Village Development

Orwell village has two quite distinct parts. The principal one is the High Street, a long street lying on an old trackway from Arrington to Barrington which runs along the foot of the chalk ridge, here at the junction of the chalk and the clay and thus at a spring-line. The church stands at the western end and immediately

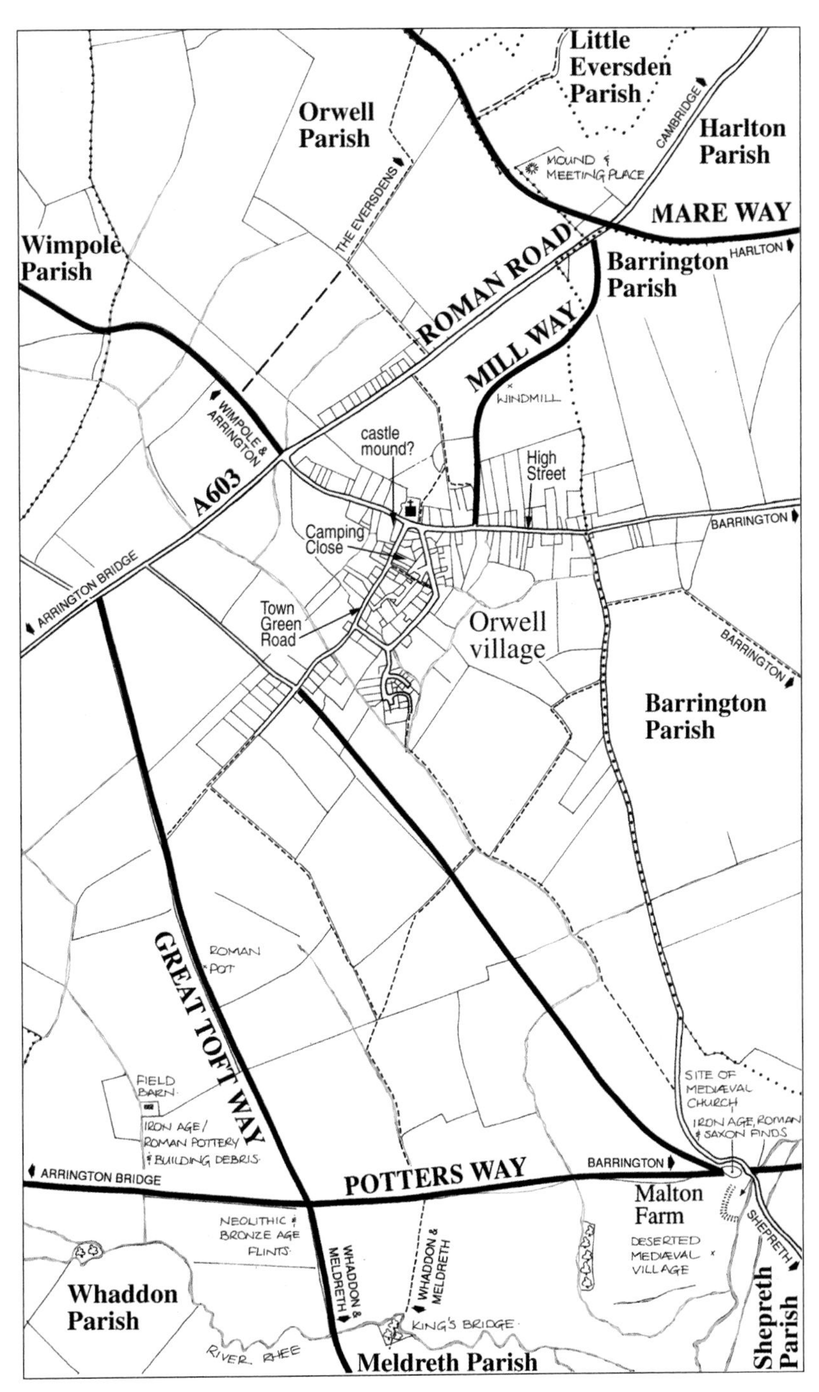

below it lies the second part of the village, now following Town Green Road. This name is all that is left to indicate the existence of a green, almost 600m long but little more than 50m wide. The green was almost certainly a deliberate addition to the village in the mid 13th century when Ralph Camoys, the lord of the manor, was granted a weekly market and annual fair in 1254. Neither the fair or the market was a success, the fair being last mentioned in the 16th century. As a result the green was gradually built over or enclosed. For example, in 1655 'Camping Close', at the north end, where village football had once been played, was given to a young student lawyer, Thomas Butler, in 1605 in exchange for legal help for the villagers in protecting access to grazing land. What remained of this green in the 19th century, a long narrow section in the centre, was divided up at Enclosure. Material from excavations has, however, indicated an older and different form of village arrangement in Late Saxon times, with occupation evidence of that period being found not only at the east end of High Street, but also towards the southern part of the later green, maybe indicating a settlement made up of distinct hamlets.

Though the population of 20 was small at Domesday it grew steadily without the obvious serious setbacks which affected smaller parishes on clay. There were 56 people taxed in Orwell and Malton in 1327, and 46 families in 1563. There were a total of 375 people in 1801, jumping to 800 in 1871, partly due to coprolite mining. It fell after that, before growing to 1070 with new housing in the late 20th century.

The church is built on high ground in a commanding position. The rectory was a sinecure after the 14th century and attracted eminent Cambridge scholars who sometimes acted as benefactors, for example founding a school in the 18th century. There are descriptions of the vicarage being in disrepair in the 16th and 17th century. Wealth of the rectors is illustrated by one, Richard Anlaby, who paid for the rebuilding of the huge chancel in about 1398 in memory of a lord of the manor of Orwell who was also the tutor to Richard II, and who had been executed ten years earlier. The chancel roof, elaborately decorated with carved bosses and painted shields, was reconstructed by an 18th century rector.

Nearly all the population of Orwell was dependent on agriculture apart from a period in the late 19th century when coprolite mining brought prosperity and population growth. A survey of 1627 notes:

The land is most field grown arable except some pastures around the town and the soyle is rich and the sole commodity is corne and some small parcells of saffron grounde...The hunting, hawking and fowlinge is there present for the Kinge's pleasure when he stays at Royston. The fishing is of a small river... belonging to the Manor for half a mile in length.

Land near the river was meadow as it was too wet for ploughing except for a short time in the late 20th century, and there were orchards around the town in the post-medieval period. Cleaning and repairing ditches and building new ones are recorded parish duties, and the brook to the south of the village was straightened into a drain by 1837 when the parish was enclosed.

Orwell Church.

Papworth Everard

Papworth Everard, a very small parish of 468 hectares, lies on clay apart from a patch of gravel near the church. It is in rolling countryside that rises from about 30m above sea level in the north to 70m along the Cambridge-St. Neots ridgeway which runs just within the southern parish boundary. Other boundaries are furlong edges, except for a minor road from Hilton to Eltisley which is the boundary with Papworth St. Agnes. The landscape was always fairly well-wooded, and Papworth Wood, perhaps the wood that is mentioned in Domesday Book, still stands east of the Hall. Ermine Street runs through the centre of the parish. There are several small streams, one of which rises near the church and created a valley which attracted the first settlers. The open fields were enclosed in 1826. In Domesday Book its name is *Papeuuorde,* or 'Pappa's Enclosure', 'Everard' being added in the 12th century, after the lord of the manor, Evrard de Beche.

Middle Ages

A circular moat in the grounds of Papworth Hall is probably an ornamental feature created during landscaping works for the 18th century park. An ice-house was built nearby. There are fragmentary remains of another moat to the north-west of the church, fed by a stream and now covered by trees. It is shown on Enclosure and Tithe maps as semi-circular, but this may be due to later changes. This is the most likely site for the manor house, which is mentioned from about 1300. By the 16th century a building known as the Manor House stood next to Ermine Street, on the east side, and

Papworth Everard Church and hollow-way.

in the late 18th century this humble Elizabethan farmhouse was replaced with a neo-classical mansion, Papworth Hall, set within a park to the east of the road.

Village Development

The original village was built near the church, which is on a promontory overlooking a steep valley, well to the west of Ermine Street and the present village. It was a pre-Conquest manor that was held by the de Beches from the 1160s to 1253. It probably grew up along an east-west track extending from Toseland and Yelling to the west across Ermine Street to Elsworth. Settlement was probably mainly south of the church, where pottery of 12th to 14th century date has been collected from plough-soil, and there are plough-damaged remains of house-sites. Traces of a hollow-way left by a later road which went eastwards from the church to Ermine Street can be seen within the present churchyard, which was extended for the burial of tuberculosis victims. In the 17th century Ermine Street became a turnpike road, and its use increased sufficiently for an inn, first the Red Lion and then the Chequers, now both farm houses, to be built to serve passing trade. By the 18th century the small population of the village was being attracted towards the main road and the new manor or Hall, and it is here that the present village has grown.

The population at Domesday was given as 19, and there were 45 tenants in 1279 and 85 tax-payers in 1377. This fell to a maximum of 15 householders in the 16th century, and about the same in the 17th, rising slightly to a total of 111 in 1801. This stayed fairly stable until the mid 19th century, and then rose to 191 in 1901. A slight fall was followed by creation of a settlement for tuberculosis sufferers in 1918, when several hundred patients and ex-patients were housed. This settlement has grown, and in 1996 the population stood at 1580.

In 1794 the manor was bought by Charles Madryll, later the MP for Cambridge, who married into enough money to build the mansion of Papworth Hall and to create a parkland setting for it. He was later responsible for enclosure of the whole parish in 1826. His family lived here until the late 19th century. A millionaire speculator, Ernest Hooley, bought the estate in 1896 and spent some of his fortune on refurbishing and furnishing the Hall and investing much money on manuring and draining the land and other improvements to the farms before he went bankrupt and was gaoled for fraud. He used the Hall for entertaining on a lavish scale. Still greater changes came after World War I when Dr. Pendrill Varrier-Jones acquired the Hall and moved his tuberculosis patients from a home in Bourn to create a revolutionary new settlement at Papworth.

The Settlement provided not only long-term hospital care for tuberculosis, with fresh air and good food, but offered suitable homes for ex-patients so that they could live healthy lives, which was their only hope of surviving a disease for which there was no real cure. New houses and workshops were built for these purposes. In the 1950s, after drugs to combat tuberculosis had been found, the Settlement began accepting patients with other disabilities and developed factories and work-shops to provide long-term employment on a commercial basis. The hospital continued to pioneer specialist treatments, particularly for patients with heart, chest and lung diseases, and in 1979 it began heart, and later heart and lung, transplants, for which it has an international reputation.

Papworth St. Agnes

Papworth St. Agnes, now a small parish of 525 hectares, lies on clay except for a patch of gravel east of the church. The land rises to 45m on Lattenbury Hill in the north and to 60m on a ridge in the south, but in between it is fairly flat and only about 20 to 30m above sea level. Its western boundary is a brook which flows from Nill Well, an iron-rich spring that is shared with Graveley and Hilton, and its eastern boundary was moved to follow Ermine Street in 1895. Previously the eastern half of the parish was in Huntingdonshire, showing that the parish was earlier than the creation of the counties. Its fields seem to have been enclosed by 1600. In Domesday Book it is not differentiated from Papworth Everard, and 'Agnes' was added later, after a lady who held the manor in 1160.

Middle Ages

A rectangular moat west of the village street was probably the site of the manor house for Papworth St. Agnes' principal manor, Russells. The service owed for this manor was feeding the poor, which may have been the reason that 'Saint' was added to Agnes' name. The Russells estate was inherited by William Malory in the early 15th century, and the family bought up most of the village. In 1546 their house was described as containing a hall, chamber, buttery and kitchen. The manor descended to another William Malory in the late 16th century, a London merchant who brought more money into the estate. He could afford a new style of home, and it was either he or his son, yet another William, who built a house that included re-used stone and surrounded it with a much larger moat and elaborate garden, close to the original moat. Some of Cambridgeshire's earliest recorded brick kilns are documented in Papworth St. Agnes in the 1530s and presumably provided bricks for this house. This manor house, which was enlarged in brick in the 17th century by the Cater family, was used as a farmhouse after 1700. It still has an ornate plaster ceiling of about 1600, and the garden features include three mounds, a long pond, and a rectangular ditched enclosure adjoining the moat around the manor house. The house became derelict in the late 20th century but is now restored.

Village Development

The minute village now consists of a thin scatter of houses of 19th and 20th century date, with several empty sites, spread along a trackway, the older housing being mainly between the manor site and the church. An earlier village may have been affected by the creation of a park around the 16th century manor, but as this fell in Huntingdonshire this is perhaps unlikely, for the pre-1895 boundary actually ran through the later manor house site, and the original moat was adjacent to the border. The church itself was originally a medieval structure that was rebuilt in the 16th century and again in the mid 19th century. The medieval road network included routes to Papworth Everard, Yelling, Graveley and Hilton, all of which are now footpaths.

Papworth St. Agnes was always an extremely small settlement. There were only about 6 villagers recorded here in 1086, possibly with a few others who cannot be differentiated from Papworth Everard, and the population had grown to 85 tax-payers in 1377. There were a maximum of 18 houses here in the 16th century, and generally only about 10 in the 17th and 18th centuries. This figure did not rise until the late 19th century, with a peak of 165 in 30 houses in 1881. After this the population fell steadily to 30 in 1975, but to prevent the village dying there was some relaxation of restrictive planning policies combined with measures taken to maintain historic buildings, and it rose to 60 in 1996.

A 19th century bakehouse still stands on the village green at Papworth St Agnes.

Shepreth

Shepreth is a small parish of 550 hectares, mostly lying on gravel soils but with underlying clay that makes many areas damp, and it is often flooded. It is flat and low-lying, especially near the Rhee and Foxton and Meldreth Brooks, which all form parish boundaries, and it rises to a maximum of about 15m above sea level. There are many other streams within the parish, some now straightened into drains, for example the Mill River which runs through the village. L-Moor near Meldreth, once common land and now a nature reserve, is a particularly marshy area. In Domesday Book the village name is *Escepride*, 'Brook of the Sheep', and a Sheep Bridge was still in use in the 17th century.

Prehistoric

A Bronze Age spearhead has been found at Frog End, and there is a group of five ring-ditches, once Bronze Age burial mounds, near the A10 in the extreme south of the parish. Flint tools and waste flakes are sometimes found in the fields.

Roman

A Roman villa near the Foxton Brook was investigated in the late 19th century. Walls of three houses, with tesserae from a mosaic pavement and brightly painted wall-plaster, along with large quantities of pottery tile, bone etc. were found. Further

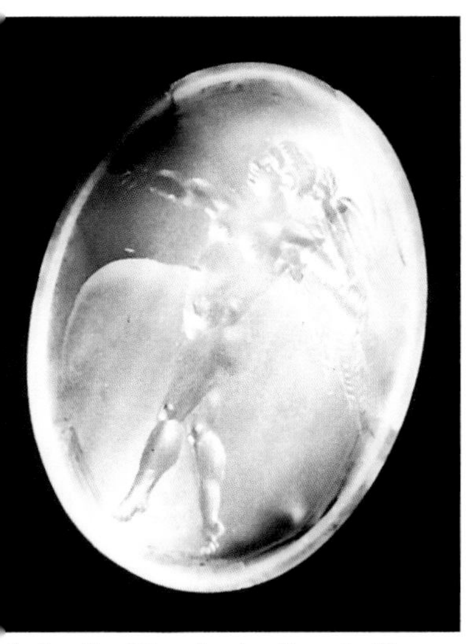

An intaglio of Eros, found at Shepreth villa.

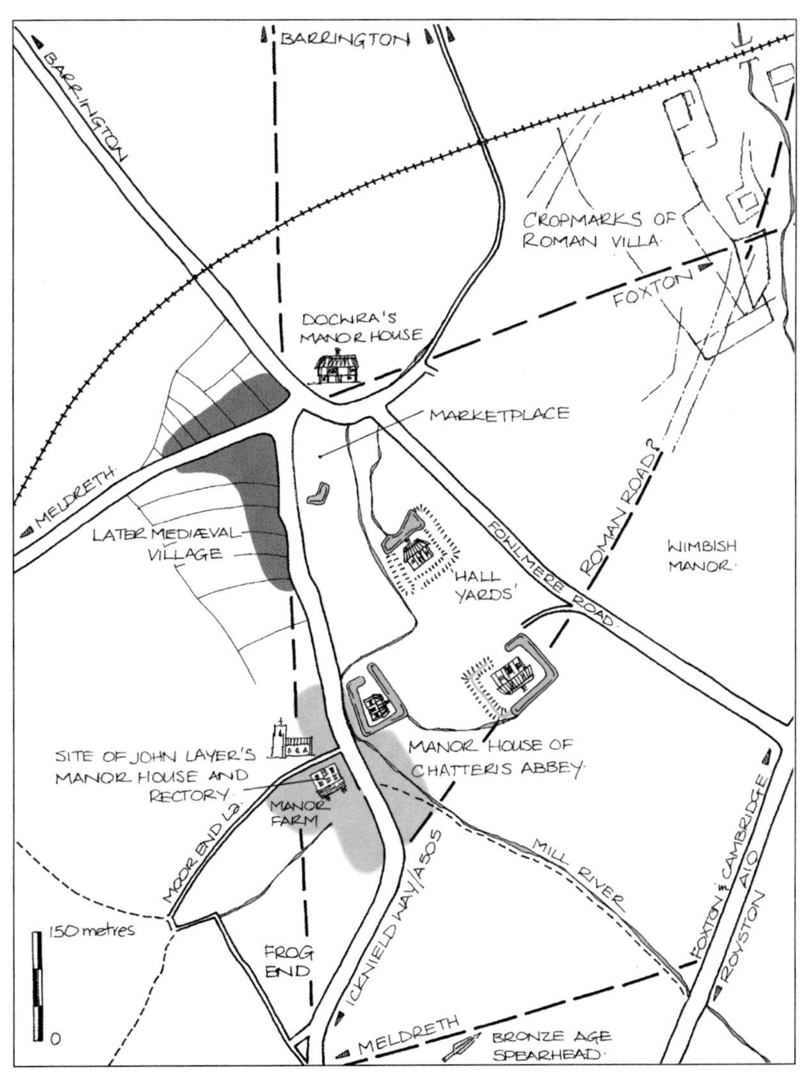

work by Rowland Parker uncovered the ground plan of the villa with its flint and mortar walls, painted plaster, tesserae, window glass, brick and tile, and also the sites of several huts. Interesting finds were an oak door in a rubbish pit and a sardonyx intaglio engraved with the plump dancing figure of Eros. This is an extremely fine piece of classical work which must have been an heirloom as it dates to the 2nd century BC, whilst all other finds are later than the Roman Conquest. A cemetery and other discoveries associated with this villa were found on the other side of the Brook, in Foxton.

Roman finds are noted regularly in this area. In 1995 Roman ditches containing settlement evidence including brick and tile as well as pot and bone were found quite unexpectedly during archaeological excavations next to the church.

Middle Ages

The manor of Shepreth was held by the Abbey of Chatteris from 1086 until the Dissolution in the 16th century. Amongst its later owners was the 17th century antiquarian John Layer. He was also the rector, so he moved across the road to the site of the rectory south of the church where he himself wrote 'John Layer... hath recently built himself a prettie house'. That house was largely rebuilt in the 19th century, but the present one retains a decoratively moulded ceiling beam of about 1500 and also Jacobean woodwork that probably came from Layer's earlier house.

The local lord of the manors that became Docwras and Wimbish, Sigar, remained unchanged after the Conquest. Both manors were later given to the preceptory of the Knights Hospitaller at Shingay, who held them until the 16th century. Their tenants probably lived in the moated site of Hall Yards. The moat is shallow, dry and largely infilled with rubbish and the interior is also much disturbed. In 1976 a collapsed building faced with large clunch blocks on sand, with rubble infill, was revealed when the interior was bull-dozed. Possibly this was the chapel for which a licence was given in 1280. Just south of Hall Yards are the damaged remains of another moat, and south-east of this is a more regular rectangular moat. These probably surrounded successive houses for Tyrells Manor.

Village Development

The original village is likely to have been near the church, next to the site of the main manor house, which belonged to the Abbess of

Chatteris. This would be on the line of a Roman road which leaves the A10 at Foxton, where it was revealed in recent excavations, passes Shepreth villa to the south, and runs through Meldreth to join Ermine Street near Bassingbourn. The route may have been later disrupted by the grounds of Hall Yards and Wimbish Manor, which were also built along it, and no doubt constant changes of thoroughfare were required in this marshy landscape.

In the 14th century the manors of Docwras and Wimbish were divided, and when Docwras manor house was burned down in 1401 it was rebuilt on its present site to the north, near a cross-road with routes to Meldreth, Barrington, Foxton and Fowlmere. The de la Haye family who held the manor had been granted a market charter earlier in the 14th century, and it may well be that this northern area, now the main part of the village, was seen as more suitable for commercial growth.

In Domesday Book there are 30 (150) inhabitants of Shepreth, and in 1377 there were 147 poll-tax payers. 35 households were recorded in the 16th century, and this had only increased to 46 families containing 202 people in total by 1801. In 1891, following growth that was encouraged by the flourishing coprolite industry licensed in 1870 and 1885 there were 89 houses, and steady growth continued, partly due to the opening of a cement factory and the presence of a railway station. In 1996 720 people lived here.

After Enclosure in 1823 the area around the Tyrells moats was made into a park and was landscaped with belts of trees, water features (no doubt modifying the moats), and picturesque lodges and summerhouses.

Shingay cum Wendy

Even after the two parishes of Shingay and Wendy were combined in 1957 the parish remained a fairly small one of 725 hectares. It lies mainly on clay, with alluvium near the Rhee, its northern border, and along the stream which separates the two parishes. There is a small island of chalk in the south-east, now part of Bassingbourn Airfield. The area is flat, low-lying and well-watered and this is reflected in the Domesday names, *Sceningeie*, or 'the low-lying land of the people of Scene' and *Wendeie*, 'the low-lying land by the winding stream'. The eastern boundary is Ermine Street. Enclosure of open fields began in the 13th century and was complete by 1600.

Prehistoric

A Mesolithic axe was found on the field surface near the Roman site (below), a Bronze Age arrow-head came from land adjacent to the Rhee, and there was a small scatter of worked flints from Church Farm, also adjacent to the river.

Roman

There is a major Roman site on Ermine Street in the north-east corner of Wendy which extends into adjacent parishes (see **Wimpole**). Within Shingay the evidence points to substantial buildings and industrial and religious sites. Pits containing 1st and 2nd century pottery were found during road widening at Wendy Lodge, many pots (some complete) were found when a house was built, and drainage trenches in the angle between the road and river revealed gravel paths, floors of rammed chalk and earth, building materials including stones, tile fragments and daub, and much pottery of the 2nd to 4th century. Artefacts from this area include bronze and lead slag, cosmetic implements, glass, a knife-handle, spoon, horse-harness, brooches, and coins. Small-scale excavations revealed pits, ditches, gullies, beam-slots, cobbled road and yard, walls, and evidence for iron-working. A sheet of lead with beaded decoration found just south of this site may be part of Roman christening vat.

Middle Ages

The village of Shingay was dominated by a Preceptory of the Knight Hospitaller from its foundation in th 12th century until the Dissolution in 1540. The Knights Hospitaller were religious order that had been founded during the Crusades to provide medical support for crusaders. They were initially based in Palestine, the in Rhodes which they defended against the Turks, and they were responsible for the defence of Malta Their wealth came from estates in Europe, administered through communities known as preceptories In Cambridgeshire they held land in 43 parishes, including Cambridge, in addition to owning all of Shingay. The Shingay preceptory was also responsible for estates in Bedfordshire, Buckinghamshire, Essex, Hertfordshire and Huntingdonshire Religious and military power, in addition to great wealth, legal privileges and connections outside Britain gave them political influence but also made them disliked locally.

Shingay became one of the richest preceptories in England. At first it included women, the Sisters of St. John. On its manor in Shingay it had two dovecotes, a watermill, a windmill and a church. One of its unusual privileges was that it could bury people not entitled to consecrated land, such as criminals and suicides, and John Layer records a 'Fairy carte' which fetched executed corpse from Cambridge. In the 16th centur one of the heads of the Order fough in the Siege of Rhodes, another served in Malta and the last one was executed by Henry VIII, accused of sympathising with Catholic rebels.

Local unpopularity made the Preceptory a target during the Peasants' Revolt. Men from Cambridge joined the band of John Hanchach c Shudy Camps (the chief leader of th Cambridge rebels, later beheaded) burn the manor of the Hospitallers, and they 'brought away a chalice ar vestments and other clothes for bed and some horses' and more goods were stolen in later attacks. Damage must have been quickly repaired an he Preceptory continued to have a trong economic influence on South Cambridgeshire.

Earthworks on the site of the Preceptory survive in pasture, includng a deep, wide moat around the utlines of foundations of buildings, vith traces of the depopulated illage, water management systems ntended to fill the moat and fuel the nill-race, and ridge and furrow outide the moat. Subsequently, after he Dissolution, the Preceptory vithin the moat was used as a country ouse known as Shingay Hall, and vas substantially altered in the 17th entury. It was demolished in the late 8th century. The village church was ulled down in about 1697 and was eplaced with a chapel whose ruins vere finally removed in 1836.

One of the manors in Wendy, Gambons, had a moated site in Lordhip Spinney. It was surrounded by a ery substantial rectangular moat vith three possible fishponds and is till partially wet. Holders of the nanor are known from the beginning f the 12th century. By 1382 it had assed by marriage to William Gambon, whose family held it until its sale o Robert Clopton of Clopton in the ate 15th century.

At Vine Farm there are traces of medieval moat which was superseded in the 17th century by a great ouse built by Thomas Wendy of Haslingfield when he bought the illage, and later his widow lived here. This house was demolished in he 19th century but the present Vine Farm, a 17th century timber-framed uilding, was part of this estate.

The original medieval church of Wendy, much of which had been rebuilt in the 16th century, was in poor repair after only forty years, and was demolished and rebuilt in the 18th century. By the 19th century it was too dangerous to use and a new one was built on the same site. Still the foundations were not adequate for the subsoil and it too was pulled down in 1957. Only the churchyard now remains.

A sketch by William Cole of the chapel which stood at Shingay in the 18th century.

The Preceptory of the Knights Hospitaller from the air, 1967. Note its position near the Rhee, the wide water-filled moat, building foundations inside the moat, and ditches and house-sites outside.
© Cambridge University Collection of Air Photographs.

Village Development

The original village of Shingay seems to have been near the river, just west of the remains of the Preceptory, where crop marks show the regular lay-out of a small settlement. Its church stood within the Preceptory, suggesting the village extended there too. However, the Hospitallers' policy of enclosing open fields, which they completed here in the 15th century, depopulated Shingay, and the village was virtually cleared by 1452. From a Domesday population of 18 it fell to 15 tax-payers in 1327 and six households in 16th century. This figure rose again to a peak of 142 in 1851, but it has continued to fall since then. In the 19th century houses were built around Manor Farm and along the road to Bassingbourn, but few of these now survive.

Wendy was built around a church, with a small green near Church Farm, and roads run to Croydon and Bassingbourn as well as to Shingay and Ermine Street. The main street ran south of its present route, without the bend. Remains of the earlier village on both sides of the main road are visible on the ground, although many are ploughed and can only be recognised from the air.

Robert Clopton, owner of Gambon's manor in Shingay in the late 15th century, bought additional land in Wendy, and this all passed to the Chicheleys of Wimpole through the marriage of his daughter. The Chicheleys also acquired the Hospitallers' Shingay estate in the 17th century, by which time they owned all Wendy and were in a position to enclose even more of the fields. The whole village was sold to Thomas Wendy of Haslingfield (the name must be coincidental) in the mid 17th century. Enclosure of the whole parish was complete by the late 17th century, after which it was known principally for its dairy farming though there was also a flock of sheep. In 1794 Vancouver states 'The land in general... consists chiefly of rich pasture employed in the feeding of ewes and lambs with milch cows'. This pattern changed in the later 19th century when much of it was arable land again.

The population of Shingay was only 17 at Domesday, with 14 tax-payers in 1327. In 1377 there were 166 adults spread between both Shingay and Wendy. There were 16 households in Shingay in the 16th century and afterwards this only rose very slowly to a peak of 154 in 1851. The population began falling in the late 19th century and this pattern has continued. The combined population in 1996 was 90.

Steeple Morden

Steeple Morden is a large parish of 1556 hectares. It is flat and low-lying in the north, especially near the Rhee, its northern border, but the chalk soils in the south rise up to 55m above sea level along Ashwell Street and then to 85m along the southern-most ridge, which is followed by a route of the Icknield Way. Its open fields were enclosed after an Award was made in 1816. In Domesday Book it is simply *Alia Mordune,* 'the other Morden', but in the 13th century 'Steeple' had been added, after a church steeple which fell in 1703 and was replaced in the 1860s.

Prehistoric

Round barrows were numerous on the chalk grassland along the Icknield Way until the 19th century when ploughing began there. At least 30 are visible as ring-ditches, showing as crop and soil marks. A small chalk quarry at Ashwell Station exposed a ring-ditch as a complete circle of black soil 19m in diameter. The ditch had obviously been very truncated by ploughing as it was only 25cms deep and no finds were made. There is also a hint that a barrow was a prominent feature here in Anglo-Saxon times, for there is a record that Anglo-Saxon jewellery was found at Ashwell Station, suggesting re-use of an earlier burial mound.

Ring-ditch at Ashwell Station, Steeple Morden.

Middle Ages

Cheneys Manor, as it was later known, stood at Gatley End, at the southern end of the parish, at the head of Cheney Water and adjoining Ashwell Street. This manor had been given to Winchester Cathedral in 1015 and returned to royal hands in 1136. A manor house is mentioned between 1325 and 1422 when it was held by the de Cheyney family, one of whom was Governor of the Channel Islands. This house, which was demolished by 1626 to be replaced by a 17th century building which still stands at Lower Gatley Farm, probably stood in the moat shown in the Enclosure Map as a completely enclosed square 90m across with a wet ditch but no building. By 1980 only fragments of the ditch survived and it was being used as a rubbish dump.

Another part of Winchester's manor became known as Brewis Manor, after the de Brescy family who held it from before 1205 until at least 1349. In 1369 this manor passed to Thomas Haselden, steward of John of Gaunt and holder of estates in several parishes, particularly in Guilden Morden. His position made him especially unpopular, and during the Peasants' Revolt in 1381 his properties were targeted for attack in both Guilden and Steeple Morden. There were at least two assaults in Steeple Morden, and 'insurgents entered his manors and houses, destroyed them and carried away horses, cattle, jewels and other goods to his utter ruination'. The value of stolen goods was claimed to be an astounding £1000, and Brewis Manor must have seen much of this damage A manor house is recorded again in 1470 and 1546, and it probably stood on the site of Morden House, now a field of earthworks west of the church. In 1662 it was taxed as a large house with twenty hearths, but was pulled down in the 18th century. Afterwards, the estate was sold to the Hardwickes of Wimpole, who owned about half the parish at Enclosure.

Steeple Morden church, drawn by William Cole in the late 18th century.

Two moated sites are shown on the Enclosure Map at the other end of the parish at North Brook End, both of which have now disappeared. One, west of the road, had a building in the centre of a rectangular moat with two entrances. East of the road a large moat surrounded two buildings. A medieval hall with a 17th century extension still stands at North Brook End.

Village Development

Like Guilden Morden, Steeple Morden was probably always a scattered village made up of separate hamlets, some of which were spread along Hay Street. These were mostly joined up by 19th century expansion. They include Brooke End, Morden Green, and the main settlement around the church, rectory and manor house. The most scattered hamlets are Gatley End on Ashwell Street, over a mile south of the village, where there were many houses in the 13th century and where cottages were being built in the 18th century, and North Brook End, half a mile to the north, which was known as 'Glitton', or 'sticky place' before 1200. After a railway station opened in 1850 a small settlement grew up near to it. Unusually for this area, but similarly to Guilden Morden, the village does not seem to have been greatly influenced by the east-west routes of the Icknield Way, but its main street, also like Guilden Morden's, was part of a through-route that left the old Cambridge-Oxford road east of East Hatley, ran south-west to Tadlow and on to the Icknield Way.

Steeple Morden had a large population of 55 in Domesday Book, and there were 95 tenants, perhaps 475 people, in 1279. This figure was down to 249 adults in 1377. In the 16th century 44 households were assessed for tax, and the population rose to 206 adults in 1676. In 1801 430 people lived here, after which there was a steep rise to 1018 in 1871, from which peak it fell below 700 until the late 20th century. Developments since the 1960s have led to a population of 1090 in 1996.

Considerable numbers of sheep at Steeple Morden were recorded in Domesday Book, throughout the Middle Ages and in later years, with 1540 still counted in 1885. These were mostly in the south of parish where permanent grassland was sold in 1809 as never having been broken by ploughing. After Enclosure most land was drained and ploughed. Coprolite mining employed many labourers in the late 19th century, otherwise, straw plaiting by women was the only industry recorded until the 20th century.

Tadlow

Tadlow is a small parish of 683 hectares which lies entirely on clay. The land rises from the Rhee, the southern parish boundary, to between 30 and 40m above sea level in the village and to 60m in the extreme north. The open fields were enclosed at an early date. In Domesday Book Tadlow is *Tadeslaue*, or 'Tada's burial mound', although there is no

Medieval hall at North Brook End, Steeple Morden.

Tadlow Granary, Wandlebury.

evidence for any prehistoric settlement or burials in the parish.

Middle Ages

Tadlow Manor was held by Picot, sheriff of Cambridge, after the Conquest, and his descendants granted it to Fulk FitzWarin, renowned as a rebel against King John. In the 17th century it was acquired by Sir George Downing, with the rest of Tadlow, and it eventually passed to Downing College, Cambridge, who held it until 1947. The manor house stood at Tadlow Bridge Farm, close to the Rhee. The site is badly disturbed by a farmyard and only fragmentary overgrown ditches survive. This manor house had accommodated the lord of the manor in 1295 but was ruinous in the 1520s. Attempts to rebuild it failed because of poor foundations, and it was moved to another site.

The Manor of Hobledod's, named after the family who held it in the 13th and 14th century, had a manor house within a moat to the east of the church. It passed through the hands of, amongst others, the Hinde family of Madingley before its sale to Sir George Downing. A modern house has now been built within the moat.

The manor of Pincote, where a substantial hamlet developed, was given to the Gilbertine priory of Chicksands in Bedfordshire and was sold by the Crown in 1554. Sir George Downing bought it in 1683. The Priory's manor house would have stood in the square moat with an outer enclosure now standing in empty countryside in the north of the parish. Arable fields around it are scattered with medieval pottery, and the outlines of ditches, banks and cobbled floors could still be seen in the early 1970s. Nearly all the pottery is 14th century or earlier, after which this inhospitable area was deserted. The moat was cleaned in the early 1980s, and now once again holds water.

Two buildings of interest in Tadlow were Tadlow Towers, an 18th century folly built for George Downing and demolished in 1960s, and Tadlow Granary. The granary has been dated to 1415 by tree-ring dating. It was pulled down at the same time as the folly, but the timbers were saved by the Avoncroft Museum of Buildings and Cambridge Preservation Society and moved to Wandlebury, where the Granary was re-erected in 1981.

Village Development

Until modern development since the 1960s, Tadlow was practically a deserted village with little more than a handful of dwellings along a street that, by this time led nowhere except as a track, although it had earlier been on a through-route that went south to Guilden Morden, Steeple Morden and the Icknield Way, and north-east to East Hatley and the Cambridge-Oxford road. The village appears to have once comprised two adjoining parts, though it is not certain if these are of the same date. At the extreme north end there was once a triangular green, with the church on a high promontory overlooking the west end of the village, and Hobledods Manor house to the east. Most of this green has been lost but the sites of medieval houses, hollow-ways and paddocks bounded by ditches are still visible. To the south of the green the rest of the village lay along the north-south street leading to Tadlow Bridge Farm.

Judging from the remains of former houses, now destroyed by ploughing, which lay on the west side of the old street, as well as the regular nature of the closes on both sides of the street and traces of former back lanes, this part of the village was planned in early medieval times. Support for this idea is provided by the fact that the two medieval east-west through-routes across the parish seem to have had no effect on it. To the north, the old 'Ridgeway', as it was known in the 14th and 15th centuries, continued a track from Croydon and Clopton along the hillside to Wrestlingworth. The 'Portway', which ran parallel to the river, crossed the village street at right angles, yet no development ever took place along it. In 1826 the turnpike road from Cambridge to Biggleswade was opened, cutting through medieval house-sites near the church, and the old routes went out of use.

The hamlet of Pincote, over a mile to the north, was first recorded in 1176 as an independent settlement. This was a linear hamlet by the side of a small brook, with the moated site at its south-eastern end,

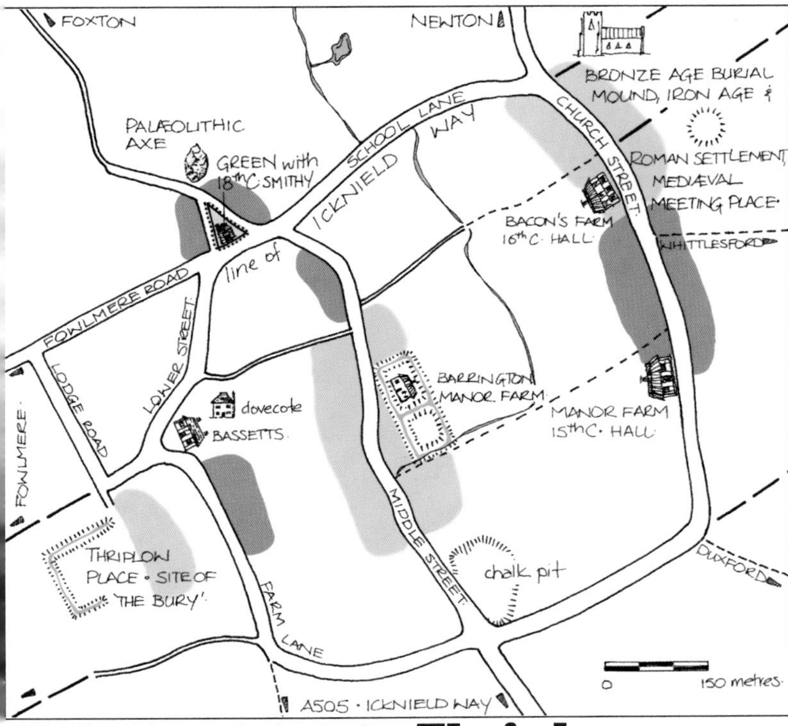

where tiles and pottery in plough-soil indicate the sites of medieval houses which were deserted in the 14th century.

Tadlow's heavy soil and low population perhaps encouraged early enclosure of land both for pasture and for arable farming in small closes from the 15th century, and the process was complete by 1750 when a map of the parish was made for Downing College. Ridge and furrow left by the open fields of medieval agricultural can still be seen on the ground as can the shorter straight ridge and furrow within hedged fields which is typical of post-enclosure ploughing. This is also noticeable from the air as soil marks, especially around Pincote.

Thriplow

Thriplow is a medium sized parish of 966 hectares, mostly lying on chalk. The land rises from about 20m above sea level in the north to 50m in the south, and there is a local high point of 30m just east of the village. The village itself is low-lying and on a spring-line described in the 17th century as providing a 'store of sweet and wholesome springs', and is on an outcrop of Melbourn Rock, or clunch, used for building and for making plaster. The chalk soil yields large flints which can still be seen used in the church and in garden walls. Its open fields were enclosed after an Award made in 1846. In Domesday Book Thriplow is *Trepeslau*, or 'Tryppa's burial mound', perhaps a reference to the large prehistoric barrow next to the church.

Prehistoric

A small Middle Palaeolithic axe was recently found near the Green, and others came from the track leading to Whittlesford, and the A505, near the Duxford border. The village lies on routes of the Icknield Way, heading for a crossing-place in Whittlesford, and the A505 in the south of the parish is another route. A Neolithic axe and a ceremonial axe made of jadeite were found in the village, but it is the areas which were grassland until Enclosure, around the A505, that are really prolific in flints of this date, with several hundred tools and worked flints reported. Tools include axes, arrow-heads, blades, scrapers and awls.

Many flint tools of Bronze Age date have been found in the same area which was once well-known for its prominent burial mounds. In the 19th century the London to Cambridge road, before it reached Fowlmere, was described, as a 'good enough road now, though passing through very exposed and open countryside, with tumuli, the solemn relics of a prehistoric race, forming striking objects on the bare hillsides and the skyline'. In the mid 19th century, R C Neville observed the effect of Enclosure on the heath's barrows; 'the plough and spade of the husbandman have encroached on their limits and curtailed considerably their fair proportions', but he was still able to see how they stretched in a line for nearly six miles. He investigated thirteen of these barrows. One contained an inhumation with a fragment of pottery, bone pin and horse-jaw, one a cremation with horse-bones and another had both an inhumation and a cremation urn. Others were just noted as 'containing burnt bones, with fragments of pottery, but no remains of importance or value'. None of these excavations were more than trenches through the mounds, so many of the burials must have been lost.

The only barrow to be examined in modern times was a once-prominent mound near the church, after which the village is supposedly named. It had been levelled in the 1840s, and by the time it was excavated in 1953 it was only visible as a crop mark, patches of chalk and stones and a slight rise on the crest of the hill. There was still sufficient evidence to show that the main burial was an inhumation and that the mound was enlarged in the Late

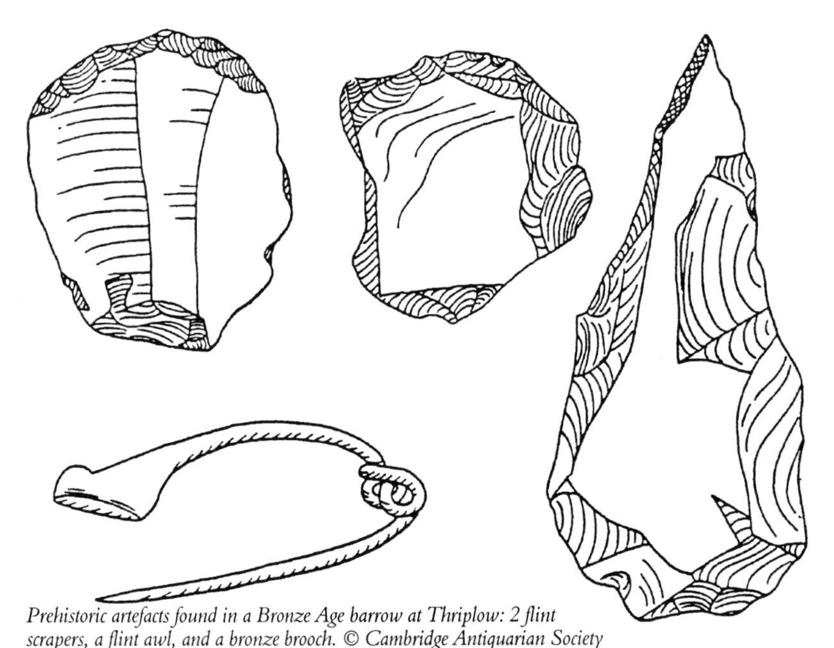

Prehistoric artefacts found in a Bronze Age barrow at Thriplow: 2 flint scrapers, a flint awl, and a bronze brooch. © Cambridge Antiquarian Society

Bronze Age to cover at least thirteen cremations, some of which had been in urns. The mound was surrounded by deep wide ditch which contained over 400 flint flakes and tools and, in its upper fills, large quantities of domestic refuse of Iron Age and Roman date.

Ground beneath the mound contained a sherd of Neolithic pottery and the whole site is remarkable for its constant re-use and the way in which this barrow, in a landscape where such features are not uncommon, acted as a focal point for settlement, presumably reflecting its significant and prominent position on the Icknield Way. This position, and the importance still attached to the prehistoric mound may also have led to the siting of the church here. The barrow was probably also used as an official meeting place for the ten villages that make up the 'Hundred' of Thriplow.

Middle Ages

In Middle Street, in the centre of the village at Barrington Manor Farm, are the dried up remains of a double moat. The present house of this manor, just west of the moat, still contains parts of the 16th century building which replaced the medieval manor house of the Barrington family, who held it from the early 13th century until its sale in the mid 16th century. Afterwards it was used as the vacation home for the Master of St. John's College. In the 17th century it was owned by Sir Christopher Hatton, who may have been responsible for the formal gardens which can still be seen. Much of it was pulled down in the late 18th century. St. John's College also acquired an estate from the bishop of Ely, based on the present Manor Farm on Church Street. This was used by the Fellows during times of plague in Cambridge and still contains the structure of a 15th century hall with a 16th century cross-wing, much enlarged in the 17th century. Another house that was once the centre of a medieval manor is Bacon's Farm on Church Street. At Bacon's, all that remains of a medieval hall is a cross-wing which has been dated by its tree-rings to 1549. The remainder was rebuilt in the 17th century. The Bacon family held the manor, which was owned by Ely, in the 14th century, and the Tyrrells, who were responsible for additions to it, in the 17th century. Bassetts is another medieval house, with 16th and 18th century additions. There was once a 17th century dovecote in its garden. Bassetts is thought to be a guild house, from which social and charitable services were provided for the village on a co-operative basis.

Thriplow Place dates to 1680-1713 when it was built by the Bening family, but its site is The Bury, the manor house for an estate held by Ely from the late 10th century until 1600. There are no traces of the bishops' house, which was recorded in 1279 and said to be ruinous in 1356. Three sides of a moated site survive, but these may be a later garden feature.

Bacon's Farmhouse, Thriplow. Photograph by Beth Davis.

Village Development

Despite its location on two or perhaps three of the east-west routes of the Icknield Way, the street pattern of Thriplow bears little relation to them. The village comprises three separate sections running roughly north to south which, with the Icknield Way routes, form a grid-like pattern. However, until recent development, there was virtually no occupation along the ancient routeways. The easternmost part of Thriplow is Church Street, set just below the prominent hill on which the church and the site of the prehistoric burial mound lie. The central section is Middle Street, on lower ground on the opposite side of an ill-drained valley to Church Street. At its north end it enters a small triangular green on which stands an 18th century smithy. The westernmost part of Thriplow is Lodge (previously Blacksmiths) Road. The lane which leaves the north end of the green formerly extended to Foxton. All the older village houses are within this grid, spaced along the main north-south streets with plentiful open areas, or else are around the green. By the time of Domesday Book, Ely owned a large estate based on its manor house at The Bury. The church, presumably also in existence in the 11th century, was at the opposite end of the village, and there may have been a settlement nearer to it. A much smaller estate was owned by the powerful Essex lord, Geoffrey de Mandeville, after the Conquest, and this was based on Barrington's Manor in the centre of the village. Thus Thriplow consisted of at least two and possibly three centres, connected by a well-planned street pattern that probably dates back to Saxon times.

Though the parish of Thriplow is larger in area than its neighbours its population has always been modest and fairly stable. At Domesday it was 27, there were 80 tenants in 1279 and 25 tax-payers in 1327. In the 16th century 42 householders were recorded, rising to a total population of 320 in 1794, and 520 at its peak in 1851. This number fell to 386 in 1951 and was 780 in 1996, but these last figures include about 200 inhabitants of Heathfield, formerly part of RAF Duxford and now the Imperial War Museum.

The Old Smithy, Thriplow in 1975.

Sheep were important to the economy, with every manor having a sheep-walk and Ely, for example, owning 1000 sheep here in the 13th century. Pasture fields near to the village and on the Moor east of the church were enclosed in the 17th and 18th centuries. Thriplow Heath was grazed as common land, although there was progressive enclosure, in this case for arable farming. In 1846 the Moor was drained and ploughed, and the remainder of the Heath was enclosed.

Toft

Toft is a small parish of 535 hectares, lying on clay except for the village itself which is on a ridge of gravel. The ground rises from 25m above sea level along the Bourn Brook, now its southern boundary, although until 1985 Toft extended south of the Brook to take in a small area of ancient settlement. The land then rises to a height of 70m near the northern boundary, which was agreed with Hardwick at Enclosure in 1815. Its eastern and western boundaries were trackways running from the Cambridge-St. Neots road to the Bourn Brook. In Domesday Book its name was the same as today's, simply meaning 'small farmstead '.

Roman

Seven skeletons with part of a Roman lamp and a metal plate were found by labourers digging gravel in 1851 between the church and the Bourn Brook, near the Lot Way.

Village Development

Toft, like Thriplow, has been influenced by its position on two north-south and two east-west routes which have given it the superficial appearance of a planned grid. The north-south routeways consisted of

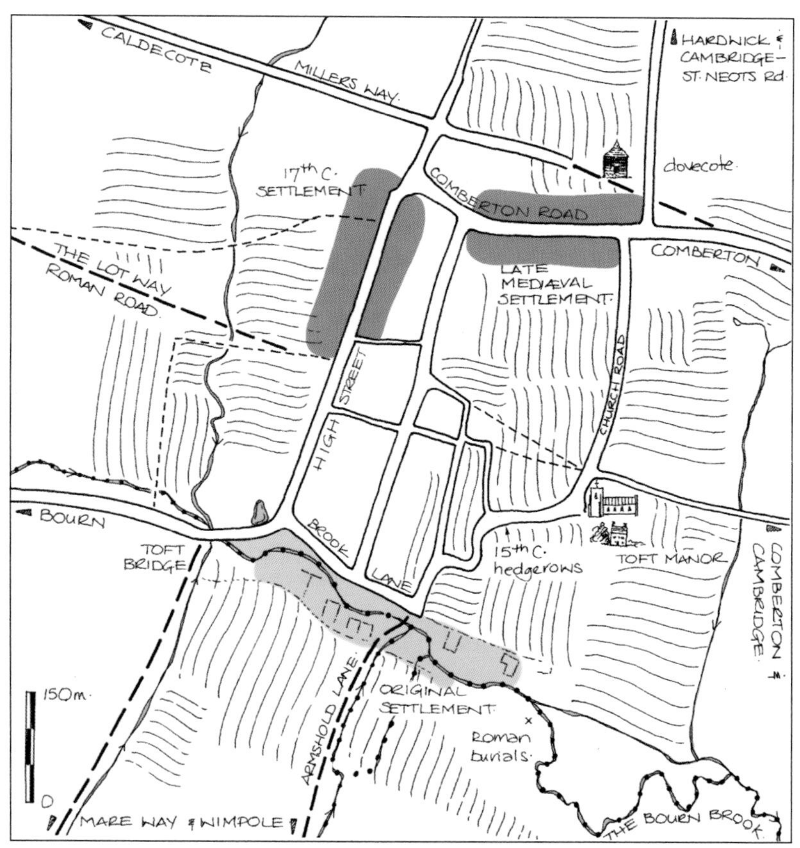

Armshold Lane, an ancient route from Arrington Bridge through Wimpole to Hardwick and the Cambridge-St. Neots road, forming the parish boundary between Kingston and Great Eversden along the way, and a parallel road to the west, now High Street, which is probably later in date. East-west routes were the Lot Way, running close to the Bourn Brook for most of the way from Grantchester to Barton, Comberton, Toft, Caldecote, Bourn and Eltisley from at least Roman times, and the later Millers Way to the north of this route. Later village roads had to respect the open fields, and therefore also developed geometric arrangements. One example of this is the zig-zag route from the church on Lot Way to the river-crossing which came into use later in the Middle Ages, probably in the 15th century on the evidence of surviving hedgerows, using a head-land between fields of ridge and furrow. This route may reflect increased use of a long-distance route from Cambridge to Oxford which passed through Toft.

The earliest settlement at Toft is likely to have been in the two small areas on either side of a crossing-place of the Bourn Brook where slight remains of house sites are visible as earthworks, which explains why this area south of the Bourn Brook was within the parish of Toft. Much of Toft belonged to Ely from the 10th century, and development here was probably encouraged by the Abbot. The church on Lot Way, and the manor house immediately to the south of it relate more closely with this site than with the present village. Toft has an unusual history in that its population fell early in the Middle Ages, and the majority of the present village was used for agriculture, now reflected in the amount of ridge and furrow which survives, but it flourished later on, especially in the 17th century. It was during this period of growth that new housing was built on land that had once been part of the open fields, particularly along the western side of the High Street.

The Domesday population of Toft was fairly dense for its size at 23, but decline in population began early, with only 76 poll-tax payers in 1377 and empty tenements recorded. There were 24 tax-payers in the 16th century, rising to 50 families in the 17th century, but only 173 people at the end of the 18th century. The population rose significantly in the first half of the 19th century, reaching a peak of 380 in 1851, but then it fell until new housing was built from the 1950s, leading to a population of 560 in 1996.

Whaddon

Whaddon is a small parish of 620 hectares, lying on chalk over clay apart from alluvial soils along the Rhee, which forms its northern border. The land is almost flat, rising only from about 20 to 25m above sea level, with the village itself on a slight slope. On the south-east the parish is bordered by Hoback Stream, which also fills some of the village's many moats, and the western boundary is Ermine Street. Most of the parish was enclosed by the 18th century, well before an official Award was made in 1841. In Domesday Book, Whaddon is *Wadune,* or 'Wheat Hill', which may refer to some unusual feature in the parish, for it is otherwise a poor description.

Prehistoric

A Neolithic axe was found near the Rhee and there was a scatter of prehistoric worked flints just north of the present village. In 1995 archaeological investigation in the centre of the village revealed numerous square pits, ditches and an oven or hearth with dating evidence ranging from earliest to latest phases of the Iron Age.

Roman

The Roman posting station at Arrington Bridge (see **Wimpole**) extended into the north-west corner of Whaddon, and remains associated with it have been found within this parish.

Anglo-Saxon

A suggestion of possible Early Anglo-Saxon burials at Whaddon is a report that, when the basin in Wimpole's great Avenue was being dug in the 18th century, many bodies and iron fragments were found. These are not far from recent discoveries of 6th century burials in Wimpole.

Middle Ages

The moated site at Manor Farm, south-east of the church, was probably where the house for a pre-Conquest manor that was given to Ely in 970 stood. This estate, along with other Saxon estates in Whaddon, passed to Hardwin de Scalers, one of William's leading knights, after 1066. Hardwin's sons divided his vast estate, which had been based at Caxton, between them, one moving his administrative centre to Little Shelford and the other to Whaddon, where the site at Manor Farm remained one of the main residences for his descendants and was the head of a large holding of Cambridgeshire estates until 1593. The south arm of this moat is an impressive feature, 8m wide and still water-filled. In the 17th century the Tempest family, one of them a colonel in Cromwell's army and MP for Cambridge, lived there, and it was at about this time that John Layer wrote 'there is a pritty old auncient gentlemanlike howse uppon this lordship and somewhat repaired by Mr. Tempest the now owner.' The manor was sold to Edward Harley of Wimpole, and then to the Pickering family. Its house was leased out in 1753 and demolished in the 19th century. The site was later ploughed, and crop marks show sites of buildings in its interior although it has now been grassed for a golf course.

Ladybury moated site at the north-east end of Bridge Street originally had three enclosures and

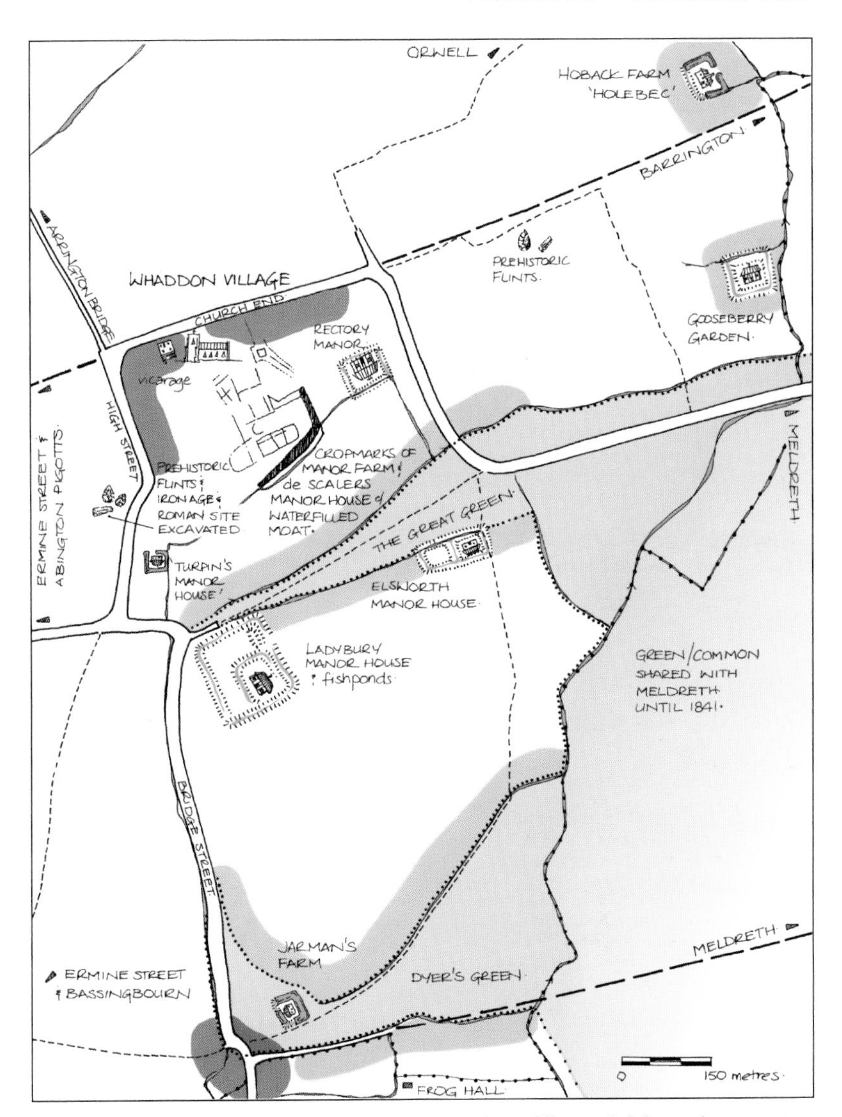

two internal fish ponds. It was recognisable as a deserted moat in 1948, but it has now been ploughed flat. Its manor had been held by Warin de Soham in 1210, passing by marriage to the de Scalers of Manor Farm from the 14th century. Another moated site that was recorded as an empty small square moat in 1948 was the house of Turpins Manor, a pre-Conquest estate that was named after the family who held it from the 13th to the 17th centuries, after which it was sold to the Tempests at Manor Farm. This stood at Town Farm on the High Street, where now only a dammed portion of the stream survives. Elsworth Manor house, at the south side of the Great Green is now only recognisable from the air as a double enclosure. In 1459 it was given to a Chantry of Wimpole Church, and it later passed to the Earls of Oxford at Wimpole. Even the rectory lay in a rectangular moat, of which the southern arm remains. A rectory was recorded in 1359 and the present house still retains a late medieval structure.

Other moated sites in Whaddon include Jarmans, a sub-rectangular moated area on the southern edge of the parish which was filled and levelled in the 1960s, Gooseberry Garden,

A dovecote and part of the moat at Rectory Farm.

which was a deserted rectangular moat in 1948, of which one arm now remains, and Hoback Farm, mentioned as *Holebec* in 1224, which still has a rectangular wet moat.

Village Development

The medieval village was based on two east-west routeways, the more northerly of which ran past the church and Hoback Farm and crossed the Rhee near Malton on its way to Barrington, the more southerly passing Manor Farm and then running to Meldreth. West of the village these tracks joined together and crossed Ermine Street at Whaddon Gap, continuing to Abington Pigotts where they were the principal village street. These tracks run to either side of Whaddon's Great Green, a huge area of common land dating back to Saxon times that was shared with Meldreth until 1841. Even the church and Manor Farm, both presumably Saxon foundations of Ely, are later than this common and encroach on one side of it. Due to the lack of later development distinctive areas of medieval settlement are still recognisable in Whaddon around the green. Of these, Whaddon village was the main part, and includes Manor Farm, the Rectory that was given from its estate, and traces of deserted medieval houses along the more northerly of the two routeways. Dyers Green, to the south, was a separate hamlet with its own green, probably also of Saxon origin and encroached upon by medieval housing, and it is possible that this also lay on an east-west route that linked the northern end of Bassingbourn with the southern end of Meldreth.

The population recorded in Domesday Book is high, 43, but afterwards Whaddon stayed a small village. In 1377 there were 170 taxpayers, and there were 33 households recorded in the 16th century. This figure stayed fairly constant, reaching only 220 people, marginally above the 1086 figure, in 1801. There were modest gains in the 19th century, to 384 in 1871, partly thanks to coprolite digging, but afterwards it fell, to 196 in 1951. The population rose to 540 by 1996, largely due to the presence of service families from Bassingbourn Barracks.

In the 18th century most of Whaddon belonged to the Hardwickes of Wimpole. The north-west corner of the parish was made part of Wimpole's landscaped park, and land near the river was run by the Wimpole estate with its land in Shingay and Wendy as 'the Dairies', where rich pastures were used for dairy cattle.

Whittlesford

Whittlesford is a moderate sized parish of 793 hectares, lying on chalk apart from alluvium near the Cam along its eastern border, and areas where gravel overlies the chalk. Much of the parish, including the village, is low-lying, less than 20m above sea level, and was liable to flood, but land in the south and west rises gently to about 30m. There were several areas of poor soil in the parish, and these were kept as common grassland that was known as moor. These include land lying near the river, to the north and west of the village and along the stream fed by springs known as Nine Wells that marks the border with Thriplow. The parish boundary with Little Shelford was not fixed until Enclosure in 1815 when land previously shared by the two parishes as common land was divided. The southern boundary is the present A505, a line of the Icknield Way that crosses the Cam at Whittlesford Bridge. In Domesday Book, Whittlesford is *Witelsforda,* or 'Witel's ford', a reference to the village's origin at a crossing-place of the Cam.

Bronze Age beaker found at Whittlesford. © Cambridge Antiquarian Society.

Prehistoric

Near the Cam Mesolithic flint tools and waste flakes have been found, and many more dating to Neolithic and Bronze Age times have been found in freshly ploughed soil near the river and along the A505 near Thriplow. One Neolithic axe is known, and a Bronze Age burial found near the station was accompanied by a pottery beaker. Ring-ditches close to the Nine Wells include remains of the Roman Chronicle Hills but some are probably of pre-Roman date.

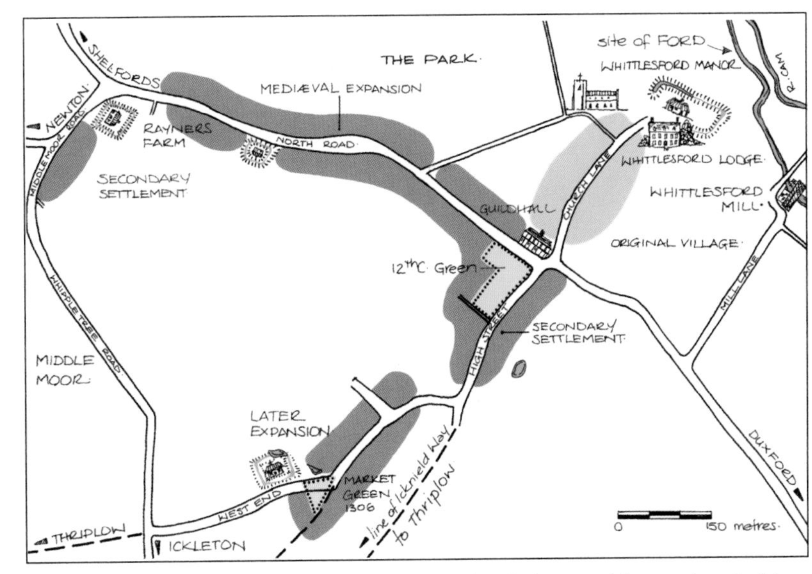

Roman

The Chronicle Hills, three prominent burial mounds, appear as landmarks on the 1836 Ordnance Survey map even though they had been deliberately levelled by labourers in 1818 in order to clear more land for arable cultivation after the Enclosure of Got Moor. A contemporary newspaper account described the discovery of four skeletons with broken sherds of red and black pottery in the largest mound, which had been 8ft high and 27ft in diameter. Two lower mounds that formed a straight line with this central one were flattened at the same time, and a thick wall of flints and pebbles parallel to them was also removed. Two low mounds 100 yards to the north contained deep graves made with flint and pebbles surrounded by circular walls. In one grave-pit were two skeletons, probably in a box as there were traces of wood and many large iron nails, with an iron knife and fragments of a bronze vessel. In the other mound were another two skeletons, one of whom had an iron spear, and more nails. The closest parallel to these burials are the early Roman cremations that were often buried in boxes with vessels suitable for feasting. Perhaps these had originally been of that type, but had been robbed of anything valuable, and possibly had had later burials added, a common Anglo-Saxon practice.

The barrows were part of an important Roman site that included a large villa and the buildings associated with it. Elsewhere in the parish, especially within the village and near the river, there are scatters of Roman pottery sherds indicating the sites of other Roman settlements.

Obscene Anglo-Saxon or medieval carving on outside of Whittlesford Church tower.

Anglo-Saxon

The church contains two fragments from Late Anglo-Saxon grave-covers. The obscene carved stone that is now built into the outside face of the tower below the clock is possibly Saxon but is perhaps later and may be the sole survivor of a series of carvings illustrating the seven deadly sins. The church is near the river and the manor house, and was once within the village, though it is now isolated on the north-eastern edge.

Middle Ages

A large rectangular moated site north of the church and close to the river was the manor house for Whittlesford Manor, held by the

Whittlesford Guildhall.

Tony family, who inherited it from Judith, niece of William the Conqueror. This moat, which lay in an important area of medieval settlement known from archaeological discoveries, was at the end of the original village street and blocks access along that street to the river crossing. In the 16th century the house was rebuilt, and its chalk foundations were recently uncovered. Later it was sold to John Huddleston of Sawston Hall, and in the late 18th century to the Hollicks, a successful milling family who owned half the parish at Enclosure. They demolished the moated house and replaced it with Whittlesford Lodge, which stood outside the moat, with stable blocks within it, the lodge being pulled down in 1858. Their descendants, the Tickells, sold most of the estate to the Pembertons.

Portions of Whittlesford Manor were held separately later in the Middle Ages, and their tenants constructed moats around their houses. Rayner's Farm, in Middle Moor, for example, was built in 1472, from the evidence of tree-rings in the floor-joists, and is built on the site of an earlier house that once stood within a moat. Another moat exists on the west side of North Road, and traces of a third lie in West End.

Whittlesford Guildhall was built co-operatively by some of the villagers and provided charitable, social and religious services for its members. In later years it served as a poor-house and a school-room for the village. Its roof is supported by a crown-post made from a whole small tree that was felled in 1489. Carpentry techniques demonstrated in this building are very similar to those in Rayner's Farm. Both are lavish buildings in their use of high quality timber and, together with the repairs to the church which were undertaken by villagers at this time, they show how Whittlesford had recovered from the horrors of the 14th century.

Duxford Chapel, which lay within that parish until the line of the A505 was changed, was founded in about 1200 as a small hospital that was run by a prior and monks. It was intended to give medical help to the poor, but its position by the bridge on a major route of the Icknield Way also involved it in providing hospitality to travellers. In the 14th century it was rebuilt as a chapel, and was in use until the Dissolution. Later it was used as a barn, and had to be extensively restored after 1947.

Rayners Farm, Whittlesford.

Village Development

The original village lay at a crossing-place of the Cam near to the point where two separate routeways running east from Thriplow converged before reaching the ford. Whittlesford thus consisted of a single street, now Church Lane, with the manor house and the church at the east end near the ford.

Perhaps in the 12th century a large L-shaped green was added at the west end of the original village, together with a further linear extension, now High Street, to the west. At the same time, or a little later, the original village was cleared away in order to increase the amount of land for agriculture immediately around the manor house. As the population increased in the 13th century the new green was largely built over and the village continued to expand westwards along the northernmost of the two routeways, now West End. When, in 1306, the then lord of the manor obtained permission to hold a market at Whittlesford, no green existed and he was forced to lay out a new triangular green at the far end of West End. This too was later partly built over. There were also at least two minor hamlets at Whittlesford, lying north of the main village alongside the Moor. These were gradually expanded to become part of the village.

In 1086 there were 33 people recorded in Whittlesford, but in the 13th century this figure had grown to 105, perhaps 525 people in all. Exceptionally wet weather in the early 14th century would have had a disastrous effect on this low-lying village, and in 1377 there were only 142 adults still here. There were 49 households recorded in the 16th century, 88 in the 18th century, and a total of 416 people in 1801. The population rose steadily throughout the 19th century, for there was some industrial work, such as Maynard's agricultural machinery factory, vinegar-brewing and artificial manure works available in the village, and also within walking distance at Sawston. In 1891 there were 891 people living here, which later fell to a minimum of 720 before rising to 1530 in 1996, growing in the years after 1950 with the benefits of good road and rail communications to London, Cambridge, and other centres, and industrial growth within Whittlesford and surrounding parishes.

Wimpole

Wimpole is a medium sized parish of 1013 hectares, lying mostly on clay. It is low-lying, around 30m above sea level, except for a quite sharp rise to 70m on the ridge of Mare Way which forms most of northern border. The Rhee flows along part of the southern boundary, and other boundaries are formed by Ermine Street and the Cambridge-Arrington Bridge road. There is no Enclosure Award for Wimpole, because its open fields had been gradually enclosed by successive owners of the Hall before the 19th century. Its name in Domesday, *Winepola*, or 'Wina's Pool', refers to a feature of general wetness, now lost in the extensive ornamental landscaping works that have been a major element in Wimpole's countryside since the 17th century.

Prehistoric

Three circular Iron Age huts, 12-13m in diameter, were found next to the A603, where a gas compressor station now stands, when a gas pipeline was laid across South Cambridgeshire in 1994. Pottery indicated a Late Iron Age date of the 1st century BC to the 1st century AD.

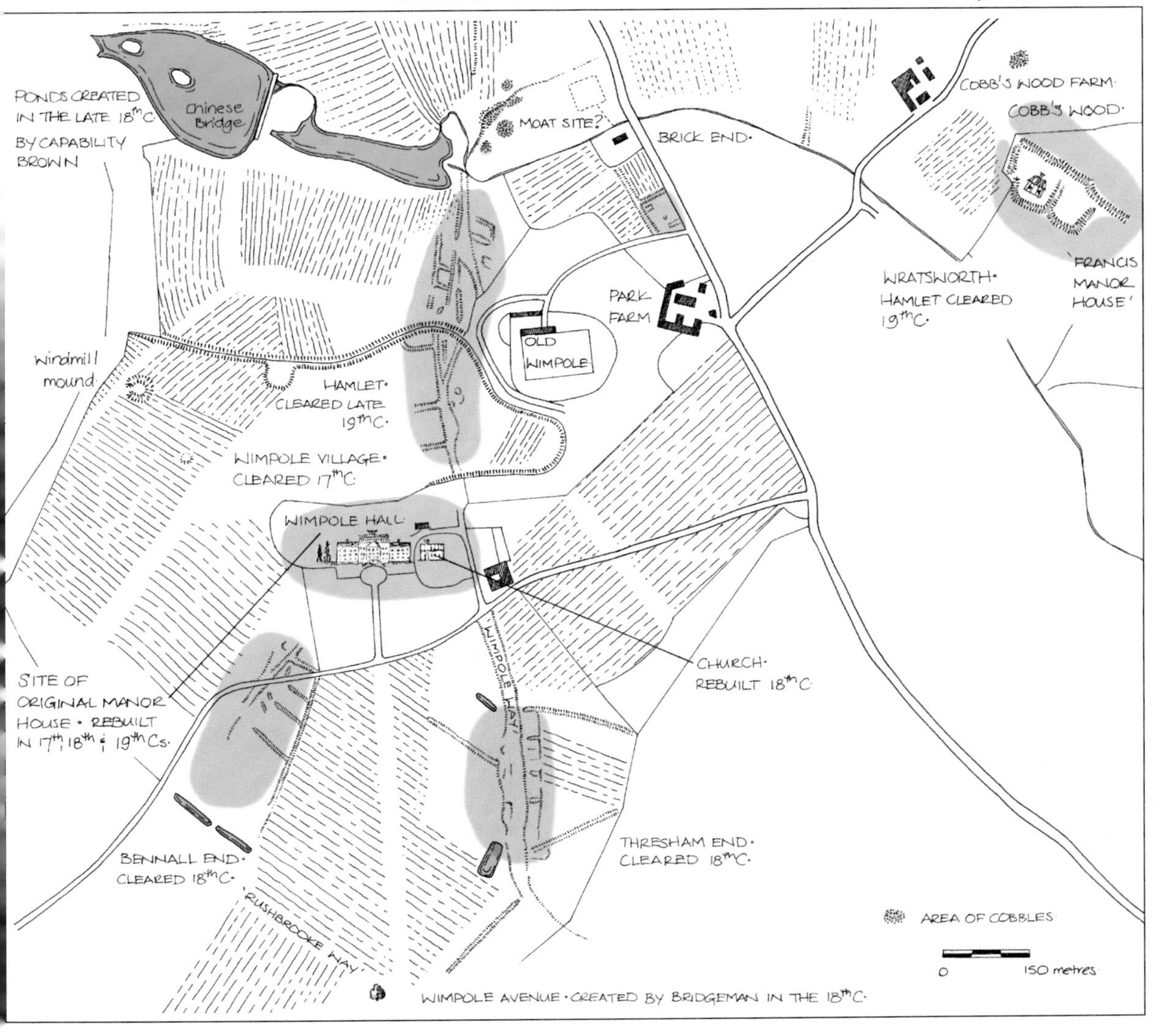

Iron Age hut excavated in 1994 at Wimpole.

Roman

The junction of two major Roman roads at Arrington Bridge was the site of a posting station, providing rest, refreshment, change of horses and communication for official travellers, and, no doubt, a welcome stopping place and overnight accommodation for others. Construction of a swimming pool at Wimpole Lodge revealed foundations of stone and clunch, with much Roman pottery, coins and the skeleton of a horse. This is clearly part of an extensive site, for similar remains are known from Wendy, Arrington and Whaddon, at the same cross-roads.

Excavations to the north of this site have revealed cobbled yards and ditched enclosures that had been paddocks, garden plots and residential sites, starting use in the late 2nd century and being re-organised about three times before the early 5th century. There was evidence for blacksmithing, and leather and bone-working on the site, as well as agriculture. Animal bones included an unusually large number of horse, in addition to cattle, sheep and pig. Artefacts found included many hobnails and two iron heel-plates, door-hinges and key, linch-pins, a reaping hook, spear, chisel, iron-slag, and occasional personal items such as a brooch, pins, knives, spindle-whorl, buckle and razor, in addition to building materials, querns, glass and coins. The site was peripheral to the main complex as no actual building were found, despite evidence for several nearby. Roman cremation urns were reported during World War II near Cambridge Road Farm. Not far from here was the Iron Age site noted above, where there were also large Roman ditches and enough pottery to indicate continued occupation of the earlier site.

Anglo-Saxon

An unexpected discovery during the excavations at Wimpole Lodge was a small cemetery of the 6th century. One middle-aged woman was buried with a necklace of 17 amber and 3 glass beads, a bronze annular brooch on her shoulder and bronze wrist-clasps by each hand. Bones of at least seven other skeletons were recovered, including three newly-born infants, an adult male with a knife, an adolescent and fragmentary bones. The Roman site had been abandoned for over a century but its ditches, ruined buildings and Roman roads would still have been obvious.

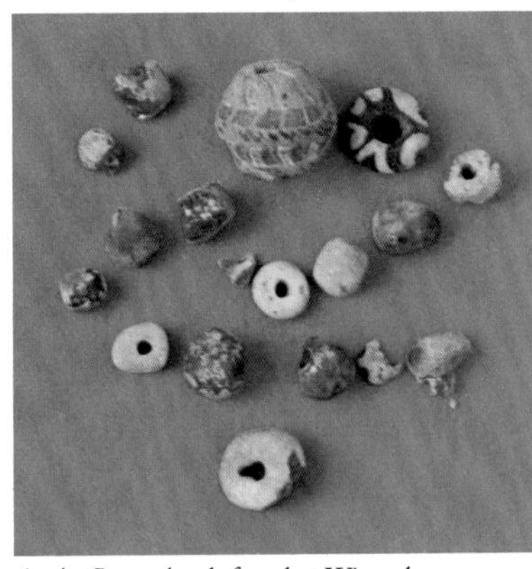

Anglo-Saxon beads found at Wimpole.

Village Development

Wimpole originally consisted of a number of separate small hamlets, at least six and possibly more. Unlike other villages, for reasons which are not understood, these hamlets survived through to the mid 17th century. One lay around the Hall and church, two more lay to the south and south-west, another lay to the north, and at least one and perhaps two more further north again on the edge of the present parish. A further hamlet and possibly two more existed on the east of the parish near Cobbs Wood Farm. In Domesday Book these numerous hamlets are described under the three separate names of Wimpole, Wratworth and Whitwell, though by the 17th century they each had their own very different names which included Brick End, Bennall End and Thresham End. In fact the medieval landscape, which had had a high Domesday population of 57, seems to have been over-populated rather than the reverse, and there were still 173 tax-payers in 1377. One of the Wratworth manors, Francis, was based on Cobbs Wood, where there is a double moated site. Field-walking inside and outside this moat has revealed medieval pottery, much of it 12th to 13th century, cobbled surfaces and chalk foundations. Geoffrey Cobbe, lord of this manor, was convicted of leading rebellious peasants in the Peasants' Revolt, but was given a royal pardon and his estate was returned to him. His son sold Francis Manor to the Wimpole estate, but Wratworth was held independently until 1686.

From the 16th century onwards successive families had the will and

Interior of Wimpole Hall, which became a centre of culture and elegance in the 18th century. Photograph by Cambridgeshire County Council, 1983.

Wimpole Hall and Park from the air, showing the remains of ridge and furrow. Photography by Geoffrey Robinson.

ability to acquire land in compact blocks and to treat it as a resource for pleasure and status rather than for economic gain, even though they may bankrupt themselves and depopulate the landscape in the process. To begin with, the village of Wimpole, where there was a manor house, church and settlement around the later site of Wimpole Hall, was given to Henry Chicheley, Archbishop of Canterbury, in the 15th century by a lady of the manor. It descended to Sir Thomas Chicheley, a well-connected courtier and supporter of Charles I. Sir Thomas rebuilt the Hall in brick and removed the village from around the church, replacing it with ornate formal gardens which can still be traced as slight earthworks and fragmentary avenues. 'Thomas Chicheley,Esq., lord of this village, is now erecting an extraordinary curious neate house near the antient site', commented John Layer, at the time. The combined populations of the Wimpole hamlets still totalled 41 families in the 16th century. Subsequent owners were further up the social scale, being first the Earl of Radnor and then the Duke of Newcastle. Daniel Defoe's comments on the 18th century Hall are not complimentary: 'Wimple Hall, formerly built at vast expense, by the late Earl of Radnor... is situated in a very dirty Country and the Gardens and Buildings are both in a very bad Taste'. The Duke's daughter married Edward Harley, Earl of Oxford, who employed Charles Bridgeman to change the formal gardens into 'parkland', almost as formal in its way, with rectangular ponds and avenues, one over two miles long and extending beyond the estate and including an octagonal water-filled basin in Whaddon. This avenue is still a distinctive feature of the Cambridgeshire landscape. Although killed by Dutch elm disease in the 1970s, it has been replaced and should last another two centuries. Two areas of settlement in the south and west were removed for this design.

Harley was a very cultivated man, and Wimpole at this time became a centre for the intelligentsia, with scholars, antiquaries, writers and poets making lengthy stays. His greatest creation was the Harleian Collection of books and manuscripts, which became the core of the British Library. However, overspending left the Earl in debt, and Wimpole was sold to the Earl of Hardwicke in 1739. He began further aggrandisement of the Hall, and a new style of landscaping. Flowers and formal beds were replaced with a small park surrounded by a ha-ha, to keep grazing animals near the house without barriers to spoil the view. Fashions in garden design had a short life in the 18th century, and within twenty years the next earl followed national trends, employing 'Capability' Brown to change the landscape into his vision of what nature might have intended. This meant enlarging the parkland area to the north and removing another medieval hamlet, joining Bridgeman's ponds into a curving lake and planting belts and clumps of trees on the arable fields. These, with his medieval style 'ruin' or folly, are major characteristics of Wimpole today.

Even this scale of work was not left alone for long, as the next earl engaged the leading landscape gardener of the early 19th century, Humphrey Repton, to introduce newer fashions, including a return to small formal gardens for the plants then being introduced into England, and he increased the parkland in the east, which removed the last surviving hamlet. Surrounding countryside was part of the Park's setting, and a long winding avenue towards Cambridge was planted for the benefit of visitors from the University. A few years later, in the 1840s, a row of Jacobean-style cottages, were built for estate workers at New Wimpole. In 1801 there were 202 people living in Wimpole, and this grew fast to 583 in 1831, before declining fairly steadily to 160 in 1996.

Foreclosure of a mortgage in the late 19th century left the estate with the Agar-Robartes family of Lanhydrock House in Cornwall, to where much of the Hall's furnishings were removed. In the 1930s Wimpole was sold to Captain Bambridge, whose widow, Elsie Bambridge, daughter of Rudyard Kipling, was virtually a recluse for the latter part of her long life, and the Park enjoyed benign neglect. In particular, her insistence that rabbits must not be killed led to distinctive grass swards that were the delight of naturalists, though the despair of gardeners and farmers. She left the Hall, Park and the surrounding farms to the National Trust in 1976. Economic pressures led the Trust to follow farming practices of that time and to start improving the fertility of the grassland, including re-seeding and harrowing areas of ridge and furrow and settlement, before better conservation policies led to management programmes for sympathetic restoration of formal features (lakes, woods, folly, etc.), and conservation of archaeological remains.

Bibliography

Abbreviations

CCC Cambridgeshire County Council; CAU Cambridge Archaeological Unit; CLHC Cambridgeshire Local History Council; CUP Cambridge University Press; PCAS Proceedings of the Cambridge Antiquarian Society; TCHAS Transactions of the Cambridgeshire and Huntingdonshire Archaeological Society; VCH The Victoria County History of the County of Cambridge and the Isle of Ely.

The following works on the archaeology and history of Cambridgeshire have been used extensively, and so have not been listed separately under each village.

Babington, C., *Ancient Cambridgeshire*, Deighton Bell and Co., 1853, 1883.

Fox, C., *The archaeology of the Cambridge region*, CUP, 1923.

Gardner, R., *History, gazeteer and directory of Cambridgeshire,* R. Gardner, 1851.

Haigh, D., *The religious houses of Cambridgeshire*, CCC, 1988.

Hart, C., *The early charters of England*, Leicester University Press, 1966.

Malim, T., *Archaeology on the Cambridgeshire county farms estate*, CCC, 1990.

Meaney, A., 'Gazetteer of Hundred and Wapentake meeting places of the Cambridge Region', *PCAS 82*, 1993.

Munby, L., *Fen and upland*, Swavesey Village College, 1961.

Palmer, W.M., *John Layer of Shepreth*, Cambridge Antiquarian Society, 1935.

Palmer, W.M., *The Peasants Revolt in 1381,* Cambridge Antiquarian Society, 1935.

Palmer, W.M., *William Cole of Milton*, Galloway and Porter, 1935.

Rackham, O., *Trees and woodland in the British landscape*, Dent, 1976.

Rackham, O., *The illustrated history of the countryside*, Weidenfield and Nicholson, 1994.

Reaney, P.H., *The place-names of Cambridgeshire and the Isle of Ely*, CUP, 1943.

Richens, T., *The history of the fields in ten West Cambridgeshire parishes*, CLHC, 1970.

Taylor, C.C., *The Cambridgeshire landscape*, Hodder and Stoughton, 1973.

Widdowson, E.M., ed. *Cam or Rhee,* private, nd.

Essential reference books that have been widely used

Royal Commission on the Historical Monuments of England, *West Cambridgeshire*, HMSO, 1968.

For Arrington, Barrington, Barton, Bourn, Boxworth, Caldecote, Caxton, Childerley, Comberton, Conington, Coton, Croxton, Croydon cum Clopton, Dry Drayton, Eltisley, Gamlingay, Grantchester, Graveley, the Eversdens, Harlton, Haslingfield, the Hatleys, Kingston, Knapwell, Little Gransden, Lolworth, Longstowe, Madingley, Orwell, Papworth Everard, Papworth St. Agnes, Tadlow, Toft and Wimpole.

VCH III, 1948.

For descriptions of earthworks.

VCH V, 1973.

For Arrington, Barrington, Barton, Bourn, Caldecote, Caxton, Comberton, Coton, Croxton, Eltisley, the Eversdens, Gamlingay, Grantchester, Hardwick, Harlton, Haslingfield, Hatley St. George, Kingston, Little Gransden, Longstowe, Orwell, Shepreth, Toft, and Wimpole.

VCH VI, 1978.

For Duxford, Ickleton and Whittlesford.

VCH VII, 1978.

For Roman sites.

VCH VIII, 1982.

For Abington Pigotts, Bassingbourn cum Kneesworth, Clopton, East Hatley, Fowlmere, Foxton, Guilden Morden, Harston, Hauxton, Melbourn, Meldreth, Newton, Great and Little Shelford, Shingay cum Wendy, Tadlow, Thriplow and Whaddon.

VCH IX, 1989.

For Boxworth, Childerley, Conington, Dry Drayton, Elsworth, Girton, Graveley, Knapwell, Lolworth, Madingley, Papworth Everard and Papworth St. Agnes.

A major source of information has also been the Cambridgeshire Sites and Monuments Record. This wa originally created in 1974 from records kept by the Ordnance Survey and various museums and individual and since that time it has been augmented with results of excavations, aerial photography, fieldwor metal-detecting and casual finds. It is maintained by the Archaeology Section of the County Council, and ca be consulted by appointment.

Abington Pigotts

De Courcy Ireland, M., *History of Abington Pigotts with Litlington*, private, 1937.

O'Connor, B., *The coprolite industry: Abington Pigotts*, private, 1993.

Fox, C., 'Early Iron Age settlement at Abington Pigotts', *Prehistoric Society of East Anglia,* 1924, 211-33.

Arrington

Taylor, A., 'A Roman lead coffin with pipe-clay figurines from Arrington, Cambs.', *Britannia* 24, 1993, 191-22

Barrington

Foster, W.K., 'Account of the Excavation of an Anglo-Saxon cemetery at Barrington, Cambridgeshire', *PCA* 5, 1883, 5-32.

Malim, T., *Excavation of an Anglo-Saxon cemetery at Edix Hill, Barrington, Cambridgeshire,* forthcoming.

Malim, T., 'Prehistoric and Roman Remains at Edix Hill, Barrington', *PCAS,* forthcoming.

Barton

Page, R., *The decline of an English village*, Davis Poynter, 1974.

Walker, F.G., 'On the contents of a tumulus excavated at Lord's Bridge near Cambridge', *PCAS 12,* 190 273- 284.

Walker, F.G., 'Report on the excavations at Barton', *PCAS 12*, 1908, 96-313.

Bassingbourn

Alcock, J.P., 'The Bassingbourn Diana: a comparison with other bronze figurines of Diana,' *PCAS 79,* 199 39-44.

Burleigh, G., 'The Mile Ditches near Royston', *Hertfordshire Past*, 1980, 24-9.

Ellison, D., *A Bassingbourn collection,* private, 1977.

Ellison, D., *Warin de Bassingbourn fortified his manor*, private, 1982.

O'Connor, B., *The coprolite industry in Bassingbourn*, private, 1993.

Robinson, S., *History of Bassingbourn*, private, 1977.

Bourn

Liversidge, J., 'Roman burials in the Cambridge area', *PCAS 67,* 1977, 23, 24.

Greenwood, M., *The chronicles of Bourn*, private, 1994.

Stevens, W.G., 'Bourn Hall and the de la Warr family', *CLHC Bulletin* 24, 1994.

Taylor, A., 'A Roman stone coffin from Stuntney and a gazetteer of similar coffins from Cambridgeshire *PCAS 73*, 1984, 16, 20.

Boxworth

Jordan, W. and Downing, J., *The Boxworth, Conington and Fen Drayton Chronicle*, Swavesey and Distric History Society Publications, 1991.

May, S.C., 'Three Earthwork Surveys', PCAS 81,1992, 43-9.

Parish, C., Extracts from Boxworth, private, 1990.

Caxton

Brown, J., *Caxton: now and then*, Brookside Press, 1984.

Hunter, J. and Taylor, C.C., *Report on archaeological investigations of land at 95 Ermine Street, Caxton Cambridgeshire*, CAU, 1984.

Palmer, W.M. *Some notes on Caxton,* Cambridge Chronicle, 1927.

Taylor, A., *Castles of Cambridgeshire*, CCC, 1984, 15.

'hilderley
ysons, D. and S., *Magna Britannia, Cambridgeshire 1808*, EP Publishing Ltd., rp 1978, 164-6.
/alker, F.A., *Childerley,* private, 1879.

'he Chishills
Iorant, P., *History and antiquities of the county of Essex*, Vol. II, 1768, 606-609.

'omberton
oreman, R., *Comberton village handbook*, private, 1981.
osthuizen, S., 'Medieval settlement plans in West Cambridgeshire: a re-examination', *Landscape History*, forthcoming.

'onington
ɔrdan, W. and Downing, J., *The Boxworth, Conington and Fen Drayton Chronicle*, Swavesey and District Local History Society Publications, 1991.

'oton
owle, K., *Coton through the ages*, private, 1992.

'roxton
rown, A. E. and Taylor, C. C., 'Cambridgeshire Earthworks Surveys VI', *PCAS 82*, 1993, 101-8.

'roydon cum Clopton
lexander, J. 'Clopton: the life-cycle of a Cambridgeshire village', *East Anglian studies*, Heffer, 1968, 48-70.
almer, W. M., 'A history of Clopton, Cambridgeshire', *PCAS* 23, 1933, 3-60.

)ry Drayton
'ambridge Archaeology Field Group, 'A survey of Dry Drayton Park, Cambridgeshire', *PCAS* 72, 1982/3, 88-9.
Iarden, D. B. and Taylor, A. F., 'A Saxon glass beaker from Dry Drayton, Cambridgeshire', *PCAS* 71, 1981, 89-93.
ekulla, M., 'Enclosure at Dry Drayton', *CLHC Bulletin*, 1975, 3.
ekulla, M., 'Excavations at Dry Drayton', *PCAS* 70, 1980, 13-45.

)uxford
Brown, A. E. and Taylor, C. C., 'Cambridgeshire earthwork surveys II', *PCAS* 68, 1978, 69-72.
'leary, R., In *St.Neots to Duxford 900mm gas pipeline 1994*, ed. by I.P. Brooks, Engineering Archaeological Services, 1995, 351-84.
Evans, C., *Archaeological investigations at Duxford* (Rpt 40), CAU, 1991.
Powell, F. and R., 'Excavations of St. John's Church, Duxford', *PCAS* 72, 1982/3, 44-7.
Schlee, D. and Robinson, B., *An archaeological evaluation of land adjacent to Duxford Mill, Duxford* (Rpt 113), CCC, 1995.
Sutherland, T.L. and Spoerry, P., *Archaeological evaluation at Moorfield Rd, St. John's Street, Duxford* (Rpt 110), CCC, 1995.

Elsworth
Evans, E., *The church and village of Elsworth, Cambridgeshire*, private, 1995.

The Eversdens
Oosthuizen, S., 'Medieval Settlement Plans in West Cambridgeshire: a re-examination', *Landscape History,* 1998.

Fowlmere
Fox, C. and Palmer W.M., 'Excavations in Cambridgeshire dykes: Bran or Heydon Ditch', *PCAS* 27, 1925, 16-42.
Hill, D., 'The Cambridgeshire dykes II: Bran Ditch - the burials reconsidered', *PCAS* 66, 1976, 126-8.
Hitch, D.E., *A mere village*, Hitch Publications, 1993.
Lethbridge, T.C. and Palmer, W.M., 'Excavations in the Cambridgeshire dykes VI: Bran Ditch' *PCAS* 31, 1927-8, 78-96.

Murphy, B.P.J., 'Excavations near the Round Moat, Fowlmere', *PCAS* 15, 1977, 69-77.

Palmer, W.M., Leaf, C.S. and Lethbridge, T.C., 'Further excavations at the Bran Ditch', *PCAS* 32, 1930 54-6.

Spoerry, P., *Medieval and later occupation in Fowlmere* (Rpt 102), CCC, 1994.

Welsh, K., *Excavations at Bran Ditch 1993* (Rpt 94), CCC, 1994.

Yorke, A.C., 'Fowlmere notes: some forgotten ways', *East Anglian Notes and Queries 10,* 1903, 4-6, 19-2 113-7, 184-6.

Yorke, A.C., 'A village in the making', *PCAS* 15, 1911, 281-99.

Yorke, A.C., 'The round moat at Fowlmere', *PCAS* 12, 1908, 114-9.

Foxton

Brooks, I.P. In *St. Neots to Duxford 900mm gas pipe-line 1994*, ed. by I.P. Brooks, Engineering Archaeologic Services, 1995, 48-55, 205-330, 558-632.

Fox, C., 'Excavations at Foxton, Cambridgeshire', *PCAS* 25, 1924, 37-49.

Parker, R., *The common stream*, Paladin, 1976.

Macaulay, S., *Herod's Farm, Foxton* (Rpt 118), CCC, 1995.

Gamlingay

Brown, J., *Gamlingay: 600 years of life in an English village*, Cassell, 1989.

Girton

Arnold, C.J. and Wilkinson, J.C., 'Three Anglo-Saxon cremations from Girton, Cambridgeshire', *PCAS* 7 1984, 23-7.

Cam, H., 'The hamlet of Howes', *The Girton Review*, 1944, 34-7.

Croft, P., 'An Iron Age and Roman cropmark site at Girton', *PCAS* 67, 1977, 3.

Hollingworth, E.J. and O'Reilly, M.M., *The Anglo-Saxon cemetery at Girton College, Cambridge,* CUP, 1925

Grantchester

Fox, C., 'Anglo-Saxon Monumental Sculpture in the Cambridge District', *PCAS* 23, 1922, 21-3.

Howard, F.G., 'On some recent discoveries in Grantchester church', *PCAS* 4, 1877, 63-5.

Saltmarsh, J., *The open fields of Grantchester*, private, nd.

Teulon, N.P., 'Report on the objects of antiquarian interest found in the coprolite diggings during 1917 a 1918', *PCAS 22*, 1921, 124-6.

Willmer, E.N., *Old Grantchester,* Birds Farm Publications, 1976.

Graveley

Bishop, A.M., *The short and simple annals of the poor - a history of Graveley, Cambridgeshire*, private, 1981.

Great Shelford

Taylor, C.C. ed., *Domesday to dormitory*, Workers Educational Association, 1971.

Guilden Morden

Fox, C. and Lethbridge, T.C., 'The La Tène and Romano-British cemetery, Guilden Morde Cambridgeshire', *PCAS* 27, 1926, 49-63.

Lethbridge, T.C., 'Further Excavations in the early Iron Age and Romano-British cemetery at Guild Morden', *PCAS* 37, 1936, 110-119.

Hardwick

Haselgrove, C., 'The moated site at Hardwick, West Cambridgeshire', *PCAS* 72, 1982-3, 48-54

Harston

Greene, H.C., *Harston: its history and records*, Pendragon Press, 1937.

Malim, T., 'An investigation of multi-period cropmarks at Manor Farm, Harston', *PCAS 82,* 1993, 11-54.

Pullinger, J. and Young, C.J., 'Obelisk kilns, Harston', *PCAS* 71, 1982, 1-24.

Haslingfield

Davidson, I. and Curtis, G.J., 'An Iron Age site on the land of the Plant Breeding Institute, Trumpingto *PCAS* 64, 1974, 1-14.

avis, G.E., *History of Haslingfield*, private, 1968.
ell, C. 'An open-work bronze disc from Haslingfield', *PCAS* 45, 1952, 65-6.
aslingfield Village Society, *Walk and look around Haslingfield,* Haslingfield Village Society, 1987.
lacgregor, A. and Bolick, E., *A summary catalogue of the Anglo-Saxon collections (non-ferrous metals*), Ashmolean Museum, Oxford, 1993 (British Archaeological Reports 230).
leaney, A., *A gazetteer of early Anglo-Saxon burial sites,* George Allen and Unwin, 1964, 66-7.
liller, T.E. and M., 'Edmundsoles, Haslingfield', *PCAS* 71, 1981, 41-72.
osthuizen, S., *Discovering the landscape: Haslingfield*, Haslingfield Village Society, 1996.
ullinger, J., 'Lingey Fen, Haslingfield', *PCAS* 71, 1981, 25-40.

lauxton
ughes, M., 'On some antiquities found near Hauxton, Cambridgeshire', *PCAS 7,* 1889, 23-6.
iversidge, J., 'Roman discoveries from Hauxton', *PCAS* 51, 1958, 7-17.

leydon
ox, C. and Palmer, W.M., 'Excavations in the Cambridgeshire dykes V: Bran or Heydon dyke', *PCAS* 27, 1925, 16-33.
lorant, P., *History and antiquities of the county of Essex*, Vol. II, 1768, 600-602.
oberts, G.F., *A history of Heydon*, private, 1957.

:kleton
ristowe, R.L., *Ickleton*, private, nd.
obinson, B., *Abbey Farm, Ickleton* (Rpt A34), CCC, 1994.
lundy, P.C.D., *Memorials of Ickleton in the past*, private, 1945.
leville, R.C., 'Memoir of Roman remains and villas discovered at Ickleton and Chesterford, in the course of recent excavations', *Archaeological Journal* 6, 1849, 14-7.
mith, J.T., 'Romano-British aisled houses', *Archaeological Journal* 120, 1963, 14.

'napwell
ongair, D., *Knapwell village and the church of All Saints*, private, 1978.
osthuizen, S., 'Saxon commons in South Cambridgeshire', *PCAS* 82, 1993, 99-100.
wavesey and District Society, *The Elsworth and Knapwell Chronicle*, Swavesey and District Society, 1994.

itlington
lark, J.G.D., 'A report of trial excavations at Limlow Hill, Litlington', *PCAS* 38, 1939, 170-176.
empe, A.J., 'Account of the collection of sepulchral vessels found in 1821 in a Roman ustrinum, Litlington', *Archaeologia* 26, 1836, 368-77.
obinson, M.J., *Manor Farm barn, Litlington, Cambridgeshire* (Rpt 14), CAU, 1995.

ittle Gransden
ackham, O., *Hayley Wood: its history and ecology*, Cambridgeshire and Isle of Ely Naturalists Trust, 1965.

ladingley
rown, A.E. and Taylor, C.C., 'Cambridgeshire earthwork surveys VI', *PCAS* 82, 1993, 108-11.
daniec, K., *An archaeological assessment at Madingley Hall, Cambridgeshire* (Rpt 35), CAU, 1991.
ackham, O. and Coombe, D.E., 'Madingley Wood', *Nature in Cambridgeshire*, 1996, 27-54.
ipper, J.B., 'A Late Iron Age/Romano-British settlement at Madingley, Cambridgeshire', *PCAS* 83, 1994, 23- 30.

lelbourn
leville, R.C., *Sepulchra exposita*, G. Youngman, 1848, 17-30.
almer, W.M., 'Argentines Manor, Melbourn, Cambridgeshire, 1317-18', *PCAS* 28, 1927, 16-27.
Vilkinson, J.C., 'Bronze Age barrows at Melbourn', *PCAS* 53, 1960, 55.
Vilson, D.M., 'The initial excavation of an Anglo-Saxon cemetery at Melbourn, Cambridgeshire,' *PCAS* 49, 1956, 29-41.

Newton
Davis, E.M., 'Dovecotes of South Cambridgeshire', *PCAS* 75, 1986, 77, 79.

Orwell
Ellison, D., *Orwell through the ages,* 4 vols., private, 1984.
Kempe, *et al., Malton Farm, Orwell, an archaeological survey* (Rpt 14), CCC, 1990.
Spoerry, P., *Medieval and post medieval features at Chapel Orchard, Town Green Road, Orwell* (Rpt 80), CCC, 1992.

Papworth Everard
Parker, R., *On the road - the Papworth story*, Pendragon Press, 1977.

Shingay cum Wendy
Kempe, S., *Manor Farm, Shingay, earthworks survey* (Rpt 27), CCC, 1991.
Palmer, W.M., 'Notes on the early history of Shingay, Cambridgeshire', *TCHAS I(2),* 1904, 126-41.
Shimfield, W.H., 'On Shengay and its preceptory', *PCAS* 7, 1889.

Tadlow
Black, G. *et al.*, 'The repair and dendrochronological dating of a medieval granary from Tadlow, Cambridgeshire', *PCAS* 72, 1982-3, 79-87.

Thriplow
Neville, R.C., *Sepulchra exposita*, G. Youngman, 1848, 11-17.
Taylor, C.C., 'Our neighbours - Thriplow', *Whither Whittlesford,* 1978, 3-6.
The Thriplow Society, *About Thriplow*, private, nd.
Trump, D.H., 'The Bronze Age barrow and Iron Age settlement at Thriplow', *PCAS* 49, 1956, 1-12.
Vinter, G.O., *Thriplow*, private, 1951.

Toft
Oosthuizen, S., 'Medieval settlement plans in South Cambridgeshire: a re-examination', *Landscape History*, forthcoming.

Whaddon
Oosthuizen, S., 'Saxon commons in Cambridgeshire', *PCAS* 82, 1993, 95-7.

Whittlesford
Cambridgeshire Chronicle, 12 Nov, 1818.
Gdaniec, K., *An archaeological recording exercise at Butts Green, Whittlesford, Cambridgeshire* (Rpt 104), CAU, 1994.
Miller, J., *Rayners Farm, Whittlesford, Cambridgeshire* (Rpt 87), CAU, 1993.
Taylor, C.C., 'Whittlesford: the study of a river-edge village', *The rural settlements of medieval England*, ed. by A. Aston *et al,* Blackwell, 1989, 207-27.

Wimpole
Defoe, D., *A tour through the whole island of Great Britain*, Vol. I, 3rd ed., G. Strahan, 1742, 104-5.
Horton, W. *et al.*, 'Excavation of a Roman site near Wimpole, Cambridgeshire, 1989', *PCAS* 83, 1994, 31-74.
May, S., 'Three earthwork surveys', *PCAS* 81, 1992, 39-43.
Taylor, C., In *St. Neots - Duxford 900mm gas pipeline 1994, Archaeological Report,* ed. by I.P. Brooks, Engineering Archaeological Services, 1995.
Taylor, C.C., 'Dispersed settlement in nucleated areas', *Landscape History* 17, 1995, 31.

Appendix

Population figures for South-West Cambridgeshire villages

Notes

Figures in italics are derived from the tenants and slaves given in Domesday Book (1086), tenants recorded in Hundred Rolls (1279), adults over 14 years eligible to pay the poll tax (1377), and households assessed for the Subsidy Rolls (1563) and Hearth Tax (1664). They have been multiplied to give a rough estimate of the total population at the time, but none of these figures are very accurate, and probably err on the low side. Subsequent figures are derived from census returns for the whole population and County Council forecasts for 1996, based on 1994 figures.

Coton is counted with Grantchester and Newton with Hauxton in 1086 and 1279. Twin parishes are sometimes counted together, and their figures should be treated with extra caution.

C19 - The maximum population of each village in the 19th century.

ha - hectares, approximately 2.4 acres. This relates to the size of the parish in 1996, which may not be the same as its medieval extent.

Parish	1086	1279	1377	1563	1664	1801	C19	1996	ha
Abington Pigotts	*17* / 85	-	*78* / 108	*24* / 108	*18* / 77	177	259	150	500
Arrington	*17* / 85	*41* / 205	*119* / 155	*25* / 112	*20* / 86	190	317	370	550
Barrington	*54* / 270	*107* / 535	256 / 333	*81* / 364	*81* / 348	348	727	990	914
Barton	*31* / 155	*85* / 425	*140* / 182	*25* / 112	*31* / 139	219	418	810	724
Bassingbourn cum Kneesworth	*39* / 195	-	*423* / 550	*114* / 513	*114* / 490	948	1910	3530	1536
Bourn	*76* / 380	*183* / 915	*299* / 389	*72* / 324	*85* / 365	-	973	1050	1658
Boxworth	*33* / 165	*100* / 500	*299* / 389	*17* / 76	*21* / 96	220	350	220	1053
Caldecote	*15* / 75	*62* / 310	*78* / 101	*9* / 40	*7* / 30	75	144	800	407
Caxton	*35* / 175	*83* / 415	*131* / 170	*32* / 144	*37* / 166	336	631	400	904
Childerley	*23* / 115	*45* / 225	*76* / 99	*3* / 13	*1* / 4	50	50?	30	433
Chisells	*28* / 140	-	-	-	-	380	637	620	1300
Comberton	*43* / 215	*50* / 250	*152* / 198	*30* / 135	*52* / 224	295	619	2370	785
Conington	*24* / 120	*65* / 325	*109* / 142	*26* / 117	*27* / 121	182	235	150	616
Coton	-	-	-	*21* / 94	*26* / 112	126	390	710	404
Croxton	*23* / 115	*65* / 325	*117* / 152	*25* / 112	*24* / 103	171	308	130	772
Croydon cum Clopton	*46* / 230	-	*182* / 237	*21* / 94	*25* / 107	208	545	200	1106
Dry Drayton	*52* / 260	-	*122* / 159	*31* / 139	*58* / 249	376	497	590	1008
Duxford	*37* / 185	*100* / 500	*104* / 135	*58* / 261	*86* / 370	494	881	1850	1310
Elsworth	*48* / 240	*90* / 450	*209* / 272	*53* / 238	*73* / 314	600	878	600	1534
Eltisley	*27* / 135	-	*136* / 177	*20* / 90	*34* / 146	250	504	390	800
Eversdens	*26* / 130	*46* / 230	*148?*/ 192	*34* / 153	*48* / 206	362	668	730	913
Fowlmere	*36* / 180	*100* / 500	-	*34* / 153	*44* / 189	420	616	1170	945
Foxton	*43* / 215	*68* / 340	-	*30 / 135*	*57* / 245	322	450	1140	708
Gamlingay	*65* / 325	-	*219* / 285	*50* / 225	*71* / 305	847	2063	3450	1300

Parish	1086	1279	1377	1563	1664	1801	C19	1996	ha
Girton	*34* / 170	*90* / 450	*196* / 255	*38* / 171	*35* / 150	232	470	3770	720
Grantchester	*76* / 380	*100* / 500	*177* / 230	*16* / 72	*40* / 172	294	625	560	490
Graveley	*20* / 100	*45* / 225	*94* / 122	*23* / 103	*28* / 120	156	334	250	640
Great Shelford	*13* / 65	*90* / 450	-	*60* / 270	*72* / 310	570	1000	4080	838
Guilden Morden	*51* / 255	*130* / 650	*222* / 287	*54* / 243	*71* / 305	428	1059	900	1052
Hardwick	*11* / 55	*43* / 215	*81* / 105	*14* / 63	*23* / 99	158	248	2490	600
Harlton	*20* / 100	*57* / 285	*103* / 134	*21* / 94	*32* / 138	156	335	290	508
Harston	*29* / 145	*65* / 325	*90* / 117	*38* / 171	*55* / 236	412	860	1580	709
Haslingfield	*81* / 405	*140* / 700	*271* / 352	*53* / 238	*70* / 301	387	762	1500	1228
Hatley	*41* / 205	-	*69* / 88	*13* / 58	*30* / 129	201	319	240	962
Hauxton	*27* / 135	*66* / 330	*16* / 21	*16* / 72	*28* / 120	144	270	710	207
Heydon	*30* / 150	-	-	*30* / 135	-	246	368	200	866
Ickleton	*46* / 230	*115* / 575	-	*68* / 306	*82* / 353	493	813	640	1080
Kingston	*21* / 105	-	*111* / 144	*43* / 193	*25* / 107	225	322	240	795
Knapwell	*24* / 120	*50* / 250	*73* / 95	*22* / 99	*32* / 138	97	188	110	500
Litlington	*43* / 215	-	*235* / 305	*36* / 162	*43* / 185	350	790	790	865
Little Gransden	*11* / 55	*75* / 375	*126* / 164	*26* / 117	*46* / 198	232	305	220	800
Little Shelford	*25* / 125	*60* / 300	-	*32* 144	*36* / 155	220	580	810	484
Lolworth	*16* / 230	*50* / 250	*154* / 200	*17* / 76	*22* / 95	98	170	150	450
Longstowe	*17* / 85	-	*97* / 126	*24* / 108	*27* / 116	175	296	210	643
Madingley	*31* / 151	*90* / 450	*123* / 160	*27* / 121	*35* / 150	190	280	220	840
Melbourn	*55* / 275	-	*323* / 420	*80* / 360	*101* / 434	819	1931	4220	1760
Meldreth	*50* / 25	-	*253* / 329	*47* / 211	*58* / 261	444	776	1790	976
Newton	-	-	-	*20* / 26	*29* / 130	114	220	370	420
Orwell	*20* / 100	-	*56* / 73	*46* / 207	*45* / 193	375	800	1070	850
Papworth Everard	*19* / 95	*45* / 225	*85* / 110?	*15* / 67	*15* / 64	111	191	1580	468
Papworth St Agnes	*6* / 30	*35* / 175	*85* / 110?	-	*18* / 77	11	165	60	525
Shepreth	*30* / 150	-	*147* / 191	*33* / 148	*59* / 265	202	-	720	550
Shingay cum Wendy	*35* / 175	*43* / 225	*166* / 216	*22* / 99	*20* / 86	109	296	90	725
Steeple Morden	*55* / 275	*95* / 475	*249* / 324	*44* / 189	*40* / 172	430	1018	1090	1556
Tadlow	*28* / 140	*60* / 300	*130* / 169	*15* / 198	*29* / 125	101	232	170	683
Thriplow	*27* / 135	*80* / 400	-	*42* / 189	*46* / 198	320	520	780	966
Toft	*23* / 115	*50* / 250	*76* / 99	*24* / 108	*32* / 138	173	380	560	535
Whaddon	*43* / 215	-	*170* / 221	*33* / 148	*29* / 125	220	384	540	620
Whittlesford	*33* / 165	*105* / 525	*142* / 185	*49* / 220	*73* / 314	416	891	1530	793
Wimpole	*57* / 285	-	*173* / 225	*41* / 184	*27* / 116	202	583	160	1013

Index

PLACES

Sources of Illustrations

Title Page - Roman cemetery, Litlington
Kempe, A .J. 'Account of the collection of sepulchral vessels found in 1821 in a Roman ustrinum, Litlington', *Archaeologia* 26, p368.

Contents Page - Roman key
Neville, R .C. 'Memoir of Roman remains and villas discovered at Ickleton and Chesterford, in the course of recent excavations', *Archaeological Journal* 6, p14-17.

Acknowledgements (p.ix) - Roman glass and pottery vessels
Babington, C. *Ancient Cambridgeshire*, p39.

Introduction (p.3) - Roman barrow at Barton
Walker, F.G. 'On the contents of a tumulus excavated at Lord's Bridge, Barton'. *PCAS* 12, p283.

Introduction (p.5) - Orwell Enclosure Map
County Record Office Q/RDc 52.

Introduction (p.7) - Coprolite mining
Cambridgeshire Collection.

Introduction (p.7) - Andrews' Mill, Great Chishill
British Museum Manuscript Collection.

Abington Pigotts (p.11) - combs and bronze ring
Fox, C. 'Early Iron Age settlement at Abington Pigotts', *Prehistoric Society of East Anglia*, 1924, p211-33.

Barton (p.17) - Fire-dogs
Sites and Monuments Record.

Childerley (p.28) - Estate map of, 1808
Cambridge University Library, MS Plans, 552.

Childerley (p.29) - chapel
British Museum Add. Ms.5820.71.

Comberton (p.31) - Plan of Roman villa
Babington, C. *Ancient Cambridgeshire*, p22.

Coton (p.34) - Wayside Cross
Source - Cambridgeshire Collection.

Duxford (p.39) - Iron Age pottery
Cleary, R. in Brooks, I.P. ed. *The Archaeology of the St. Neots to Duxford gas pipeline 1994*, British Archaeological Reports, British series 255, 1997, p400.

Fowlmere (p. 47) - Bran Ditch drawing
Palmer, W.M. et al 'Further excavations at the Bran Ditch'. *PCAS* 32, plate I.

Foxton (p. 50) - buckle
Fox, C. 'Excavations at Foxton, Cambridgeshire', *PCAS* 25, p44.

Gamlingay (p. 51) - flints
Walker, F.G. 'A recently discovered site at Gamlingay, Cambridgeshire'. *PCAS* 15, p66.

Girton (p.53) - milestone and lion
Babington, C. *Ancient Cambridgeshire*, pp40, 41.

Girton (p.54) - Cremation urn
Arnold, C.J. and Wilkinson, J.C. 'Three Anglo-Saxon cremations from Girton, Cambridgeshire' *PCAS* 73, p25.

Guilden Morden vase
Babington, C. *Ancient Cambridgeshire*, p60.

Guilden Morden pendant
Fox, C. and Lethbridge, T.C. 'The La Tène and Romano-British cemetery at Guilden Morden, Cambridgeshire'. *PCAS* 27, p60.

Harston (p.64) - pottery
Pullinger, J. and Young, C.J. 'Obelisk kilns, Harston', *PCAS* 71, p23.

Haslingfield (p.66) - Roman objects
Miller, T.M. and M. 'Edmundsoles, Haslingfield'. *PCAS* 71, p67.

Hatley (p.69) - East Hatley estate map, 1750
Downing College Archive.

Hauxton (p.71) - axe
Hughes, M. 'On some antiquities found near Hauxton.' *PCAS* 7, opp. p30.

Heydon (p.72) - Roman temple
Neville, R.C. *Sepulchra exposita*, p17-30.

Heydon (p.72) - Bran Ditch
Lethbridge, T.C. and Palmer, W.M. 'Excavations in the Cambridgeshire Dykes, VI. Bran Ditch'. *PCAS*, 30, p79.

Ickleton (p.74) - Plan of Roman villa
Neville, R.C. 'Memoir of Roman remains and villas discovered at Ickleton and Chesterford in the course of recent excavations'. *Archaeological Journal* 6, p14-17.

Ickleton (p.74) - comb
Archaeologia 15, p405.

Litlington (p.79) - Roman vessel
Kempe, A.J. 'Account of the collection of sepulchral vessels found in 1821 in a Roman ustrinum, Litlington.' *Archaeologia* 26, p376.

Melbourn (p.86) - urn
Neville, R.C. *Sepulchra exposita*, p17-30.

Shepreth (p.97) - intaglio
Sites and Monuments Record.

Shingay cum Wendy (p.99) - church
British Museum Add. Ms. 5810.115.

Steeple Morden (p.101) - church
British Museum Add. Ms. 5820.57.

Thriplow - Prehistoric artefacts
Trump, D.H. 'The Bronze Age barrow and Iron Age settlement at Thriplow', *PCAS* 49, p6.

Full bibliographical details of books and articles will be found in the Bibliography on pages 115-120.